Social Interaction Between Road Users and Automated Vehicles

Dr. rer. nat. Hatice Şahin Ippoliti

Bibliografische Information der Deutschen Nationalbibliothek:
Die Deutsche Nationalbibliothek verzeichnet diese Publikation in der Deutschen
Nationalbibliografie; detaillierte bibliografische Daten sind im Internet über
http://dnb.dnb.de abrufbar.

Die automatisierte Analyse des Werkes um daraus Informationen insbesondere
über Muster Trends und Korrelationen gemäß §44b UrhG („Text und Data Min-
ing") zu gewinnen ist untersagt.

Zugl.: Oldenburg, Univ., Diss., 2025

Verlag: BoD · Books on Demand GmbH,
In de Tarpen 42, 22848 Norderstedt,
bod@bod.de

Druck: Libri Plureos GmbH,
Friedensallee 273, 22763
Hamburg

ISBN: 978-3-8423-7676-2

Abstract

Self-driving cars are currently operational in certain urban areas. Despite these designated zones presumed to be optimal, concerns over incident rates and shifting public opinion necessitate a focus on the social integration of these technologies. The ability of self-driving cars to navigate informal interactions and unexpected situations, a critical aspect of social behavior, falls short due to the absence of human-centric communication transfer in urban mixed traffic where self-driving cars and humans coexist. Recognizing the social context of traffic, the thesis aims to address the gap in social interaction and position fully Automated Vehicles (AVs) as social agents.

Achieving widespread accessibility for AVs goes beyond technological advancements; it requires successful social integration. The present thesis contends that failure to integrate the social agency of AVs during design could diminish their usability and overall success. Understanding social behavior in traffic and how AVs function as social agents is crucial to resolving interaction challenges and ensuring seamless coexistence with human road users.

The current thesis unfolds systematically. At the first stage, I lay my efforts to define and measure social behavior in traffic. Accordingly, I unveil key dimensions of prosocial behavior in traffic and analyze communication cues of drivers and pedestrians through observation of naturalistic driving data. Additionally, I address the need for quantifiable metrics by developing and validating a new scale. Specifically, components of prosocial behavior are found as being coherent with existing norms, hence following a predictable driving style and abiding by the rules, as well as deviating from rules where necessary, awareness, yielding the right of way to facilitate help and traffic flow, and expressing gratitude and apology to express socialness.

Furthermore, I investigate human behavior around self-driving vehicles to understand existing patterns and address potential challenges. By implementing a pedestrian simulator in virtual reality and utilizing gamification to introduce real costs and benefits, I create a test bed for assessing jaywalking behavior in mixed traffic with AVs. Most notably, results show that while individuals desire the defensive behavior of automated vehicles, conflict-avoidant automated vehicles may incentivize individuals to take advantage of their defensive stance and promote deviant behavior toward them.

Moreover, I seek design solutions to provide support for interaction between AVs and humans. I explore various external communication cues for self-driving vehicles and test the influence of these cues on prosocial behavior and perception in two distinct studies. Most significantly, results identify the efficacy of sympathy-eliciting cues and external displays emphasizing locomotion intention in increasing prosocial behavior and perception.

Finally, I reflect on the presented results and methods. I discuss the key findings regarding social behavior in traffic, how AVs influence human behavior with their employed driving styles, and how the interaction between AVs and humans can be eased and balanced through external and emphasized implicit communication. I further discuss the potential use of my created metrics and external communication options to enhance social interaction under current regulations and research trends. Lastly, I emphasize the limitations and future directions of my work.

In conclusion, the present thesis, rooted in understanding social behavior and perceiving AVs as social agents, contributes valuable insights. It aims to aid researchers, policymakers, engineers, vehicle manufacturers, designers, and developers in unraveling social behavior and perception in traffic, offering solutions for societal challenges and advantages in the coexistence of humans with self-driving vehicles.

Zusammenfassung

Selbstfahrende Autos werden derzeit in bestimmten städtischen Gebieten eingesetzt. Trotz dieser ausgewiesenen Zonen, die als optimal gelten, ist es aufgrund der Besorgnis über die Unfallrate und der sich ändernden öffentlichen Meinung notwendig, sich auf die soziale Integration dieser Technologien zu konzentrieren. Die Fähigkeit selbstfahrender Autos, sich in informellen Interaktionen und unerwarteten Situationen zurechtzufinden - ein entscheidender Aspekt des Sozialverhaltens - wird durch das Fehlen einer menschenzentrierten Kommunikationsübertragung im städtischen Mischverkehr, in dem selbstfahrende Autos und Menschen nebeneinander fahren, beeinträchtigt. Unter Berücksichtigung des sozialen Kontextes des Verkehrs zielt dieses Dissertation darauf ab, die Lücke in der sozialen Interaktion zu schließen und voll automatisierte Fahrzeuge (AVs) als soziale Agenten zu positionieren.

Um eine breite Zugänglichkeit für AVs zu erreichen, bedarf es nicht nur technischer Fortschritte, sondern auch einer erfolgreichen sozialen Integration. Die vorliegende Dissertation vertritt die These, dass eine fehlende Integration der sozialen Rolle von AVs während der Entwicklung ihre Nutzbarkeit und ihren Gesamterfolg schmälern könnte. Das Verständnis des sozialen Verhaltens im Verkehr und der Funktion von AVs als soziale Agenten ist entscheidend für die Lösung von Interaktionsproblemen und die Gewährleistung einer nahtlosen Koexistenz mit menschlichen Verkehrsteilnehmern.

Die vorliegende Dissertation geht systematisch vor. In der ersten Phase lege ich meine Bemühungen zur Definition und Messung von Sozialverhalten im Verkehr dar. Dementsprechend lege ich die Schlüsseldimensionen prosozialen Verhaltens im Verkehr offen und analysiere die Kommunikationshinweise von Autofahrern und Fußgängern durch die Beobachtung von naturalistischen Fahrdaten. Darüber hinaus gehe ich auf den Bedarf an quantifizierbaren Messgrößen ein, indem ich eine neue Skala entwickle und validiere. Zu den Komponenten prosozialen Verhaltens gehören insbesondere die Übereinstimmung mit bestehenden Normen, d. h. ein vorhersehbarer Fahrstil und das Einhalten von Regeln, aber auch das Abweichen von Regeln, wenn dies erforderlich ist, Aufmerksamkeit, Vorfahrt gewähren, um Hilfe zu leisten und den Verkehrsfluss zu erleichtern, sowie das Ausdrücken von Dankbarkeit und Entschuldigung, um Sozialität zu zeigen.

Darüber hinaus untersuche ich das menschliche Verhalten in der Umgebung selbstfahrender Fahrzeuge, um bestehende Muster zu verstehen und potenzielle Herausforderungen anzugehen. Durch die Implementierung eines Fußgängersimulators in der virtuellen Realität und die Nutzung von Gamification zur Einführung realer Kosten und Vorteile schaffe ich ein Testfeld zur Bewertung des Verhaltens von Fußgängern im gemischten Verkehr mit AVs. Die Ergebnisse zeigen vor allem, dass Individuen zwar das defensive Verhalten automatisierter Fahrzeuge wünschen, dass aber konfliktvermeidende automatisierte Fahrzeuge Anreize für

Individuen bieten können, ihre defensive Haltung auszunutzen und abweichendes Verhalten ihnen gegenüber zu fördern.

Darüber hinaus suche ich nach Designlösungen, um die Interaktion zwischen AVs und Menschen zu unterstützen. Ich untersuche verschiedene externe Kommunikationshinweise für selbstfahrende Fahrzeuge und teste den Einfluss dieser Hinweise auf prosoziales Verhalten und Wahrnehmung in zwei verschiedenen Studien. Die Ergebnisse zeigen vor allem die Wirksamkeit von sympathieerweckenden Hinweisen und externen Anzeigen, die die Fortbewegungsabsicht betonen, bei der Steigerung von prosozialem Verhalten und Wahrnehmung.

Abschließend reflektiere ich die vorgestellten Ergebnisse und Methoden. Ich erörtere die wichtigsten Ergebnisse in Bezug auf soziales Verhalten im Verkehr, wie AVs das menschliche Verhalten mit ihrem Fahrstil beeinflussen und wie die Interaktion zwischen AVs und Menschen durch externe und betonte implizite Kommunikation erleichtert und ausgeglichen werden kann. Des Weiteren diskutiere ich die potenzielle Nutzung der von mir entwickelten Metriken und externen Kommunikationsoptionen zur Verbesserung der sozialen Interaktion im Rahmen aktueller Vorschriften und Forschungstrends. Abschließend gehe ich auf die Grenzen und die zukünftige Ausrichtung meiner Arbeit ein.

Zusammenfassend lässt sich sagen, dass die vorliegende Dissertation, die auf dem Verständnis von sozialem Verhalten und der Wahrnehmung von AVs als soziale Akteure beruht, wertvolle Erkenntnisse liefert. Sie soll Forschern, politischen Entscheidungsträgern, Ingenieuren, Fahrzeugherstellern, Designern und Entwicklern dabei helfen, das soziale Verhalten und die Wahrnehmung im Verkehr zu entschlüsseln und Lösungen für gesellschaftliche Herausforderungen und Vorteile im Zusammenleben von Menschen und selbstfahrenden Fahrzeugen anzubieten.

Acknowledgements

Even though pursuing a doctoral degree is a very independent experience, it is by no means a single-person effort. In my journey, I had the professional and social support of many people, who made me grateful for being surrounded by such brilliant minds and kind hearts.

I'd like to thank my supervisor Prof. Dr. Susanne Boll for giving me a chance to challenge myself and switch my discipline, as well as supporting my steps through the years. I also would like to express my gratitude to Dr. Larbi Abdenebaoui, Dr. Wilko Heuten, Dr. Marion Koelle, Dr. Heiko Müller, Dr. Maria Wolters, Dr. Jochen Meyer, and Prof. Dr. Torben Wallbaum for their feedback and guidance.

The picture of the Oldenburg family is by no means complete without my esteemed colleagues and dear friends: Saja, Susanna, Ani, Mikolaj, and Micheal, to name a few! I'd like to explicitly thank Dr. Sebastian Weiß for being the absolute to-go person in any question I had during my PhD.

I feel very lucky to have worked with Dr. Debagha Dey, Prof. Dr. Shadan Sadeghian and Prof. Dr. Philipp Wintersberger who not only shared their domain knowledge with me but also a lot of laughs. I'm also thankful for all the students who contributed with their great efforts to the studies I ran during my PhD.

Lastly, I'm very grateful for the support of my family, especially my husband Tommaso, as he is my biggest supporter in the world.

Contents

1   Introduction

Automated vehicles (AVs) have made their presence known, particularly in the United States, where they're already in use as fully automated taxi services in certain regions [Kec19]. Despite the remarkable technological advancements behind them, seamless integration of them into the social fabric of traffic remains a distant goal. While traffic appears to be regulated with formal rules, humans often rely on informal interactions to navigate cooperation and resolve ambiguities. Unlike sentient beings, automated vehicles cannot engage in informal communication, beyond sending basic locomotion cues such as deceleration and stopping. Recognizing this gap, manufacturers have compensated by deploying overly cautious AVs, which, though aimed at enhancing safety and acceptance in urban traffic with various motorized and non-motorized road users such as drivers and pedestrians [HCRB21a], also lead to disruptions in traffic flow. As these conflict-avoidant AVs become more prevalent, the risk of user frustration due to frequent stops by pedestrians or impatient drivers rises, potentially undermining the long-term viability of the services of the AVs. Consequently, while automated vehicles are increasingly commonplace, they remain imperfect, prompting a search for alternative approaches to foster clearer social interactions and replace over-cautiousness in their behavior with better social embeddedness.

1.1   Automated Vehicles with Different Levels

Automated vehicles have become increasingly prevalent in our surroundings, yet what defines a vehicle as automated? The Society of Automotive Engineers (SAE) describes six levels of automation that are shaping the landscape of transportation today and in the foreseeable future (see Figure 1.1). At Level 0, vehicles lack automation and coexist alongside Level 1 and 2, where features like lane centering and adaptive cruise control offer driver support. In these levels, drivers retain primary control while benefiting from assistance features. Level 3 automation marks a pivotal shift with active engagement between human drivers and automated systems, where takeover and handover requests come into play. Recent years have witnessed the emergence of Level 3 automation on roads [Mac22].

The higher levels of automation, Levels 4 and 5, represent advancements where human intervention in driving tasks is no longer necessary. While Level 4 operates within specific traffic zones, Level 5 can navigate any environment under varied conditions. Presently, Level 4 automated vehicles function as local driverless taxis or shuttles in selected regions worldwide, sometimes with safety operators and sometimes autonomously. However, achieving Level 5 automation necessitates further technological development before widespread implementation [KS23].

This thesis focuses on automated vehicles operating at higher automation Levels 4 and 5. We specifically target scenarios where these vehicles must autonomously navigate conflicts without requiring intervention from human drivers. This approach enables us to delve into situations where both human-driven and automated vehicles confront ambiguity and must resolve it independently, without external human assistance. Consequently, we regard automated vehicles within this thesis as social agents, beyond their conventional roles as mere modes of transportation or tools controlled by humans.

Figure 1.1: SAE J3016 levels of automation diagram indicate different levels of automation and their features and characteristics in terms of task division between human drivers and automation [SAE16]. [Source: SAE International, `https://www.sae.org/blog/sae-j3016-update`, accessed 2024]

1.2 Social Interaction in Traffic

Humans are social beings. They interact with each other in everyday life, such as at work, while commuting, playing sports, and shopping, to name but a few. Through these social interactions, they communicate their intentions, emotions, and needs to each other. The need for relatedness to others is one of the fundamental psychological needs that – if satisfied – leads to positive experiences [SEKK01]. Through decades, humans have invented ways to communicate, fulfill the need for relatedness, become a part of a bigger group — a society, and care for each other. Thus, modern human life is heavily based on living in a society and interacting and communicating with each other. Social interaction with others, therefore, is not only a way to fulfill individual needs, but to create a collaboration. The behavior of individuals and how they interact with others can be propagated to a bigger group and impact society. Therefore, as a general untold rule, everyone is expected to care for each other and interact mindfully and with mutual respect in a social context. The resulting positive experiences from such behaviors are regarded as *"Prosocial Behaviors"* which were defined as *" [a] broad range of actions intended to benefit one or more people other than oneself – behaviors such as helping, comforting, sharing, cooperation, philanthropy, and community service"* [Bat12, p. 243].

Traffic is a social interaction space that is mostly regulated by traffic laws. Yet, these laws often remain insufficient to address humans' space-sharing problems [MMN+20]. In traffic situations or in countries where formal rules are non-strictly regulated, informal communication between road users fulfills an important role: bridging the necessary communication for solving cooperation problems or supporting smooth traffic flow. For instance, these can be situations where two drivers come at each other on a narrow street, where one of them has to yield the right of way to the other. In such bottleneck scenarios formal traffic rules fall short of solving the "game of chicken" [RC66] encounter and might ultimately lead to deadlocks, if they were strictly adhered to. Such space-sharing conflicts in traffic may easily result in aggressive behavior and negative experiences if parts fail to establish cooperative behavior [Ris85]. In similar scenarios, humans rely on informal communication originating from vehicle locomotion cues such as acceleration, and human-centric cues, such as gestures and eye contact. Implicit or vehicle-centric [DHP+20] communication cues can be summarized by vehicle movement patterns such as acceleration, deceleration, and vehicle distance [SF09, TVKBS05, Var98, REV+17, HR14] or flashing the headlights [Lau19]. Explicit or driver-centric communication cues are managed via eye contact [SG16, NPP+18, RJW16, GME15], body movements, gestures [Fär16, SDR17, GME15, HR14] or thanking [Lau19] of the traffic participants. In the research landscape, the benefit of informal communication under different circumstances has still been under discussion and seems to require further attention [Šuc14]. Some perspectives reevaluate the role of explicit communication in road traffic [DT17, RKT17b, LMG+21]. These researchers argue for the adoption of implicit interactions based on the kinematics of vehicles, including visual cues such as vehicle movements and auditory signals in the forms of engine and tire sounds. Nevertheless, it is still a question of when implicit communication is sufficient and when explicit communication is needed.

1.3   Prosocial Behavior in Traffic

Not only do traffic participants interact with each other when the rules are unclear, but also when the courtesy of who can go first is an option. This also extends to the interaction of e.g. vehicle drivers with other road users, such as pedestrians or cyclists. Specifically, urban traffic is a typical case for cooperation and exchange. In such traffic situations, the communication is not necessarily explicit. Still, traffic participants use more subtle signs of cooperation, such as reducing their speed when driving or walking, turning their gaze in a specific direction, or performing small gestures. These interactions can entail following traffic rules for the right of way, avoiding risky situations while overtaking, or stopping a car for an elderly pedestrian at an unprotected pedestrian crossing without traffic lights. While traffic rules offer fine-grained instructions for avoiding or handling safety-critical situations in general, many "social" situations, as in the former crossing example, are generally handled by unwritten rules that are sometimes shaped by the norms of society. In our former crossing example, the driver stops the car because she cares for the elderly pedestrian or wants to be judged as a prosocial road user. Another example could be a driver on a side road who wishes to take a turn into a busy main road without the existence of traffic lights. This driver would have to wait until another driver on the busy main road opens a gap for them to join the main road. Eventually, one of the drivers on the main road empathizes with the situation and lets the other vehicle merge. Hence, prosocial behavior becomes a key in many of the daily traffic situations and it is employed through many different behavioral expressions in traffic.

As mentioned previously, in a broad sense, prosocial behavior is defined as *"actions that benefit others"* [PRMP09] and, consequently, it comes into play in everyday traffic situations. Acting prosocially in traffic benefits all traffic participants in positive ways, and it helps to resolve traffic conflicts easily and effectively. Beyond the aforementioned examples, this happens, when searching for parking lots, when keeping the lane clear at the expense of violating traffic rules, when merging lanes effectively, and in many other situations. In the context of road traffic, prosocial behavior is defined as *"driving behaviors that potentially protect the well-being of passengers, other drivers, and pedestrians, and that promote effective cooperation with others in the driving environment"* [HHV+14]. This definition highlights essential aspects of prosocial behavior in traffic. "Wellbeing" is not only a matter of comfort but extends to safety, and "effective cooperation" has a genuine impact on the traffic system itself, ultimately influencing factors such as throughput or even emissions. A hypothetical scenario where all actors in the system act prosocial would improve safety overall. Regarding the effectiveness of the traffic system, a similar conclusion cannot be made because individuals need access to all the relevant information and could get stuck in local optima. However, this could change with the introduction of automated vehicles that replace human drivers, at least partly. Fostering prosocial behavior in mixed traffic, i.e., in road situations where both human participants and automated vehicles are involved, could create the opportunity for future traffic environments that are more cooperative and, thus, safer.

1.4 Social Interaction with Automated Vehicles

Soon, in more and more traffic areas interactions will not be limited to human users (i.e., drivers, pedestrians, cyclists, etc.) but include mixed traffic with AVs at different levels of automation [SAE16]. Future traffic systems may develop "superhuman" behavior in terms of effectiveness and efficiency [WFRS18, CBD+22], however, strategies to reach global optima may not be comprehensive for individual users with limited information access [SWRG19]. Consequently, this might pose additional requirements and foster the need to develop AVs as (pro)social actors and actively communicate and interact with other (human) traffic participants. Research has already addressed interactions between AVs and other (vulnerable) road users such as pedestrians [HCRB21b] in the context of crossing decisions [DHL+20]. In less regulated situations such as parking lots or shared traffic spaces, as formerly mentioned, drivers and pedestrians utilize a wide range of cues to communicate explicitly with each other. These cues include hand gestures, eye contact, and other body movements that are employed to resolve conflict situations but also to convey expressions of gratitude or empathy. Yet, automated vehicles lack this intuitive communication ability. This deficiency leads to situations in which pedestrians struggle to discern the intentions of AVs, and the AVs, in turn, cannot move around individuals with ease. Consequently, this limitation results in incidents where the traffic flow is disturbed, and the traffic participants are unsure of AVs' movements [BBV23]. Furthermore, AVs might lead to greater frustration in space-sharing conflicts, receiving less sympathy from other road users due to their reduced informal communication capabilities. Research in Human-Robot Interaction (HRI) emphasizes that humans treat robots as if they were social beings [KB18], which contributes not only to positive feelings such as sympathy but also negative behavior such as bullying towards them. The robots are subjected to similar social norms, for example, they are punished when they perform badly and rewarded when they perform well [BRC08]. Some researchers argue that robots are ideal targets for bullying as they are perceived as subordinate to humans, and the less intelligent they are perceived, the more likely they are to be subjected to aggressive behavior [KB18]. Assuming that AVs are similar to non-humanoid robots [LBY+20] and considering a high-level AV that cannot communicate clearly to road users, bullying behavior towards them is expected due to their reduced perception of intelligence.

To ease the communication problem with AVs, overly cautious vehicles have been deployed and released by car manufacturers in recent years. Undeniably, human trust and safety are essential before AVs are released on the streets. Nonetheless, some studies highlight the possible drawback of conflict-avoidant behavior of AVs in their interaction with humans [CRM+18, DML+21, CCB+20, FCM+18].

For instance, Moore et al. [MCSS20] report that human road users disturb driver-less cars in a Wizard-of-Oz study with obstructive behavior types, ranging from playful curiosity to aggression, to purposely stepping in front of them, which was also observed in Madigan et al. [MNF+19]. Similar behavioral patterns were also observed towards service robots [SCY+10]. Drawing on game theory, recent studies argue that if AVs are programmed with a zero-probability for collision, situations as these were to be expected [FCM+18, MB18]: The shared argu-ment is that a collision-avoidant AV will reduce other traffic participants' risk of a crash or injury when interacting with them, thereby increasing the rational utility to exploit their passive stance for individual benefit, hence leading to a "freezing robot problem" in the mixed traffic of the future [TK10]. As a counter-measure, Camara and Fox [CF20] introduced a pedestrian-AV interaction model where they suggested replacing conflict-avoidant AVs with milder space-invading AVs without introducing severe crash risks, inspired by findings regarding social factors in traffic among individuals. Overall, it seems that comprehending and deciphering the established communication "norms" or "language" among traf-fic participants is an important step in the process of designing AVs to interact effectively with others in traffic.

With a disappearing driver in the automated vehicle, in unclear situations, humans would only have to rely on the vehicle-centric signals of the AVs. Research in pedestrian - AV interaction largely addressed this issue by exploring External Human-Machine-Interfaces (eHMIs), which could assist communication between drivers and other traffic participants, and could increase the acceptance of AVs [CN16, CTSI17, DHB+20, CBR22a]. Moreover, eHMIs have been consistently found to make people feel safer when interacting with AVs [HLA+18, DWMT19, ABSK19, DCDNV+19a]. Some other studies explored trust and overtrust of Vulnerable Road Users (VRUs) in AVs [HWB19a, FMB20, HWWR20, JCT+19]. Previous works in human-AV research have explored different types of cues in different modalities, mostly visual cues such as light strips [DHP+20] and displays [MSS18] which convey information regarding the automation status, locomotion intention of the AV such as stopping [CBR22a] or courteous behavior such as yielding [DHP+20]. The effect of those cues has been studied concerning the trust and safety perception of humans [FKB20, DML+21]. Concerning making decisions to cross a street, Dey et al. [DHB+20] and Ackermans et al. [ADR+20] found that participants' willingness to cross remained higher when eHMIs were placed on the vehicle in comparison to the baseline condition where no eHMIs were introduced. Petzoldt et al. [PSB18a] experimented with front braking lights on vehicles. Though existing works show that deceleration distance and signaling yielding intent affect the crossing behavior and perceived safety, it remains unclear how these interfaces can be utilized the best in order to aid social interaction between AVs and humans.

1.5   Thesis Scope and Method

The motivation behind the present thesis is to provide solutions to interaction problems that humans and higher-level automated vehicles in urban mixed traffic may face. The current approach in the research domain seems to be emphasizing nonverbal vehicle-originated cues to convey the intention of movement in traffic. Even though many traffic situations are resolved through formal regulations, and informal communication through locomotion cues, certain situations require active communication of humans with each other through human-originated cues such as verbal communication, eye contact, or performing gestures and nods. The present work seeks to provide better interaction between humans and AVs even in those cases where human-to-human interaction is necessary to resolve conflicts or ambiguity, thus providing social interaction between them as the title suggests.

Most initial studies in this domain have focused on the acceptance of AVs and the feeling of safety in bystanders when they share the same traffic space with AVs. The present thesis pursues a different angle. While existing work mostly serves for the time frame of the initial deployment of AVs, our focus aims to tackle the problems of an emerging future where AVs are accepted, and their behavior is widely known and predictable among road users. Hence, our research aim is to benefit both users of AVs and the bystanders around AVs in traffic by making them more socially embedded. This way, AVs can be understood better by bystanders, while at the same time, users do not get frustrated by frequent stops that AVs have to make due to their over-cautiousness.

In the current thesis, we followed a generative design-driven and technology-focused approach [WK16]. Generally, we used methodologies from the fields of Psychology, Sociology, Computing Science, and Design. Due to AV's unavailability in the larger population in Germany, where we did big portions of our studies, instead of User-Centered Design, we used a combination of Design Thinking for vaguely defined problems [DAE+05] and Scenario-Based design for testing how users behave given a situation [Car03].

1.6   Research Questions, Specific Methodology and Contributions

Wobbrock and Kientz [WK16] classify HCI contributions in their work into different types. Building upon their work, the present thesis includes Empirical, Artifact, and Methodological contributions. The following paragraphs present each research question, goal, specific methodology, and contribution of the thesis.

RQ1: How can we define and measure social behavior in traffic to explore its role for road users?

Motivation: Understanding and defining social behavior in traffic is essential to inform the interaction between automated vehicles and humans. By studying social behavior, we could identify the nuanced communication patterns, gestures, and norms that govern interactions on the roadways. This understanding enables us to design automated vehicles that effectively communicate intentions, anticipate human behavior, and integrate seamlessly into the existing social fabric of traffic. Moreover, insights into social behavior can inform the development of protocols that prioritize safety, efficiency, and user experience in mixed-traffic environments. Ultimately, by defining and measuring social behavior in traffic, we pave the way for a more harmonious interaction between automated vehicles and humans on the road.

Methodology and contributions: The first research question is investigated through qualitative and quantitative methodologies used in Human-Computer interaction research. Firstly, with an ethnomethodological approach and through conversation analysis of non-verbal communication between drivers and pedestrians, explicit gesture use among drivers and pedestrians is discovered in naturalistic driving recordings (see Section 2.1). This aims at tracing the cues of social norms in traffic where formal rules vary in transparency. With this work, our **contribution** reveals the gesture use in traffic with different levels of ambiguity. Secondly, the present question is explored in a focus group of experts in automated driving (see Chapter 2 introduction). The focus group session aims to reveal today's social interaction norms in traffic and road users' expectations of the social behavior of automated vehicles in traffic, as well as measurement tools and methods for assessing and quantifying social behavior in traffic. This effort has **contributed** to the literature by listing key considerations of what defines prosocial behavior in traffic. Lastly, the development and validation of a quantifiable metric for assessing the social perception of road users is presented under the current research focus (see Section 2.2). Hence, with this extensive work, we **contribute** to the literature by creating an assessment tool to measure social behavior perception in traffic.

RQ2: What are the influences of automated vehicles on the prosocial and aggressive behavior of road users?

Motivation: Researching the influences of automated vehicles on the social behavior of road users also becomes critical for the present project. Firstly, as automated vehicles become increasingly prevalent on the roads, they introduce a novel element into the social dynamics of traffic. Understanding how the presence of automated vehicles shapes the behavior of human road users is essential for anticipating and mitigating potential challenges or conflicts that may arise. Secondly, studying the impact of automated vehicles on prosocial behavior, such as cooperation and consideration for others, is crucial for fostering a culture of safety and collaboration on the roadways. By researching these influences, we can develop strategies to promote positive interactions, enhance safety, and optimize the integration of automated vehicles within the broader context of human-driven traffic. Additionally, insights gained from this research can inform the design and implementation of policies, regulations, and technological solutions aimed at creating more inclusive, equitable, and efficient transportation environments for all road users.

Methodology and contributions: The present question seeks to explore potential changes in the social behavior of humans around automated vehicles due to various reasons such as imbalanced power dynamics between conflict-avoidant automated vehicles or overreliance on automation safety. Gamification in experimental studies approach is adopted to create a test bed in virtual reality where participants are introduced with realistic costs and benefits while playing a repetitive street crossing game in front of vehicle switch different degrees of automation (see Section 3.1). Hence, we utilized a controlled experimental study to research this topic. With this work, we **contribute** to existing works by revealing deviant behavior around overly cautious AVs.

> **RQ3:** What kind of design solutions can we provide for supporting prosocial behavior between AVs and human road users?

Motivation: As AV technology continues to advance, it is essential to ensure that these vehicles integrate seamlessly into existing traffic environments while fostering positive interactions among all road users. It is crucial to understand how design elements such as communication interfaces and behavioral cues can influence the behavior and perceptions of bystanders around AVs to create safe and efficient traffic flow. Moreover, research in this area may enable us to develop guidelines, standards, and best practices for the design and deployment of AVs that can operate seamlessly in traffic. Ultimately, by exploring design solutions to support prosocial behavior, we can pave the way for a future where autonomous and human-driven vehicles coexist harmoniously, contributing to safer, more sustainable, and more inclusive transportation systems.

Methodology and contributions: The final research question aims to offer solutions for promoting social behavior among humans and automated vehicles by enabling social communication between them. Firstly, we run a pilot study to reveal optimal timing for cueing necessary information with external interfaces in an online first-person street crossing game (see Section 4.1). Then, the promoting social behavior approach is tested through two research directions. Firstly, inspired by social cues today's human drivers place on their passenger vehicles regarding different needs (i.e. baby on board), sympathy eliciting external cues on automated vehicles are tested in terms of their performance on altering the yielding behavior of drivers on a video vignette survey (see Section 4.2). With this work, we **contribute** to literature by exploring different external cues to successfully elicit prosocial interaction. Additionally, informed by formal regulations and guidelines on explicit communication automated vehicles may express, accentuating their locomotion intention through external displays is investigated in terms of its effect on increasing the perceived social behavior of these vehicles in an ambiguous traffic scenario. We realized this on a realistic test track study by utilizing Wizard of Oz, or more specifically, Ghost Driver method [RLS+15] (see Section 4.3). This work **contributes** to existing discussions in literature by revealing the effective use of locomotion intention to elevate the social perception of AVs, an easily transferrable alternative to anthropomorphism.

1.7 Publications

This section lists the publications that constitute the main parts of the present thesis, as well as publications that contributed to the ideas expressed throughout the thesis. Publications that could be considered as backbones of the current thesis are as follows:

- **Şahin, H.**, Hemesath, S., & Boll, S. (2022). Deviant Behavior of Pedestrians: A Risk Gamble or Just Against Automated Vehicles? How About Social Control? Frontiers in Robotics and AI, 9, 885319. https://doi.org/10.3389/frobt.2022.885319

- **Şahin İppoliti**, H., Daudrich, A., Dey, D., Wintersberger, P., Sadeghian, S., & Boll, S. (2023). A Real Bottleneck Scenario with a Wizard of Oz Automated Vehicle—Role of eHMIs. Proceedings of the 15th International Conference on Automotive User Interfaces and Interactive Vehicular Applications, 280–290. https://doi.org/10.1145/3580585.3607173

- **Sahin Ippoliti, H.**, Trilck, N., Koelle, M., & Boll, S. (2023). Please, Go Ahead! Fostering Prosocial Driving with Sympathy-Eliciting Automated Vehicle External Displays. Proceedings of the ACM on Human-Computer Interaction, 7(MHCI), 1–18. https://doi.org/10.1145/3604265

- **Şahin İppoliti**, H., Weibert, A., Manstetten, D., Reimer, B., Gherson, P. & Abdenebaoui, L. (in review) Analysis of Driver and Pedestrian Gesture Use in Traffic. Automated Vehicles May Need More Than Kinematics in Ambiguous Situations. 2024

- **Şahin İppoliti, H.**, Colley M., Dey D., Habibovic A., Löcken A., Matviienko A., Müller H., Sadeghian S., Wintersberger P., & Boll S. (in review) Introducing SPAT: Development and Validation of Situational Prosocial and Aggressive Behavior Perception in Traffic Scale. 2024

Furthermore, workshops, short papers or posters that are included in the thesis are listed below:

- **Sahin, H.**, Mueller, H., Sadeghian, S., Dey, D., Löcken, A., Matviienko, A., Colley, M., Habibovic, A., & Wintersberger, P. (2021). Workshop on

Prosocial Behavior in Future Mixed Traffic. 13th International Conference on Automotive User Interfaces and Interactive Vehicular Applications, 167–170. https://doi.org/10.1145/3473682.3477438

- Şahin, **H.**, Daudrich, K., Müller, H., & Boll, S. C. (2021). Signaling Yielding Intent with eHMIs: The Timing Determines an Efficient Crossing. 13th International Conference on Automotive User Interfaces and Interactive Vehicular Applications, 5–9. https://doi.org/10.1145/3473682.3480253

- Şahin, **H.**, Vöge, S., Stahr, B., Trilck, N., & Boll, S. (2021). An Exploration of Potential Factors Influencing Trust in Automated Vehicles. In C. Ardito, R. Lanzilotti, A. Malizia, H. Petrie, A. Piccinno, G. Desolda, & K. Inkpen (Eds.), Human-Computer Interaction – INTERACT 2021 (Vol. 12936, pp. 364–367). Springer International Publishing. https://doi.org/10.1007/978-3-030-85607-6_38

Finally, publications that I co-authored or workshops that I co-organized that contributed to the ideas in the thesis are as follows:

- Lee, S. C., **Sahin, H.**, Zhang, Y., Yoon, S. H., Lee, J., Boll, S., & Wintersberger, P. (2022). A Workshop on Driving Style of Automated Vehicles in Ambiguous Driving Scenarios. Adjunct Proceedings of the 14th International Conference on Automotive User Interfaces and Interactive Vehicular Applications, 182–185. https://doi.org/10.1145/3544999.3550160

- Baby, T., **Sahin, H.**, Lee, J., Zhang, Y., Yoon, S., & Lee, S. C. (2023). What Do You Expect for Your AV? The 2nd Workshop on Behaviors of Autonomous Vehicles in Ambiguous Driving Scenarios. Adjunct Proceedings of the 15th International Conference on Automotive User Interfaces and Interactive Vehicular Applications, 264–266. https://doi.org/10.1145/3581961.3609834

- Baby, T., **Sahin, H.**, Wintersberger, P., Zhang, Y., Yoon, S. H., Lee, J., & Lee, S. C. (2024) Development and Classification of Autonomous Vehicle's Ambiguous Driving Scenario. Accident Analysis and Prevention, 200. https://doi.org/10.1016/j.aap.2024.107501

1.8 Thesis Outline

In the present thesis, Chapter 1 starts with an introduction and background of the topic, explains the thesis scope and methods, and provides a thesis outline. Chapter 2 presents how social behavior in traffic unfolds through various methods by using focus groups, observation of real interaction video data, and creating a quantifiable metric for measuring social perception in traffic. Chapter 3 investigates whether individuals change their behavior when they encounter automated vehicles through gamification and simulated environments. Chapter

4 seeks an answer to facilitate social behavior between automated vehicles and humans through external communication cues, realized by test track and video vignette studies. Lastly, Chapter 5 not only presents discussion points regarding the aforementioned chapters by focusing on the essence of social behavior in traffic, social perception of automated vehicles, and enhancing social embeddedness of automated vehicles through external communication, but also touches upon future directions and summary of research contributions.

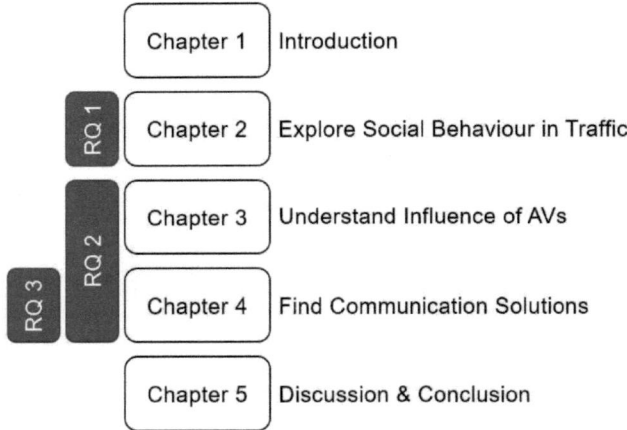

Figure 1.2: Thesis structure and corresponding chapters for investigating each research question.

2 Exploring Social Behavior in Traffic

This chapter sets the stage for the current work, highlighting the need to delve deeper into the underlying social norms that extend beyond mere adherence to formal traffic regulations. To address this, we have convened a focus group with 8 experts working in the area of automated vehicles during a conference workshop, which serves as the cornerstone of our investigation [SMS+21]. The central concern in the present focus group has been the concept of "prosocial behavior," which is becoming increasingly important as the road environment witnesses a growing diversity of users, from electronic bicycles and scooters to vehicles with varying levels of automation. While some initial research has touched upon this topic [SHE20a, HHV+14], there is currently a notable absence of systematic methodologies for its study. In the expert focus group, the primary goal was to establish a clearer definition of what constitutes prosocial behavior in traffic scenarios of today and the future, particularly those involving interactions between automated and manual vehicles and a wide range of vulnerable road users. We also intended to identify key scenarios and discuss potential evaluation methods for examining prosocial behavior.

To facilitate this discussion, we asked participants a series of targeted questions:

- Think about the last time you acted prosocial towards these traffic participants. How was the road and traffic situation? What did you do? What was your role as a traffic participant?

- What are the key features of prosocial behavior in traffic?

- Which scenarios and measurements can be applied for operationalizing prosocial behavior in traffic?

- What type of prosocial behavior is expected from automated vehicles?

These questions were used to elicit personal experiences and expert insights, allowing us to ground our exploration of prosocial behavior in real-world contexts. By asking participants to reflect on their own prosocial actions in traffic, we were able to capture a wide range of behaviors and scenarios that might otherwise be overlooked. This not only helped in identifying key features of prosocial behavior but also in contextualizing them within various traffic environments. The questions about scenarios and measurements provided valuable input for the next study phases by highlighting practical and relevant methods for evaluating prosocial behavior. Finally, discussing the expectations for automated vehicles offered a forward-looking perspective, essential for understanding how prosocial behavior might evolve as automation becomes more prevalent in traffic systems.

Consequently, the elements of prosocial behavior in traffic could be condensed into the following categories: maintaining a consistent and predictable style while driving, clearly signaling one's intentions, yielding the right of way, adhering to traffic regulations, making exceptions to the rules when necessary to resolve conflicts, and demonstrating appreciation and offering apologies when appropriate. Furthermore, results emphasized the necessity for a quantifiable metric to assess the situational aspects of prosocial behavior in traffic, which is presented in this chapter in Section 2.2. Beyond organizing focus groups, we solidified our findings by observing natural informal interactions in traffic (see Section 2.1). The parts of this chapter are submitted for publication as two distinct papers. The following section explores an ethnomethodological approach to analyze real video recordings of everyday traffic interactions.

2.1 Observing Social Interaction in Traffic with Ethnomethodology

The present section presents a qualitative video observation study for informing the use of explicit interaction cues between drivers and pedestrians in daily traffic situations with different levels of ambiguity.

2.1.1 Motivation and Related Work

Understanding today's social norms in traffic and the core aspects of human-to-human interaction has been under focus to enhance the interaction between AVs and humans [HR14, MM19]. While it is important to explore the interaction between the AV and its passengers, AV-bystander interaction has become a crucial topic and challenge to socially embedding AVs in our everyday lives [ABBK18, CRM+18, CPD+18, DML+21, MNF+19]. Bystanders are, in one sense, non-users of the AV, but they are still individuals who are affected by this technology since they share the same social space with AVs in the roadway [WMB+15]. As a specific element of this complex and dynamic interaction space, researchers have begun to focus on developing an understanding of the interaction characteristics of drivers and pedestrians (e.g. vulnerable road users) [SDR17, LMG+21, RKT17a, MM19, WFO+20]. Some studies have turned their focus to identifying the essential elements of driver-pedestrian interactions to pinpoint communication needs. For example, Lee et al. [LMG+21] ran an intercultural study in which they observed behaviors in three different locations in Europe. Results indicated that there is a heavy reliance of pedestrians on vehicle kinematic cues such as braking, distance, and speed (acceleration) when making a street crossing decisions. They further reported minimal communication via body language or eye contact. In a similar direction, Dey and Terken [DT17] reported pedestrians' reliance on implicit locomotion cues rather than explicit communication cues in a video observation study. Risto et al. [REV+17] highlight similar findings while emphasizing the need for further research into the use of explicit interactions. While reliant on somewhat weaker data showing the importance of kinematics, Sucha et al. [SDR17] highlight the importance of eye contact and explicit gestures of pedestrians in communicating with drivers while making road crossing decisions. Vinkhuyzen and Cefkin [VC16] provide a case study that illustrates the value of gestures and eye contact in the complex communication between drivers and pedestrians in deciphering the right of way. Rasouli et al. [RKT17a] conducted a large video observation study that captured the behaviors of pedestrians interacting with drivers. Results show that most of the time pedestrians send a form of nonverbal communication cue to the driver, mostly gazing towards them and 15 % of the time augmenting this with gestures such as nodding and/ or waving. This work is somewhat limited in that the interaction scenarios were not categorized in terms of the types of situations they occurred. The authors suggested that more work was needed to investigate drivers' nonverbal gestures and draw a more complete picture of the interactions. Explicit communication seems to serve a number of purposes in roadway communication. Hence, not only its functionality in conflict resolution is investigated, but also its purpose for daily social interactions which are as simple as expressing gratitude and apology. Haddington and Rauniomaa [HR14] emphasize the use of explicit cues in establishing social interaction between road users where a driver is effectively in an "iron cage" with communication limitations [Urr06].

While explicit interaction occurrences are reported to be rare in naturalistic studies, automated vehicle-human interaction research has considered eHMIs as a mechanism in which automated vehicles can compensate for missing explicit communication and perhaps by signaling a wide range of cues to augment the information provided by traditional forms of communication. Although there have been ongoing evaluations regarding the safety [HWB19a] and necessity [WD22] of eHMIs, cues have been reportedly found helpful and reassuring in multiple studies [DCDNV+19b, ADR+20, HLA+18, CFR22, FMB20]. Recent work by Brown et al [BBV23] demonstrated that AVs solely relying on vehicle locomotion cues still struggle to handle basic driving scenarios and can create confusion among bystanders and even passengers. The research leveraged data from YouTube channels. They investigated the yielding behavior of AVs as it is regarded as social behavior in traffic [HR14] that requires negotiation. They suggested a design pipeline for fluid interaction through movement between AVs and human road users.

According to Rasouli and Tsotsos [RT18b], environmental factors such as traffic signals and zebra crossings affect pedestrians crossing decisions. These findings may relate to pedestrians' reliance on formal traffic regulations in different environments. As environmental factors affect crossing decisions, they may also affect how drivers and pedestrians interact with each other. Marked crossings tend to be perceived as rather flexible and negotiable areas in traffic where the pedestrian has the right of way, but drivers can progress if pedestrians are not intending to cross. This room for flexibility incentivizes drivers to continue driving before pedestrians reach or start crossing the road [DT17]. In some countries, a great percentage of drivers fail to yield to pedestrians in such crossings [SDR17].

Hence, marked -or unprotected- crossings are deemed to be more ambiguous traffic situations when compared to more definitive situations such as stopping at a stop sign. Šucha [Šuc14] argues that social behavior is facilitated by formal rules. However, individuals do not always follow such rules due to divergences in motivation, lack of knowledge, or incongruency with infrastructure and road design. The research further suggests that ambiguity of traffic situations leads to the evolution of informal rules that help to play a role in resolving conflict. Such, informal rules are established by interaction between individuals ([HA78] as cited in [Šuc14]). Findings of Domeyer et al. [DLT+20] support this argument through a study of pedestrian-driver interactions that revealed a level of interdependence of both agents on each other's behavior. They divided the traffic scenarios into **nonintersections** where pedestrians jaywalked to cross the road, **unprotected pedestrian crossings** where no traffic or pedestrian lights existed, and **stop indicators** where clear traffic rules were present to define the right of way. The analysis looked at time and distance-based metrics to test interdependence and results indicated that most negotiations occurred in unprotected scenarios where rules were less formal. Nonintersections and stop indicators appear more as non-interaction scenarios according to the results and merely encounters without negotiation. One limitation in this analysis is the exclusion of a consideration of explicit gestures. To our knowledge, the level of ambiguity of a traffic scenario and the reliance on informal communication through explicit cues has received limited or no exploration in previous studies. As such, this study aims to support resolving problems in human-automated vehicle interaction through data-driven efforts, lay the foundation for the development of a deep learning system with real-world driving data, and share insights that contribute to the evolution of safer roads with automated vehicles.

2.1.2   Advanced Vehicle Technology Consortium Data

Data were drawn from a vehicle-pedestrian encounter dataset from the ongoing MIT Advanced Vehicle Technology (MIT-AVT) naturalistic driving study [FBG+19]. Several studies [TGS+19, DLT+22] have been conducted and published utilizing this dataset. This research aims to build upon this work through additional annotation and analysis that leverages new perspectives on video annotation to derive novel understanding of real-world vehicle-pedestrian behaviors when compared to other research. Our focus leverages this existing data given its unique synchronization of driver-facing and forward-facing video with selected vehicle telemetry and extensive existing annotations of key pedestrian and driver behaviors.

The dataset included driving data from a sample of drivers in the greater Boston area from 2016 to 2017. Details on the data collection and curation procedures including computer vision techniques initially leveraged to find scenarios of interest can be found in Terwilliger et al. [TGS+19]. The curated dataset included roughly 30-second-long naturalistic or "in the wild" driving data epochs where drivers yielded for pedestrians. Cases where pedestrians yielded for drivers are not included in the dataset as detecting these instances with only a front view camera, and limited data on pedestrian intentions is more challenging than detecting situations of a driver yielding [DLT+22]. At the onset of this project, vehicle kinematics, lead pedestrian body language such as gaze and hand waving, and pedestrian entering the scene had been manually annotated. Different traffic scenario types such as nonintersections where undesignated midblock crossings are categorized and stop indicators including red lights, pedestrian lights and stop signs, as well as unprotected pedestrian crossings labeled.

2.1.3   Naturalistic Driving Data Analysis

This section explains how the aforementioned curated data were extended by adding explicit interaction annotations including gestures and head movements.

Working from the existing dataset, a new annotation effort was undertaken for the purposes of this research. This included adding details on gestures and head movements linked to driver-pedestrian to the existing dataset. Efforts focused on a subset of videos that represent halting situations. Building from an approach rooted in ethnography for interaction design [RR18] and particularly in video analysis as an important medium for qualitative research [HHL10], an annotation effort focused on data observation without employing an initial coding framework was undertaken. We iteratively reviewed each encounter to classify, encode, and comprehensively document the actions of both drivers and pedestrians. The primary and only goal throughout this process was to gain insights into the timing and manner in which interactions unfolded.

Extending the Data with Driver Gestures

The initial curated 212 epochs in the dataset included forward camera recordings synchronized vehicle kinematics and pedestrian-related annotations. Of all these epochs, 176 of the cases were traceable to the initial raw data at our disposal. In 109 of the epochs, we were able to synchronize the inside-the-vehicle video streams excluded from the initial dataset. Upon visual inspection, one of the epochs was found as non-yielding, since the driver was parking and the presence of a pedestrian did not influence driving behavior. Another epoch where the driver did a left turn was also excluded since the pedestrian was not in conflict with the vehicle's trajectory. As such, this research focuses on 107 epochs amended to include synchronized video recordings of drivers' heads and arms (including hands). The final dataset of 107 epochs included 29 drivers (8 F - 21 M, M age = 41, $SD = 15$, range: 21 - 75).

The new video streams were inspected with Mangold Interact (version 20.9.7.0.) video annotation software (Mangold International GmbH, Arnstorf, Germany)

[Man18]. Of the epochs, 34 belonged to nonintersection scenarios including parking lots and undesignated midblock crossings (e.g., jaywalking, etc.). Fifty epochs were classified as unprotected pedestrian crossings without pedestrian lights. Lastly, 23 epochs were composed of stop indicators including stop signs, red traffic lights, and signalized crossings where pedestrian lights could be observed. To manage annotation investments, we prioritized efforts to epochs that had existing annotations tagging the presence of pedestrian waving [TGS+19], as these epochs presumably had higher chances of driver gestures. As described earlier, video analysis began without having predefined codes. As new annotations emerged, new codes were defined in the coding list. For example, starting with the code "waving", and seeing single finger movement instances in upcoming epochs, a new code of "finger movement" was created. "Nodding" and "mouth movement" were added in a similar way. After completing the initial observation of all the epochs, each epoch was reviewed against the final set of defined codes. We cross-checked the codes and annotations. Potential unclear epochs were discussed together, and mutual agreement was required for the final assignment.

Finger movements were defined as forward and backward motions of one or two fingers. A hand motion was annotated as waving when all the fingers moved in the same fashion. Nodding was single or multiple head movements upward and downward. Lastly, mouth movements included verbal communication which was rare. Afterward, finger movements, nodding, and waving were merged under the code "driver gesture". These annotations were added to preexisting annotations for analytical purposes. Analysis efforts focused on new perspectives explaining driver-pedestrian interaction in different traffic scenarios where drivers yield to pedestrians.

Bringing New Insights by Moment-by-moment Analysis

Building on Brown et al. [BBV23, BLV23] and Haddington and Rauniomaa [HR14], we conducted a moment-by-moment interaction analysis on three exemplary epochs of our data. The selection of the example epochs was based on a subjective consideration of how representative or unusual these cases were across the data (non-intersection and unprotected crossing representative, stop indicators unusual). In this context, the approach focused on specific encounter scenarios as a single fluid motion of interaction made in sequences. The methodological foundation was based on conversation analysis suggested by Goodwin and Heritage [GH90], in which the authors propose that social interaction occurs sequentially and that researchers can derive the meanings of each action at a time by observing the moments leading up to the interaction. Specifically, we adopted multi-modal conversation analysis methodology [Mon18] that extends the use of body gestures to body arrangements, group, and environmental effects. Epochs were analyzed in group data sessions [HHL10].

2.1.4 Results

The proportions of gestures in each of the categorized traffic scenarios appear in Table 2.1. In order to validate if pedestrians were aware of driver gestures, we inspected pedestrian gaze directions, average latencies between mutual gestures, and average driver gesture distances to pedestrians in different scenarios. Results show that pedestrian gaze was annotated as "towards" drivers while a driver was performing a gesture. This appears indicative of drivers' gestures being noticed by pedestrians. The average latency of mutual gesture use between pedestrians and drivers was 952 ms ($SD = 660$, range: 2633). This suggests that these gestures were following a somewhat structured communication pattern. Lastly, in driver gesture use distances, we observed an average of 15 m for nonintersections ($SD = 12$, range: 41), 17 m for unprotected crossings ($SD = 9$, range: 30), and 9 m ($SD = 7$, range: 13) for stop indicators as approaching distance. Not only do these distances seem reasonable for recognizable gestures by drivers through windows, but they also indicate a distance-related pattern of gesture use dependent on the scenario categories.

Table 2.1: Proportions of gesture in different interaction scenarios

Traffic scenario	Pedestrian	Driver	Mutual
Nonintersections	26 % (9/34)	38 % (13/34)	18 % (6/34)
unprotected crossings	34 % (17/50)	32 % (16/50)	16 % (8/50)
Stop indicators	17 % (4/23)	13 % (3/23)	9 % (2/23)

A Particular Case for Driver Gesture Use: Non-intersections

In the non-intersection scenarios, 26 % (9/34) of the epochs included pedestrians waving at the drivers. Notably, 38 % (13/34) of the observations included drivers using a gesture to indicate their yielding to pedestrians. Of all encounters, 18 % (6/34) included mutual gestures from both drivers and pedestrians.

To solidify gesture use in these conditions with an example, we described a jaywalking situation in a non-intersection scenario (see Figure 2.1). The scenario takes place on a busy urban road where cars have the right of way over pedestrians. The driver appears following a line of cars ahead, approaching a red traffic light. It is snowing, and the pedestrian on the left (#1) is wearing a hooded winter jacket, somewhat restricting their field of view. The driver starts braking to match slower-moving traffic and takes time to observe the surrounding scene. The driver first sees the waiting pedestrian (#2) wearing a cap in front of the white taxi parked on the right. Consequently, the driver waves at the pedestrian (#2) on the right to indicate yielding right of way to allow crossing. At the same time, on the left, the other pedestrian (#1) appears to have started to walk in

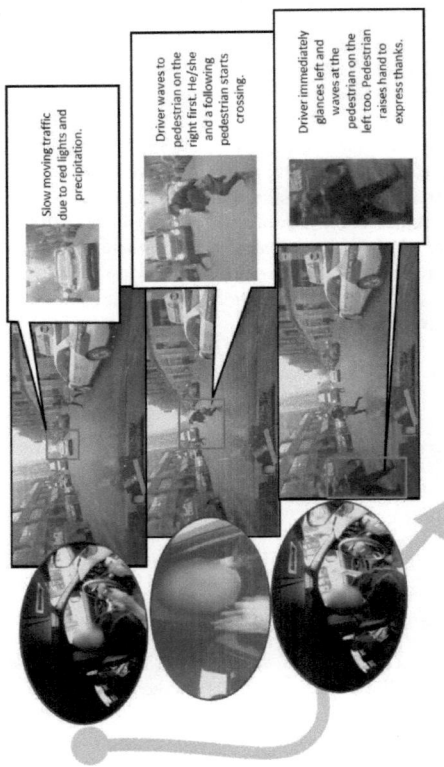

Figure 2.1: Driver waving and yielding the right of way to jaywalking pedestrians. [Source: Advance Vehicle Technology (AVT) Consortium Dataset, https://avt. mit.edu/]

the direction of traffic and then decides to wait for an indication of the right of way. After waving to the pedestrian (#2) on the right, the driver turns to the left to check on the status of the other pedestrian (#1) and waves to signal yielding. In return, the pedestrian (#1) on the left sends a soft hand raise to express gratitude. Simultaneously, a third pedestrian (#3) further ahead also starts crossing, perhaps seeing that the driver has yielded to other pedestrians, clearing the way for safe passage. Although the driver has enough space to pull forward and stop right after the crossroad, still chooses to let the pedestrians cross. Perhaps a courtesy or managing risks in a traffic situation that appears somewhat unstable. In this context, the driver acting as a considerate road user does not take on much effort or time yielding to the multiple vulnerable road users. After all three pedestrians finish crossing, the driver closes the gap without obstructing the crossroad and waits for traffic lights to turn green. Lastly, a truck driver indicating a left turn on the opposite lane waits for all pedestrians and the driver before making any movement.

Conflict Resolution and Gratitude in Unprotected Crossings

Across all unprotected pedestrian crossing scenarios, 34 % (17/50) of the epochs included pedestrians waving at drivers, and 32 % (16/50) of the epochs contained a driver gesture. Of all these epochs, 16 % (8/50) included mutual gestures by drivers and pedestrians.

A second case illustrates other uses of driver gestures (see Figure 2.2). In this example, the driver approaches an unprotected pedestrian crossing on a two-way road on a cloudy day. In the oncoming lane, a car stops for a crossing pedestrian (#1) on the left. The pedestrian (#1) thanks the other car by raising their hand. As the pedestrian (#1) starts crossing, another pedestrian (#2) on the opposite side (right of the driver) attempts to initiate crossing. This pedestrian (#2) seems unsure about moving into the lane of travel and steps backward. Perhaps, the driver's deceleration for the crossing pedestrian (#1) (on the left) does not seem slow enough. Seeing the uncertainty, the driver first waves at the pedestrian (#1) to the left and then to the hesitating pedestrian (#2) on the right side. Upon these reassuring gestures, both pedestrians, as well as a third pedestrian (#3) (entering from the left), cross the street by checking their smartphones (#1 and #2) or by talking on the phone (#3), indicative of established trust. Once the three pedestrians have moved out of the road the driver begins to accelerate.

Where Formal Rules and Vehicle Locomotion Suffice: Stop Indicators

Pedestrians waved at drivers in 17 % (4/23) of the stop indicator epochs. Drivers performed a gesture in 13 % (3/23) of the instances in these epochs. Lastly, mutual gesture use was observed in 9% (2/23) of the observations. In environments with well-defined traffic rules and signals, such as at crosswalks with traffic lights or stop signs, both drivers and pedestrians may rely on these signals to regulate behavior. The predictability of these rules reduces the need for additional communication, like waving, as both parties already know what to expect.

Figure 2.2: Driver waving and yielding to pedestrians at a pedestrian crossing. [Source: Advance Vehicle Technology (AVT) Consortium Dataset, https://avt. mit.edu/

Figure 2.3 depicts a rare driver gesture interaction in the presence of a stop sign. The driver is approaching a stop sign at a four-way junction on a two-way road on a rainy day. As the driver approaches the stop, a bus makes a right turn on the opposite lane. At this moment, a pedestrian with an umbrella speaking

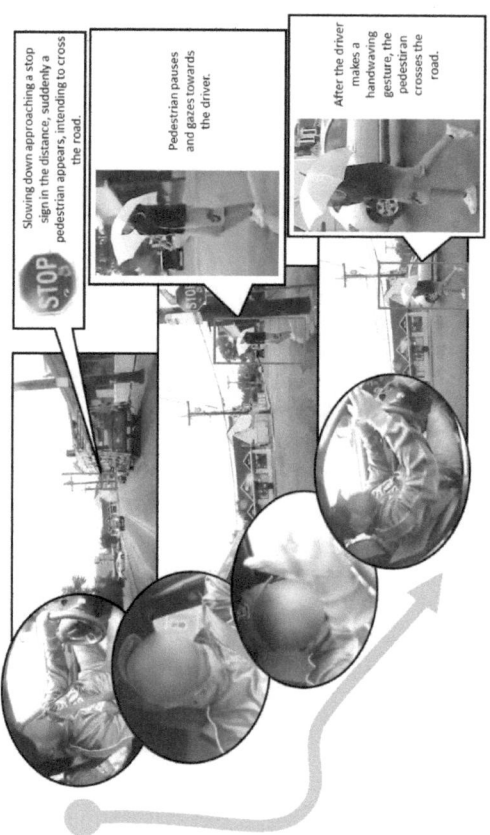

Figure 2.3: Driver stopping and waving to a pedestrian at a stop sign. [Source: Advance Vehicle Technology (AVT) Consortium Dataset, https://avt.mit.edu/

on a phone appears on the right side of the road. The pedestrian gazes towards the driver almost seemingly unaware of the stop sign or trusting that the driver will yield following traffic law. Alternatively, perhaps the crossing appears risky as the pedestrian carries an umbrella, is distracted by the phone on a rainy day, or wishes to finish the phone call. Exchanging gazes with the pedestrian, the driver waves in a manner that suggests that the pedestrian can cross. Reassured of being given the right of way, the pedestrian starts moving. Finally, the driver visually scans the surroundings and proceeds to drive after the stop.

2.1.5 Discussion

The current section elaborates on findings regarding gesture use in different ambiguous traffic situations, and it continues with their implications on AV-human interaction research. Lastly, it touches upon limitations and future directions.

From Clear to Ambiguous Traffic Scenarios

Upon reviewing three different traffic conditions, as the literature would suggest stop indicators appear to provide structure to the traffic flow while still allowing for communications between road users. Stop signs, traffic lights, and pedestrian lights help encourage drivers to yield to other road users[1]. As formal rules indicate the right of way, there is less dependency on negotiation in these situations. Since the use of stop indicators usually contains safety-critical areas with enforcement mechanisms, drivers are encouraged to follow the rules and yield to the moving traffic or pedestrians. In line with this, we observed in our study that drivers rarely use gestures in these situations. When they do choose to use gestures they tend to use them in the last seconds before arrival. This may have to do with an intent to clarify the ambiguity of deceleration, an expectation that a pedestrian could not see them earlier, or other factors such as a lack of perceived benefit of gestures in the presence of stop indicators until observing a pedestrian exhibiting signs (e.g., distraction by phone, etc.) of confusion or slow response. In essence, some assessment of ambiguity encourages a more overt expression of intentions as illustrated in Figure 2.3.

Regarding unprotected crossings, according to General Laws of Commonwealth of Massachusetts Part I Title XIV, Chapter 89, Section 11[2], if the pedestrian is on the same side of the road that the vehicle is traveling on, or if the pedestrian comes within about 3 meters of the side of the road where the vehicle is traveling, the driver must slow down or stop to allow the pedestrian to cross safely. Attention to such a statute may not dictate all drivers' behaviors. Regardless, an approaching driver should calculate an approximation of pedestrian distance in the event of an unprotected crossing to assess who has the right of way and yield if appropriate. Even with the effort to disambiguate the right of way by laws, it is likely that social norms and the behavior of drivers and pedestrians play a role in deciding who has the right of way on a more situational basis [DLT+20]. This type of

---

[1]   https://malegislature.gov/Laws/GeneralLaws/PartI/TitleXIV/Chapter89/Section9,[Online; accessed 15-August-2023]

[2]   https://malegislature.gov/Laws/GeneralLaws/PartI/TitleXIV/Chapter89/Section11,[Online; accessed 15-August-2023]

communication space calls for interdependence and explicit negotiation to assign or indicate the right of way to oneself or other road users.

Non-intersection scenarios seem to contain the most ambiguity due to unexpected pedestrian movements or lack of clear regulations (i.e. parking lots). In these situations, explicit interaction-requiring instances usually occur when pedestrians deviate from expectations, such as crossing by jaywalking. Such instances demand a new and perhaps dynamically created set of rules to be established between both sides. In a substantive number of cases, this seems to occur with explicit interaction as opposed to primarily vehicle kinematics as described in Terwilliger et al. [TGS+19].

In conclusion, the surrounding traffic environment and the clarity of roles in pedestrian-driver interactions likely reduce the need for prosocial gestures in many situations. When traffic rules and signals provide clear guidance, both drivers and pedestrians may not feel the need to engage in additional communication, resulting in the low frequency of observed gestures. However, in more ambiguous or less regulated interactions, prosocial behaviors could play a more critical role in ensuring safety and mutual understanding.

To Gesture or Not to Gesture? Situation Defines Frequency and Function

Different frequencies of gesture use were observed by pedestrians and drivers in scenarios with different levels of ambiguity. The role of these gestures appears to be situation and role-dependent. In scenarios like those described, drivers used gestures to redefine priority rules and provide pedestrians a clear indication of the right of way. In this regard, a gesture is meant to function as a conflict resolution and increase efficiency by resolving the ambiguity faster with explicit interaction. Hence, both drivers and pedestrians could continue on their trajectory without further delay. Pedestrians and drivers often exchange waves expressing gratitude for being given the right of way. For drivers, both non-intersections and unprotected crossings explicit gestures were observed over 30 % of the time. This may indicate that, as the negotiating party with less vulnerability, drivers use gestures in these situations to clarify their intention to yield the right of way. For pedestrians, unprotected crossings seem to increase gesture use for expressing gratitude even more than non-intersections. Contrary to our findings, we expected the largest amount of gratitude gestures in non-intersections as pedestrians did not by "default" have the right of way in these situations. Slightly decreased pedestrian gesture use in non-intersections could be a byproduct of the safety-critical situation of jaywalking scenarios or a bias to the type of individual who chooses to cross in such conditions. Alternatively, pedestrians prefer to quickly cross so as not to obstruct the traffic in non-intersections leaving less lingering attention to social gestures. In unprotected crossings, however, they might feel more secure and take their time crossing, which might increase the flexibility for expressing gratitude.

Results show fine-grained details around the use of gestures in vehicle-pedestrian interactions in situations with different levels of ambiguity. In all cases, drivers eventually yielded to pedestrians. Observations suggest that in some conditions, the use of gestures appears higher than what has been reported in previous studies [LMG+21, DT17]. However, results may still largely corroborate with existing literature as gesture use does not appear to be the primary way of interaction around space-sharing resolution in traffic [DT17, RKT17a]. It's plausible that as situations become more ambiguous, reliance on solely kinematic cues decreases, and individuals' use of gestures increases to resolve conflicts or to express prosocial behavior [SMS+21]. To our knowledge, no previous work has classified traffic situations according to their ambiguity and proportions of gesture use.

Cultural differences, data collection methods, and dataset specificity may likely contribute to differences in gesture use observed in this work as compared to previous studies. Cultural differences result in different social norms in traffic [LMG+21], for instance, it is plausible that drivers in the greater Boston area might be engaging with pedestrians by using gestures more often than drivers in Europe (i.e. [DT17, LMG+21]). Since observations were based on systematic video from three different synchronized perspectives annotation and analytical efforts may have focused on more minute gestures than have been reported in earlier work. The aforementioned observational studies largely relying on the third-person perspective video footage may not easily capture some interaction occurrences. Finally, while this case study provides robust documentation of gestures it only considers drivers yielding to pedestrians. How gestures are used in other types of interactions is an area of future work.

Analytical efforts of Domeyer et al. [DLT+20] appear to provide a key comparison point for the current study. Drawing upon the same dataset, Domeyer et al. [DLT+20] suggest that unprotected crossings are the scenario requiring the most mutual action and interdependency. Our results were in line with these findings. However, Domeyer et al. [DLT+20] also suggest that non-intersection scenarios were practically "noninteractions". Our results regarding explicit communication suggest the opposite in this case. Drivers use the most gestures in non-intersections and pedestrians often use gestures to thank them in non-intersections. As Domeyer et al. [DLT+20] suggest, integrating both explicit and implicit interaction cues in a single model may reveal a better approximation of interdependency between drivers and pedestrians in these situations.

Limitations and Future Directions

As this work was performed on a naturalistic driving dataset it did not have a homogeneous distribution of traffic conditions across drivers. The work considers an unequal number of conditions and as such we opted for a qualitative analysis approach to gain meaningful results from the available data and only reported descriptive statistics of explicit gesture use in different scenarios to illustrate potential trends in the data. We consider this study as an ethnographic case study among drivers in the greater Boston area and believe that the findings shed new light on the importance of human-human interaction in different roadway scenarios by dissecting the fluidity of motions and behaviors between drivers and pedestrians. In this sense, road situations belonging to the same category were similar. Yet, each scenario is unique with a specific location in space and unique communication between two road users.

Despite limitations, it is believed that natural recordings allowing for scientific considerations of observed roadway behavior are valuable resources [RT18b]. These examples and qualitative insights derived in this work provide new valuable contributions to the literature as few efforts have systematically assessed naturalistic driver and pedestrian gesture use. In future steps, an interplay between explicit gestures and implicit kinematic cues can be investigated to reveal how these communication channels influence each other and work together in the fluidity of the actions.

Lastly, our analysis is based initially on the probing of driver and pedestrian gestures. Our results begin to provide the insight needed to contribute to the design of AV-human interaction. Future regulations and cultural changes may also greatly affect how people perceive and interact with AVs. Doing a natural observation in a systematically collected naturalistic dataset between self-driving vehicles and human road users may be an opportunity to draw out more specific insights regarding AV-human interaction and the use of or lack of gestures in encounters.

2.1.6 Conclusion

This research explored the frequency of driver and pedestrian gesture use in roadway scenarios with different levels of ambiguity through qualitative video observation of natural driving recordings and the development of case studies. The systematically collected dataset enabled us to observe the interrelated details of the vehicle interior and external view recording pedestrians and the road environment. Results highlighted the change in frequency of gesture use in different scenarios the relationship to roadway ambiguity and the change in function of gesture use dependent on the role of the road user. Consequently, we found that drivers tend to use gestures to resolve conflicts, especially in non-intersection scenarios where pedestrians either jaywalk or are in a parking lot. Furthermore, we realized that pedestrians use gestures to thank drivers mostly in unprotected pedestrian crossings where they have more suitable conditions for social interaction. These insights not only highlight the social norms of human-to-human interaction in today's road environment but also point out in which daily traffic scenarios self-driving vehicles may need to communicate beyond locomotion cues to resolve space-sharing conflicts.

2.2   Quantifying Perception of Social Behavior

After running focus groups and natural driving video observation studies, we concluded that social behavior is a part of daily traffic. Yet the current research stage does not possess a quantifiable metric to work on the social perception of road users including non-human traffic participants. Hence, we addressed this gap and took the challenge to create our metric to measure the situational social perception of road users. The current section unfolds the stages of scale creation and validation process, finishing with a discussion of findings.

2.2.1   Motivation and Related Work

This section provides background on relevant research regarding the essentials of prosocial behavior in general and in the traffic context that is not covered in the thesis introduction (see Section 1.3), followed by former approaches to measuring social behavior in traffic with self-assessment tools.

Prosocial behavior requires an interpersonal dynamic and different forms of acts. Volunteering, helping, and cooperation encapsulate the essence of such behavior [SG15]. Any prosocial act needs to be interpreted in its social context by judging the effect of the action on the recipient/s [DPSP17]. Hence, situational factors and the outcome of prosocial intentions become essential in the perception of prosocial behavior. Seeking an answer to the question "Why do individuals help?" has led to several evolutionary and social development theories. For instance, Batson [Bat10] introduced the empathy-altruism hypothesis to explain the underlying cognitive mechanisms for acting prosocial and helping others. Batson suggested that the first step of acting prosocial is establishing empathy with the recipient, which is followed by the helper evaluating the recipient's magnitude of the need. As the perceived need for help increases, the chances of helping the recipient will also increase [Bat10]. An alternative model of explaining prosocial behavior was raised by Piliavin et al. [P+81]. Their arousal: cost-reward model starts with physiological arousal in the form of distress after a helper sees a recipient in need. Accordingly, the helper chooses to act prosocial to release their distress. However, the helper also weighs the costs and benefits of helping the recipient. The lower cost of helping the individual and the higher cost of the recipient not receiving help increases the chances of acting prosocial [P+81].

Prosocial and aggressive behavior in traffic have been investigated in several previous works. Harris et al. [HHV+14] defined prosocial behavior in traffic as the act of safe driving that will protect road users, including drivers themselves, pedestrians, cyclists, and other motorized road users. This way, the authors suggested that effective cooperation among road users can be established. To understand the essence of social norms in traffic, Eckoldt et al. [EHL+16] conducted an online study asking participants for examples of their experience with positive, negative, and prosocial behavior in traffic from the recipient and helper perspectives. They found that giving the right of way to a pedestrian was a common answer to prosocial behavior experiences. Furthermore, Sikkenk and Terken [ST15] investigated under which conditions individuals were more willing to give their right of way to vulnerable road users such as an elderly lady or a mother and a child. Their survey revealed that the personal driving style and vulnerability of the recipient influenced individuals' driving decisions.

There have been attempts to foster prosocial driving behavior with storytelling and norm-activation [Sch77] by providing positive feedback. Knobel et al. [KHM+13] introduced a gentleman character to nudge drivers to act more prosocial with pleasure. They reported positive comments and increased motivation from the drivers who tested the system. With a similar attempt, Wang et al. [WTHR16] suggested utilizing like and dislike icons for elevating driver-to-driver interaction and establishing a social behavior feedback mechanism. To carry the body of prosocial behavior research in future mixed traffic where humans and AVs coexist in the same interaction space, Sadeghian et al. [SHE20a] tested how prosocial AVs were perceived when they indicate communication cues in different traffic scenarios and in the presence of different vulnerable road users. Expressing different degrees of politeness via communication cues in fostering prosocial behavior towards AVs was also investigated in an intercultural study. In their study, Lanzer et al. [LBY+20] found that polite communication cues increased the acceptance and trust of AVs in Chinese and German samples. Additionally, the effect of bidirectional communication in the context of pedestrians and AVs has been evaluated. Colley et al. [CBR21] found that if the AV acknowledges and thanks for a wave gesture of the pedestrian to let the AV pass, this is seen as positive and leads to improved perceived intelligence. Some related work also indicates that pedestrians will cross in front of AVs despite it communicating not to stop [CBR22b]. This shows that fostering prosocial behavior in traffic against aggressive behavior is a worthy effort to pursue in order to have a better traffic experience for all in future mixed traffic.

Measuring Social Behavior in Traffic

There are existing **self-evaluation** tools for measuring social behavior in traffic. One of the early examples is the Driver Behavior Questionnaire (DBQ) [RMS+90], which is based on the theoretical framework of "generic error modeling system" [Rea90] and measures self-assessment of aberrant driving behavior (lapses, errors, violations) with 50 items. While it has been proven to be a reliable tool in accident risk prediction, it does not capture other behavioral components, such as attitudes and emotions. To address these limitations, Taubman-Ben-Ari et al. [TBAMG04] suggested the Multidimensional Driving Style Inventory (MDSI), a multidimensional omnibus measure of driving style capturing behaviors, attitudes, and emotions. Yet, this scale has the same theoretical basis as the DBQ and is, as such, rather focused on errors and negative aspects of driving. Examples of other scales that mainly capture such aspects of driving are the Driver's Stress Profile (DSP) [Lar96], Driving Anger Scale (DAS) [DOL94], Driving Behaviour Inventory (DBI)[GMG+89, GDM+93], Aggressive Driving Behavior Scale (ADBS) [HHN03], and Drivers' Attitudes of Right-of-way Questionnaire (DARQ) [HMC23].

In more detail, the DSP scale captures four broad dimensions with 10 items each: competition, anger, impatience, and punishment. The DAS captures situation-specific anger and, therefore measures how angry drivers feel in 14 situations when they encounter hostile gestures and discourtesy, illegal or slow driving examples, and other situations where drivers may feel and express anger. The DBI assesses psychological components of driver stress and consequent driving performance, determined through interactive effects of driver's assessment of traffic demands, appraisal of personal competence, and selection of behavioral strategies to cope with stress. The ADBS is an 11-item scale that includes hostility, hyper-competitiveness, and aggressive driving-related thoughts and emotions as measures. The DARQ is a tool for self-evaluating drivers' negative right-of-way attitudes using three dimensions: cognition, behavioral tendency, and emotion. Notably, attitudes measured with the DARQ are believed to be good predictors of prosocial and aggressive driving behaviors. The higher the correctness of drivers' right-of-way attitudes, the higher the level of prosocial driving behavior and the lower level of aggressive driving behavior [HMC23].

To fill the gap by measuring positive driver behaviors, Özkan and Lajunen [ÖL05] suggested the Positive Driver Behavior Scale (PDBS), emphasizing the importance of considering not only what drivers did in traffic but also what drivers intended to do in traffic. It is a self-assessment 14-item scale that captures positive driver behaviors that are not necessarily associated with coded traffic rules or safety practices (e.g., caring for the road environment, helping other road users, being polite, etc.). In addition, there are existing measurement tools that serve as a self-evaluation for both prosocial and aggressive driving behavior. For instance, Harris et al. [HHV+14] developed the Prosocial and Aggressive Driving Inventory (PADI) to enable drivers to report their own driving behavior in two opposite dimensions: safe (prosocial, measured by 17 items) and unsafe (aggressive, measured by 12 items). Furthermore, Ward et al. [WFO+20] created a questionnaire specialized in self-evaluation of driver's behavior towards cyclists. Similar to PADI, this questionnaire contained prosocial and aggressive driving statements in its items to be provided as a self-assessment tool for drivers.

Not only the driver, but also pedestrian behaviors were put in focus in previous research. Notably, the most frequently used scales for self-evaluation of pedestrian behavior are based, or inspired, by the corresponding scales for driver behavior (see Vandroux et al. [VGJ+22] for a more detailed review). The Scale of Pedestrian Behavior (SPB) [MD97] was based on the DBQ and captured the same dimensions: lapses, errors, and violations. After being used in several studies, this scale was further developed by Granié et al. [GPG13] into the Pedestrian

Behavior Scale (PBS), capturing 5 dimensions of pedestrian behavior: violations, errors, lapses, aggressive behaviors, and positive behaviors. In its original form, the PBS consisted of 40 items. However, a shorter version consisting of 23 items was also developed. This scale is widely used today in research on pedestrian behaviors (e.g., [DSD+17]), including a study on interactions between cyclists and AVs [NVVF+20]. Another example of a self-evaluation scale for pedestrian behaviors is the Pedestrian Behavior Questionnaire (PBQ) [DSD+17], which is a slight modification of PBS and consists of 23 items. Since its introduction in the USA, PBQ has been used across the globe (e.g., in China, Mexico, the UK, Kenya, and Thailand). In addition, it has served as the basis for the Pedestrian Receptivity Questionnaire for Fully AVs (PRQF) [DSD+17], which consists of three dimensions: safety, interaction, and compatibility. Not only behavior-related questionnaires but also other types of evaluation tools were used for measuring social behavior in traffic. For instance, Sadeghian et al. [SHE20a] explored how different traffic scenarios and different road user roles affect the perception of prosocial interaction by using the Traffic Climate questionnaire [SRE+19]. Schwarting et al. [SPAM+19] utilized the Social Value Orientation (SVO) Questionnaire for how the social behavior of AVs can be shaped in different traffic situations. SVO is developed as a slider measure to allocate resources between oneself and others and derive individuals' competitiveness, altruism, prosocialness, and individualism [MAH11].

In summary, many scales mainly address drivers and driver behavior which limits their use in a single road user perspective. Furthermore, the majority of the existing metrics are formed with general statements that restrict their use in various experimental designs with **situational differences** such as if another road user expresses road rage, or if the person is under time pressure. Moreover, items with self-assessment statements reveal what type of road user characteristics one has, rather than helping to dissect how individuals perceive the social behavior of other road users in specific circumstances. In other words, the aforementioned tools are not tailored for situation specificity of other person perceptions [Pat11] that would be essential for understanding how individuals perceive the social behavior of others in different situations. Since these scales can not be utilized to evaluate how **other** human and non-human road users are perceived socially in specific situations, we decided to develop "SPAT", Situational Prosocial and Aggressive Behavior Perception in Traffic Scale, a novel measurement instrument without the aforementioned limitations. Even though our initial aim was to create a quantifiable metric for evaluating social perception of AVs, we believe SPAT will be useful in many different combinations of road user interactions in the future (i.e. cyclist - delivery robot; driver - e-scooter rider; pedestrian - cyclist, or even self-evaluation under different situations).

2.2.2 Creation of SPAT

The creation and evaluation of SPAT followed a multistep process. In total, the creation process involved one workshop, several group meetings and external meetings with statistical and linguist experts, a pre-study with different participants, and an online vignette survey (see Figure 2.4). The evaluation included construct and external validation of SPAT by running a confirmatory factor analysis and using the scale in another experiment with different conditions. Generally, we followed the suggestions described by Boateng et al. [BNF+18] for the creation and evaluation of the new scale. **In overview**, we started with *item development* in group and linguist meetings, which aimed at the identification of the domain, item generation, and content validation. We then continued with the *scale development* step by applying a pre-testing of questions in terms of their clarity and validation of ground truth scenarios which represent very prosocial and aggressive traffic situations with 11 participants. Then, we released a large online survey and discussed item reduction and factor extraction steps with a statistical expert. Furthermore, we tested factorial validity by running a confirmatory factor analysis as the first step of *scale evaluation*. Finally, we tested the external validity of the scale under different experimental conditions and contexts to investigate whether the scale can be generalized to measure the social behavior perception of road users not only in tested scenarios but also in other traffic situations. Details are described in the following sections.

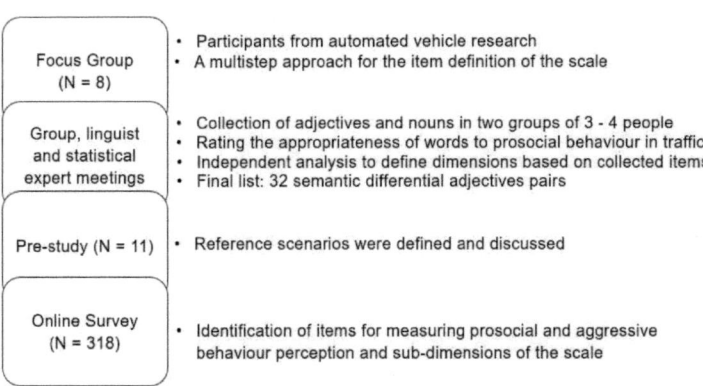

Figure 2.4: Overview of methodology: (1) one focus group, (2) several group meetings and external meetings with statistical and linguist experts, (3) a pre-study with different participants, and (4) an online vignette survey.

Focus Group, Expert Meetings and Pre-study

Firstly, we conducted a workshop [SMS+21], which aimed at discussing individual experiences of prosocial behavior in traffic, defining the key features of prosocial behavior in traffic with examples, exploring new interaction paradigms to support prosocial behavior in traffic (scenarios and measurements), exploring the behavior of prosocial AVs of the future, and defining new interaction paradigms to evaluate prosocial interaction between AVs and humans. In the workshop, eight participants working in the area of automated vehicle research discussed the above-mentioned topics. A need for a quantifiable evaluation of situational evaluation of prosocial behavior in traffic was raised as one of the results of the workshop.

Based on the workshop outcomes, we followed a multistep approach for the item definition of the new scale we aimed to create (see Figure 2.4). After discussing different definitions of prosociality, the first group meeting involved collecting as many words as possible in two groups of three and four people. The collected words were recorded for each group for future reference. Following the word collection, both groups engaged in independent analysis to define potential factors or dimensions based on the collected words. Afterward, the results were shared with the other group. Each group presented their results during this phase and elaborated on their findings. The whole group then discussed the findings, with the aim of identifying similarities and differences in the results. The initial list included 44 nouns and 75 adjectives. Then, the top 5 suggestions from Power Thesaurus [3] were added to the list for each word. After that, we rated the appropriateness of all words to prosocial behavior in traffic on a 7-point Likert scale (1 = "not related at all" to 7 = "very related"). Words with a mean lower than 4 were excluded. Before the next step, for the versatility advantage, a consensus on forming the items in semantic differentials using positive and negative polars of adjectives was reached. Hence, we pre-clustered the words, and all words were converted to positive and negative adjective pairs using OpenAI Playground with GPT-3 [4], which yielded more consistent outcomes than manual-formation of the pairs. Then, we consulted with a linguist expert who is a professional skills trainer (English for Academic and Professional Purposes for 13 years). In the first meeting, some of the repetitive words were removed by the expert. The shortened list was sent to 23 respondents, including us and our colleagues, for a short evaluation round of the item pairs in terms of their relatedness to prosocial and aggressive behavior in traffic. Thereafter, 65 items scored on average 4 and above regarding their appropriateness to the topic were re-discussed with the language expert. Less appropriate items, according to the expert's suggestions and our suggestions were removed. Lastly, 32 items were shortlisted as the items to be evaluated for the scale. These items were semantic differentials, therefore

---

[3] https://www.powerthesaurus.org/
[4] https://platform.openai.com/playground

showing adjective antonyms in each item (e.g., cautious — reckless) (see Table 2.2 for the item set).

Figure 2.5: Scenarios are categorized as prosocial and aggressive on the horizontal axis and participant perspectives are divided on the vertical axis. Scenario 1: Prosocial Driver yielding the right of way to the participant from the pedestrians' perspective. Scenario 2: Aggressive driver taking the right of way of the participant at a pedestrian crossing. Scenario 3: A prosocial pedestrian yielding the right of way to the participant from the driver's perspective. Scenario 4: An aggressive pedestrian attempting to annoy the participant in the driver's perspective.

Afterward, reference scenarios were defined and discussed. Then, we ran a pre-study with eleven participants (Age: $M = 26.24$, $SD = 5.32$; driving experience in years: $M = 5.82$, $SD = 4.81$). In this study, participants were given a pilot version of the online survey, and they followed the instructions to evaluate the behavior of the described road user with listed items. They were interviewed to assess the clarity of the instructions and the items. None of them reported confusion regarding the shortlisted items or the instructions. Furthermore, they were asked to evaluate how prosocial or aggressive each scenario was according to their views, and how to increase prosocial or aggressive perception of the situations. Upon their suggestions, we refined and finalized highly prosocial and aggressive behavior scenarios to be used in the large survey. These ground truth scenarios included a pedestrian perspective interacting with an aggressive driver, a pedestrian perspective interacting with a prosocial driver, a driver perspective encountering a prosocial pedestrian, and, a driver perspective interacting with an aggressive pedestrian (see Figure 2.5). The motivation for using ground truth scenarios is to ensure that item loadings are indicative of factors that explain prosocial or aggressive behavior. Then, more vague conditions in a different experimental setup between automated vehicles and human drivers were utilized to test the validity of the scale which would indicate its sensitivity to reveal social perception differences in various situations beyond ground truth scenarios (Section 2.2.3). Each ground truth scenario followed the descriptions below:

- Scenario 1: "Imagine you are a pedestrian, and you want to cross the street at a place where there aren't any traffic lights or a pedestrian crossing. It is raining heavily, and you are getting wet because you do not have an umbrella. You need to run across the road to the shelter. However, you cannot immediately cross the road because a car is approaching. There is no other traffic on the road, but you have to wait until the car - which has the right of way - has passed. Yet, the driver of the car slows down, stops, and lets you cross the road first with a smiling face."

- Scenario 2: "Imagine you are a pedestrian and want to cross the street at a pedestrian crossing. You would have the right of way. But an approaching car honks, revs its engines, and accelerates, even though the driver clearly sees you, and prevents you from crossing the street. It is a very rainy day and the driver splashes you with a puddle of muddy water. As the car passes by, you notice that the driver and the passenger look at you mockingly as they enjoy the loud music in their car."

- Scenario 3: "Imagine you are driving a car in a city center, stopping at a zebra crossing. As this street is crossed by many people, you have already spent some time waiting. A single pedestrian approaches the crossing when you finally think you can continue driving. The pedestrian acknowledges that you have already waited, gives you their right of way, and steps back to allow you to pass."

- Scenario 4: "Imagine you are driving a car in a city center, stopping at a zebra crossing. As this street is crossed by many people, you have already spent some time waiting. A single pedestrian approaches the crossing when you finally think you can continue driving. Although the pedestrian has seen you waiting for quite some time, they insist on their right of way and cross. They walk extra slowly with the clear intention of annoying you."

Finally, we conducted an online vignette [AB14, AS10] study with 318 participants from `prolific.co` that were pre-selected from the US to control the effect of cultural biases in a single culture.

Online Vignette Survey Overview

An online within-subject vignette survey was conducted to evaluate SPAT, intended to measure the perceived social behavior of any road user, including pedestrians, drivers, cyclists, and AVs. Ethical approval was given by the ethics committee of the host institution. The study aimed to identify suitable items for measuring prosocial and aggressive behavior and to establish the factorial structure of the scale. It is worth noting that we did not have theoretically predefined facets of prosocial and aggressive behavior, so an exploratory factor analysis was appropriate at the first stage. Participants were asked to evaluate fictional situations (i.e., this was a fixed-situation design). Content analysis and appropriate statistical methodologies were employed to select items judiciously. An exploratory factor analysis was performed to investigate the number of dimensions that can be discerned. This was performed on 50% of the sample, created by randomly splitting the measured sample into two parts. Afterward, a confirmatory factor analysis cross-validated the suggested factorial structure on an independent sample (second half after split). Lastly, a separate test track experiment in the form of a bottleneck traffic scenario was employed to evaluate the external validity of the scale (see Section 2.2.3).

Sample

318 participants from the USA (Age: $M = 41.6$, $SD = 14.2$, range: [19, 80]; Gender: 154 F, 153 M, 10 Non-binary, 1 Prefer not to tell) took part in the online survey. On average, they have had a driving license for 11.10 years ($SD = 15.65$) and they spend 2.48 hours ($SD = 6.07$) on daily travel including walking, cycling, driving, and public transport. Participants were compensated with \$7.25 per hour. Most of them drove their cars either every day or multiple times a week. All participants had a high proficiency of the English language (B2 = 4, C1 = 12, C2 = 302). They volunteered to participate in the survey from Prolific database, where their demographics matched the requested sample in the survey.

Procedure

The online survey was implemented via LimeSurvey and `prolific.co`. Participants could participate in the study through a computer, laptop, or tablet. At the onset, participants were greeted and provided with information regarding the survey's duration and methodology. Upon giving consent, participants answered demographic questions as a first part of the survey, to ensure they met the sample criteria. Subsequently, participants were introduced to the general setting which was introduced with the following text:

"The second part of this survey evaluates a new scale measuring prosocial and aggressive behavior in everyday traffic. Please read the definitions below carefully:

Prosocial behavior in traffic is defined as acting by taking the **well-being** of **other traffic participants** into account and **promoting effective co-operation** with others, such as drivers, passengers, pedestrians, and cyclists. Acting prosocial in traffic **benefits all traffic participants** in positive ways. It also helps to resolve traffic conflicts easily. This happens, for example, when searching for parking spaces, when merging lanes *on the highway, when letting pedestrians cross the road, or when thanking someone. **Aggressive or antisocial behavior** in traffic can be defined as opposite behavioral patterns, such as **acting and driving offensively, putting other people in danger, or acting selfishly in traffic.***

In this part, we will provide you with some traffic scenarios. Please read each scenario from the beginning until the end, as some of the scenarios are similarly structured."

Then, scenarios were presented with a pseudo-randomized order of four traffic situations accompanied by descriptive images (see Figure 2.5). This means that participants saw each scenario only once in a randomized order. They were required to respond to the developed survey items, which were also presented in a pseudo-randomized order. They firstly read the instructions of how to use the scale on each page, then viewed the image description and text description of the scenario. Consequently they were asked to imagine themselves being in the scenario from the first person perspective and evaluate the behavior of the other person on the scenario by using 32 adjective pairings. Upon completion of the tasks, they were reimbursed via their platform accounts. In total, eight attention checks were added. Participants could give open feedback per situation and at the end of the survey. The survey was conducted in English and lasted approximately 15 minutes.

Data Analysis

Data analysis was conducted with R 4.2.3. All packages were up-to-date in April 2023. We employed the packages EFATools version 0.4.4 [SG20], psych version 2.3.3 [Rev19], and eRm version 1.0-2 [MH07]. The analyses of Kaiser–Meyer–Olkin (KMO $= .89$) and Bartlett's test of sphericity suggested that the data were suitable for orthogonal factor dimension ($\chi^2(496) = 3597.50$, p $< .001$) [TFU13]. In addition, the analysis was performed with Varimax rotation to facilitate the factor interpretation [BS11]. Confirmatory factor analysis was performed with the lavaan package version 0.6-16 [Ros14]. Results were visualized with semPlot version 1.1.6 [Eps15].

Results

This section describes the results of exploring and evaluating the factorial structure of SPAT. It describes statistical modeling details on the exploration and confirmation samples, which are created by a random split of the survey participants. Exploratory and confirmatory factor analysis results are described in separate subsections in the following.

Exploratory Factor Analysis

Firstly, all inverted items were reverted by multiplying the answers by -1 and adding 8. Then, each scenario evaluation was randomly split into 2, namely as exploration and confirmation samples. Each exploration sample scenario evaluation was inspected with scree tests and parallel analysis by using the factoring method weighted least square to reveal the factor structure in ordinal variables [Li16]. The scenario describing a prosocial driver yielding the right of way to the participant from the pedestrian's perspective revealed two factors. Another prosocial scenario where a pedestrian yielding the right of way to the participant from the driver's perspective indicated four factors. The scenario where an aggressive driver acted rude when participants were in the pedestrian's perspective revealed three factors. Similarly, the scenario where an aggressive pedestrian on the zebra crossing acted rudely toward the participant from the driver's perspective indicated three factors. Upon closer inspection of the factor loadings, it was observed that the scenario with a 4-factor structure had only one item loading onto one of the factors. Hence, we concluded that most of the scenarios revealed three factors. In accordance with Comrey and Lee [CL92] and Hair JR et al. [HjATB98], we defined the factor loading cutoff threshold as 0.45, which is suggested as a fair threshold for our sample size. Afterward, we ran a factor analysis with three factors for each scenario. From the items passing the cutoff value for each factor, we checked for recurring items across scenarios.

Consequently, to ensure the robustness of the items across scenarios, we retained the items with recurring loading patterns in all four scenarios. When this criteria did not reveal multiple items, we retained the items recurring in three or at least two different scenarios. As a result, we obtained the listed items in Table 2.2 for each factor. We did not have theoretically predefined expectations about the factors prior to exploratory factor analysis. Inspecting the items contributing to each factor, we reached a consensus on naming these three emerging factors as Socialness (S), Coherence (C), and Awareness (A). Items contributing to multiple factors were notated with the combination of the shortened letters (i.e., SC9 for Acceptable - Unacceptable, meaning item number 9 contributes to both socialness and coherence).

Confirmatory Factor Analysis

In total, 23 items fulfilled the above-mentioned criteria of the explorative factor analysis. These items were further inspected in the confirmation sample (see Table 2.3 for descriptive statistics). By following section 4.3.2. in Mair [Mai18], the Partial Credit Model (PCM), which can be applied to ordinal scales with unequal answer categories, was adopted to inspect item fit. The PCM was run for each factor in each scenario, followed by inspection of item fit indices based on the following criteria: If an item had low p-values in at least three scenarios and if infit and outfit t-values were beyond the +- 2 threshold, then the item

Table 2.2: Set of items and their factor loading values on each scenario

Item	Sn1			Sn2			Sn3			Sn4		
	F1	F2	F3	F1	F2	F3	F1	F2	F3	F1	F2	F3
S1 Cooperative - Competitive	0.870			0.782			0.633			0.646		
S2 Helpful - Unhelpful	0.706			0.768			0.754			0.831		
S3 Considerate - Inconsiderate	0.831			0.757			0.479			0.856		
S4 Courteous - Impolite	0.778			0.724			0.617			0.832		
S5 Prosocial - Antisocial	0.837			0.695			0.612			0.781		
S6 Supportive - Unsupportive	0.835			0.827			0.487			0.777		
SC7 Beneficial - Harmful	0.624	0.652		0.633	0.472		0.604	0.497		0.586	0.488	
SC8 Reasonable - Unreasonable	0.586	0.711		0.615	0.634		0.797			0.701	0.499	
SC9 Acceptable - Unacceptable	0.591	0.695		0.626	0.613		0.775			0.696	0.537	
SC10 Detrimental - Beneficial (i)	0.575	0.717		0.769			0.485	0.523		0.695	0.495	
C11 Reckless - Cautious (i)		0.684			0.676						0.680	
C12 Safe - Unsafe		0.803			0.638						0.604	
C13 Trustworthy Untrustworthy		0.634			0.536			0.649				
C14 Rational - Irrational		0.677			0.756						0.620	
C15 Caring - Uncaring					0.511			0.682			0.478	
CA16 Mindless - Mindful (i)		0.505			0.632	0.525					0.474	0.588
A17 Unexpected - Expected (i)			0.991						0.687			
A18 Predictable - Unpredictable			0.600						0.629			
A19 Ungrateful - Thankful (i)						0.521			0.615			
A20 Aware - Unaware						0.618						0.790
A21 Inattentive - Attentive (i)						0.753						0.805
A22 Acknowledging - Ignoring						0.798						0.717
Compliant - Non-compliant*		0.644			0.511						0.544	

(i) inverted item, *Compliant to rules - Non-compliant to rules excluded after PCM analysis. Sn1: Prosocial driver, Sn2: Antisocial driver
*Sn3: Prosocial pedestrian, Sn4: Antisocial pedestrian. F1: Socialness, F2: Coherence, F3: Awareness, Cross-loading items are excluded in further steps. Retained items are marked in **bold**.*

was removed, and PCM was repeated without the non-fitting item. Based on this criteria, only the item "compliant to rules - non-compliant to rules" was removed from the factor Coherence. Since items SC7 - SC10 and item CA16 cross-loaded on two factors, they were also excluded in further steps to optimize a simple structure. Following this procedure, 6 items from Socialness, 5 items from Coherence, and 6 items from Awareness factor were selected based on the above-mentioned statistical criteria to constitute a 17-item SPAT scale (see Appendix 5.6).

A confirmatory factor analysis was then applied to confirm the three-dimensional factor model in the confirmation sample (see path diagrams of each scenario in Figure 2.6, and appendix 5.6 figures 2, 3 and 4). For readability purposes, only Figure 2.6 with prosocial driver scenario are displayed in the main part of the section and the rest were added to the appendix. These figures include standardized factor loadings representing the relationship between latent variables, -or factors- (socialness, coherence, and awareness), and the observed variables (items). Loadings closer to 1 indicate a stronger relationship between the latent factor and the observed variable, while values closer to 0 suggest a weaker relationship. The path diagrams further indicate the loadings of the latent variables socialness, coherence, and awareness onto the higher-order latent variable perception. Values range from -1 to 1, where 1 indicates a perfect positive relationship, -1 indicates a perfect negative relationship, and 0 indicates no relationship. Lastly, the diagrams include error variances attached to observed and latent variables, capturing variability that is not explained by relationships specified in the model.

Factor loadings in the prosocial driver scenario (Scenario 1) indicated a strong relationship between factors and items, except for A17 ($\lambda = 0.40$) and A18 ($\lambda = 0.48$) in Awareness factor. All latent factors had substantial loadings onto the overall, higher order Perception factor, indicating that the commonality across all these factors can be interpreted as overall social perception ($\lambda \geq 0.94$). Aggressive driver scenario (Scenario 2) revealed strong relationships between latent factors and items, except for A20 ($\lambda = 0.34$) and A21 ($\lambda = 0.47$) in Awareness items. Coherence and Socialness lower order latent variables load onto overall Perception substantially ($\lambda \geq 0.81$), while Awareness and overall Perception relationship seemed weaker in this scenario ($\lambda = 0.58$). The third scenario, which included a prosocial pedestrian revealed strong relationships among latent factors and items except for A17 ($\lambda = 0.15$) and A18 ($\lambda = 0.28$) in Awareness factor. All latent factors load onto overall Perception positively ($\lambda \geq 0.94$). Lastly, Scenario 4, which included an aggressive pedestrian indicated strong relationships between latent factors and items except for A20 ($\lambda = 0.33$) and A21 ($\lambda = 0.46$) in Awareness factor. All latent factors load onto overall Perception positively ($\lambda \geq 0.73$).

To evaluate the fit of the confirmatory factor model for each scenario, we inspected the statistic, the Comparative Fit Index (CFI) (should be ≥ 0.95), the Root Mean Squared Error of Approximation (RMSEA) index, including 90 % CI (≤ 0.10 for upper and ≤ 0.05 for lower bound), and the Standardized Root-Mean-Square Residual (SRMR) (≤ 0.08) (see Table 2.4). These fit evaluation criteria are described in section 2.4.1., p. 44 in Mair [Mai18]. According to these criteria, each model for each scenario had good CFI values (≥ 0.974), however, none of their RMSEA upper (≥ 0.115) and lower bounds (≥ 0.087) and SRMR values (≥ 0.086) were within the proposed threshold values, indicative of poor fit. Although a 2-factor model without Awareness factor seemed to be increasing model fittings, the three-factor model was kept for the sake of preserving the theoretical breadth of the scale.

Lastly, to inspect the correlations of the factors across scenarios, we returned to the entire sample and estimated a model for each factor including each scenario (see Figure 2.7, and Appendix 5.6 Figures 5, and 6). For better readability, Figure 2.7 including the path diagram for the Socialness factor can be viewed in the main part, while the latter two are added in the appendix. The correlations between scenarios for factor Socialness were weak ($-015 \leq \lambda \leq 0.09$). Similarly, correlations between scenarios for the Coherence factor were weak ($0 \leq \lambda \leq 0.06$). Finally, weak correlations among the scenarios for factor Awareness were also observed ($-0.02 \leq \lambda \leq 0.02$). These results highlight that despite the situation specificity of the traffic scenarios that do not correlate with each other, the internal consistency of SPAT is very high and sensitive to measure social perception in various traffic scenarios we explored in the survey.

Table 2.3: Descriptive statistics of survey scenarios for overall and sub-dimensions scores

Scenarios	Composite Average	Socialness	Coherence	Awareness
Sn1	6.14 (1.51)	6.69 (0.86)	6.18 (1.36)	5.56 (1.87)
Sn2	1.75 (1.45)	1.22 (0.71)	1.30 (0.77)	2.65 (1.92)
Sn3	6.14 (1.43)	6.65 (0.76)	6.27 (1.14)	5.51 (1.86)
Sn4	2.28 (1.62)	1.55 (0.95)	2.06 (1.31)	3.19 (1.93)

Average scores and standard deviations in parentheses.

Sn1: Prosocial driver, Sn2: Antisocial driver, Sn3: Prosocial pedestrian, Sn4: Antisocial pedestrian.

Table 2.4: Confirmatory factor analysis performance measures on each scenario

Scenarios		df	p	CFI	RMSEA 90% CI lower	RMSEA 90% CI upper	SRMR
Sn1	374.216	116	0	0.99	0.105	0.132	0.099
Sn2	345.392	116	0	0.974	0.098	0.126	0.117
Sn3	302.879	116	0	0.99	0.087	0.115	0.086
Sn4	424.659	116	0	0.975	0.117	0.143	0.104

CFI: Comparative fit index, SRMR: Standardized root-mean-square residual, Sn1: Prosocial driver Sn2: Antisocial driver, Sn3: Prosocial pedestrian, Sn4: Antisocial pedestrian.

2.2.3 External Validation of SPAT

SPAT was used in an experimental study to assess its external and ecological validity. This experiment was designed as a controlled test track study. Detailed study info and other findings beyond SPAT can be found in Section 4.3. In the following sections, we present brief study details and SPAT evaluations.

Study Overview

24 participants (8 f, 16 m, age [20 - 67], $M = 30.21$, $SD = 13.44$ years) were asked to drive their own cars and pass through a naturally narrowed path with two parked cars on each side (see Figure 2.8B). As they approached a narrow path, a Wizard of Oz AV with a ghost driver [RLS+15] controlling the manually driven car (see Figure 2.8D) reached the narrow area on the opposite side. An LED matrix as an external communication interface was attached to the radiator grills of the vehicle (see Figure 2.8A). This interface either was off as a baseline condition or indicated deceleration or acceleration intention with moving bars inside or outside (see Figure 2.8C). The design of the interface was introduced to participants before the experiment began since we did not test for intuitivity, but rather behavior changes when participants knew the meaning of the message given by an AV. The ghost driver arranged her driving style to match the conditions indicated by the external interface, which was on from the beginning until the

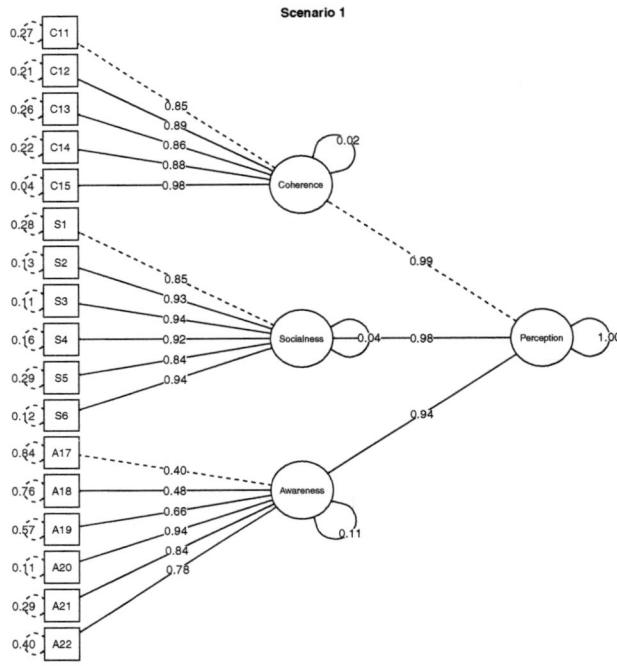

Figure 2.6: Path diagram of Scenario 1. Participant from the pedestrian's perspective encounters a prosocial driver. Items are presented as squares with their associated error variances and latent variables as circles with their associated variances and covariance (edge). The values on the arrows are the loadings.

end of the trial. Furthermore, the ghost driver observed the average speed of the participant in order to meet around the narrow area. The average speed of a ghost driver in baseline condition was 12 km/h, unless the other driver was very slow or very fast. Lastly, the ghost driver left enough time and distance to enable the participant to make the decisive move regarding who would cross the narrow path first. Consequently, participants would use SPAT (with the exploratory set of 32 items in a pseudo-randomized order) to rate how they perceived the AV socially after each of 9 pseudo-randomized encounters via a tablet (3 repetitions of 3 conditions).

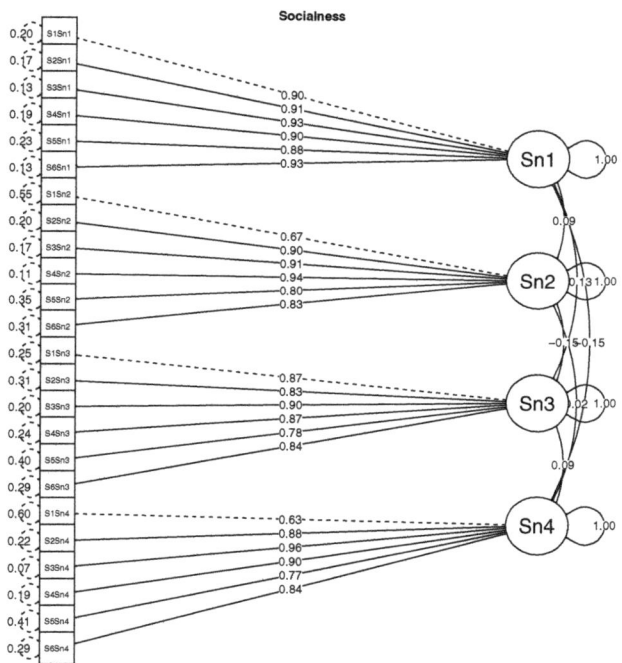

Figure 2.7: Path diagram of factor Socialness and correlations of each scenario. Items are presented as squares with their associated error variances and latent variables as circles with their associated variances and covariance (edge). The values on the arrows are the loadings. Notation example: S1Sn1 indicates item S1 from Scenario 1.

Data Analysis

SPAT evaluations regarding the AV in three different conditions were inspected with linear mixed-effects models (LMM) by using `lmer` function in R package lme4 version 1.1-27.1 [BMBW15]. Composite average SPAT scores and subdimensions were entered as the outcome variable for each model, where higher scores meant perceiving the other road user as more prosocial (items were inverted for better interpretability). The results in the following section include 17 final items. External interface conditions (eHMI Acceleration, eHMI deceleration, baseline) were added as fixed effects. Within-subject variance, sex, and age-related variability were added as random effects factors.

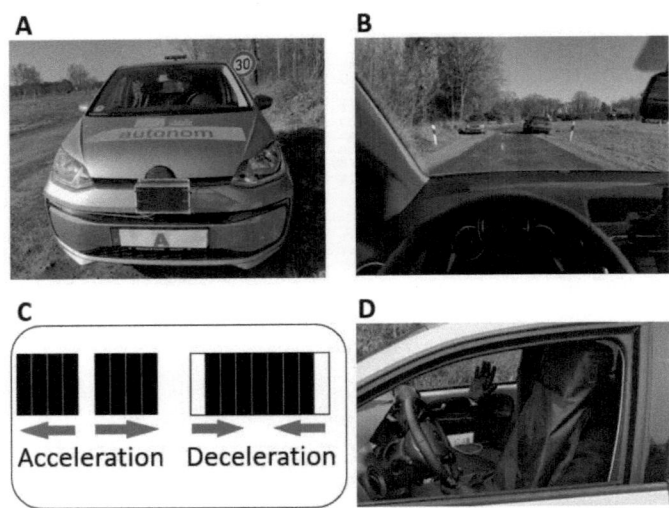

Figure 2.8: A: Wizard of Oz AV used in the study. The eHMI in the form of an LED matrix is attached above the covered license plate. **B**: Participant perspective while approaching the bottleneck scenario. **C**: Acceleration and deceleration intention cues. The white bar extends from the middle to the sides on acceleration, while it merges in the middle on deceleration intention. **D**: Ghost driver hidden under a car seat costume.

Results

Table 2.5: Driving choices and descriptive statistics of experimental conditions for each SPAT score

Conditions	# of times passed/waited	SPAT Composite Average	Socialness	Coherence	Awareness
Baseline	32/40	4.87 (0.91)	4.81 (1.05)	4.99 (0.95)	4.84 (0.82)
eHMI Acceleration	19/53	5.17 (0.70)	5.05 (0.89)	5.30 (0.73)	5.19 (0.61)
eHMI Deceleration	64/8	5.43 (0.74)	5.60 (0.76)	5.38 (0.80)	5.28 (0.84)

Average scores and standard deviations in parentheses.

The indication of deceleration intention significantly increased the probability of AV being perceived as prosocial in contrast to baseline in composite scores ($\beta = 8.70$, $t(199.98) = 3.46$, $Pr(> |t|) < .001$). However, indication of acceleration intention did not predict a meaningful change in prosocial perception compared to baseline ($\beta = 4.19$, $t(199.98) = 1.67$, $Pr(> |t|) = .09$). In line with composite scores, Socialness dimension of SPAT showed significant social perception scores when AV indicated deceleration intention ($\beta = 4.58$, $t(199.54) = 4.58$, $Pr(> |t|) <$

.001), while in acceleration intention condition, no difference compared to baseline was found ($\beta = 1.27$, $t(199.54) = 1.27$, $Pr(> |t|) = .20$). Coherence dimension of SPAT indicated that participants found the behavior of AV significantly more coherent in deceleration eHMI conditon ($\beta = 2.09$, $t(189.99) = 2.31$, $Pr(> |t|)$ $< .02$). Yet, acceleration eHMI condition did not predict a significant increase in coherence perception when compared to baseline of no indication ($\beta = 1.59$, $t(189.99) = 1.78$, $Pr(> |t|) = .076$). Lastly, compared to the baseline condition of no eHMI, AV indicating deceleration ($\beta = 2.77$, $t(200.55) = 2.93$, $Pr(> |t|)$ $< .01$) and acceleration intention via eHMI significantly increased participants' perception of AV's awareness ($\beta = 2.23$, $t(200.55) = 2.36$, $Pr(> |t|) < .05$) (see Table 2.6).

Table 2.6: Linear Mixed-Effects Model results of eHMI conditions on composite SPAT scores and SPAT sub-dimensions of Socialness, Coherence, and Awareness

Predictors	Composite Average	Socialness	Coherence	Awareness
(Intercept)	34.84 ***	17.20 ***	16.66 ***	14.23 ***
eHMI Acceleration	4.19	1.28	1.60	2.24 *
eHMI Deceleration	8.71 ***	4.58 ***	2.10 *	2.78 **
Random Effects				
σ^2	227.15	35.97	28.89	32.26
τ_{0_0} ID	0.00	0.00	0.15	0.00
τ_{0_0} age	23.93	4.83	2.40	1.03
τ_{0_0} sex	0.00	0.00	0.00	1.23
N ID	24	24	24	24
N sex	2	2	2	2
N age	17	17	17	17
Observations	216	216	216	216
Marginal r^2 / Conditional r^2	0.053 / NA	0.094 / NA	0.027 / NA	0.043 / NA

*** $p < .001$, ** $p < .01$, * $p < .05$
Note: *LMM Estimates and Random Effects are reported for composite average scores and Socialness, Coherence, and Awareness dimension scores of SPAT.*

2.2.4   Discussion

The current section incorporates how SPAT is intended to meet an emerging evaluation tool need, what its sub-dimensions reveal regarding their impact on prosocial and aggressive behavior judgment of individuals, further discussion regarding construct and external validity study, and limitations and future directions of the current study.

Situational Prosocial and Aggressive and Behavior in Traffic Scale (SPAT)

Existing social behavior in traffic scales are tailored predominantly for drivers and their general road user characteristics (i.e., DAS [DOL94], PADI [HHV+14], DBQ [RMS+90], MDSI [TBAMG04], DSP [Lar96], DBI [GMG+89], ADBS [HHN03],

DARQ [HMC23]). Sometimes they are developed for pedestrians (i.e., PBS [GPG13], PBQ [DSD+17], SBP [MD97]) and cyclists [WFO+20]. As specific and useful as they are when these tools are used according to their purpose, they seem to have three drawbacks that limit their usability in evaluating the social behavior of others in traffic.

Firstly, these evaluation tools help self-assessment of the social behavior of traffic participants from a general perspective, using them in experiments with different social conditions would not be ideal in revealing situational differences among traffic conditions being investigated. For instance, if a person answers a set of self-assessment questions regarding their overall driving characteristics under different traffic situations (i.e. driving on the highway or in slow-moving traffic), they would be expected to answer these questions similarly as the tool is developed for revealing general driving style tendencies. However, in certain situations (i.e. if they are in a hurry, or if another driver expresses road rage), individuals might be deviating from their usual driving characteristics. Hence, a requirement for a situational assessment of social behavior in traffic has emerged in our work [SMS+21]. SPAT is aimed to be used as an assessment tool for revealing such situational differences in traffic in terms of the social perception of road users. Therefore, individuals' social receptivity to behavioral or vehicle design-related changes could be evaluated in different traffic situations.

Secondly, a large body of the existing scales are designed as self-assessment tools such as all the aforementioned ones, and these scales are not developed to be used for understanding how individuals perceive another road user's behavior in its social context. For this reason, SPAT is intentionally developed as a scale with semantic differential items (i.e. reckless — cautious) in order to abstain from using statements in the first-person singular such as 'I find cyclists as reckless when they cut in front of me'. This way, SPAT could be used for evaluating other users' prosocial or aggressive behavior from an individual's perspective.

Thirdly, with the development of micromobility, we could foresee that an expansion of traffic participant perspectives beyond drivers, pedestrians, and cyclists in social behavior evaluation tools will be essential. Hence, an inclusive assessment tool that could be suitable for any road user perspective would bring a lot of ease to the current body of research evaluating social behavior in traffic. By formulating the items as adjectives and not using specific statements such as 'Cyclists who cut in front of other people are reckless.', we did not contain the use of the scale for specific road users and widened its use cases. Therefore, the versatility of SPAT even enabled us to assess how individuals perceive the social behavior of a non-human traffic participant, an AV.

Key Ingredients for Prosocial Perception in Traffic: Socialness, Coherence, and Awareness

Upon closer inspection of where perceptual differences regarding the social behavior of other road users stem from, SPAT revealed three factors. Accordingly, the general social outlook of the road users, coherence -or rationality- of their behavior, and awareness regarding the impact of their actions on the situation help individuals to set their judgments on the prosocial and aggressive behavior of other road users in traffic.

Socialness

We could observe that social qualities such as being cooperative and helpful play a key role in the social judgments of individuals even in a strictly formally regulated social space, in traffic. This should not come as a surprise to researchers working on this topic, as it has been accepted that traffic is a social domain [BBV23] even though it is mainly regulated by formal rules. Social cues such as eye contact, gestures, and verbal communication are a part of everyday traffic, especially when the rules become vague or situations get more ambiguous [SDR17]. Moreover, existing questionnaires such as PDBS [ÖL05] already integrated the socialness dimension into their work by emphasizing helping and being polite when measuring positive driving behavior. As in any environment in which humans exist, traffic situations require and welcome social interaction between road users through prosocial behavior. Hence, being considerate, supportive, and courteous alongside other items we detected on this factor affect individuals' prosocial perception of other road users. Without this component, it would be difficult to bring the cooperative traffic environment that individuals feel content with by solely relying on traffic rules.

Coherence

Having stated that solely relying on traffic rules does not encapsulate the prosocial behavior in traffic entirely, it still comprises a great part of it. Existing scales such as PADI [HHV+14] and DARQ [HMC23] integrate traffic rules related-items to measure individuals' self-evaluation of social driving. Acting in accordance with rationality in traffic, following traffic rules, and moving in a safe and trustworthy manner seem to be an important factor in evaluating a road user's behavior as prosocial or aggressive. Therefore, we named this factor "coherence" to indicate being rational and coherent with existing rules. This is why, we may have received some open feedback regarding the first scenario that even if the behavior of the driver who is yielding their right of way on a priority road is prosocial, it is expected that everybody follows the rules, therefore conflicts are resolved in a more usual way. Similarly, in the third scenario where a pedestrian gives their right of way at a pedestrian crossing, participants found the behavior as prosocial. Yet, it would not be an aggressive decision even if a pedestrian insisted on their right of way, as using one's right of way is an expected behavior, and it falls under traffic rules.

Awareness

We could observe that being aware of one's own actions and intentions plays a vital role in deciding the social behavior of other traffic participants. This component seems to be as important as the actual outcome of the behavior while making social judgments. In line with Dovidio et al. [DPSP17], participants seemed to interpret prosocial or aggressive behavior in its social context. In each situation, sometimes the intention and awareness of the participant, and other times the outcome of the other road users' behavior played a bigger role in perceiving their behavior as prosocial or aggressive. For example, some participants stated in the open feedback section in the prosocial driver scenario that, even if the intention is prosocial, the outcome could be hazardous to the traffic environment by suddenly stopping on a 50 km/h road. In the aggressive pedestrian scenario, some participants stated that even if the pedestrian follows the rules and has the right of way, the intention of the pedestrian annoying them made their judgment regarding the participant as very aggressive. Hence, it seems that prosocial behavior in traffic cannot be stripped from the awareness and perceived intentions of road users by simply considering the outcome of the action as a beacon of social behavior. Rather, both behavioral intentions and behavioral outcomes play a role in social perception, however, their proportion of importance seems to be dependent on the situation specificity.

Construct and External Validation of SPAT

We used four traffic scenarios with two different perspectives and two different types of road users to lay judgments on. These enabled us to pick the best working items across these traffic situations. When we look at the confirmatory factor analysis results, we see that all CFI values have good indicators (≥ 0.95). However, RMSEA and SRMR values seemed to fall behind the conservative thresholds with the 3-factor model of the data. (Table 2.4) [Mai18]. Facing the tradeoff between theoretical breadth and internal consistency, we opted for theoretical breadth by retaining the 3-factor model over the better-fitting 2-factor model where the awareness factor would be excluded. Furthermore, when we tested for correlations across scenarios, we observed that our scenarios were distinctive from each other. This indicates that SPAT is sensitive to situation specificity, holding internal consistency across different scenarios of prosocial and aggressive traffic situations.

We tested the external validity of SPAT by setting up an experimental study between drivers and an AV in a game-of-chicken [RC66] -or bottleneck- [RB21, RAB20b, RPSB19, RDB21a] situation in a controlled test track study. Bottleneck situations could be considered as one of the optimum traffic situations to evaluate the social behavior of traffic participants as it requires active negotiation regarding who will take the priority of crossing the narrowed area first. In this situation, when the AV indicated its deceleration via an external display, drivers on the other side of the narrowing perceived the AV as more social, coherent, and aware, compared to the times the AV did not indicate its locomotion intentions. Furthermore, when the AV indicated its acceleration intention with the external display, drivers perceived the AV as more aware. In both acceleration and deceleration intention signaling cases, participants might have attributed AV's intention cues to its *awareness* since an intelligent vehicle attempted to actively communicate with them. Furthermore, they might have found the behavior of AV as *coherent* when it indicated its deceleration with a display since it is the rational behavior they expected of a self-driving vehicle yielding the right of way to humans. Another interesting finding of the study was that deceleration, -giving the human driver the right of way- was perceived as more prosocial. This finding is in a similar direction to Sadeghian et al. [SHE20a], that equipping AV with communication cues leads to a more prosocial perception of the vehicle. Overall, these results seem to be in accordance with the literature and SPAT sub-dimensions seem to be in harmony with expected results. Hence, we could conclude that the emphasized differences we observed in socialness, awareness, and coherence perception of the AV in this experiment highlight the discriminative power and usability of SPAT in different traffic situations. In other words, we could confirm the external validity of SPAT in detecting the prosocial perception of road users and being sensitive to situational differences.

Limitations and Future Directions

Although the validation step was conducted outdoors using a real car, it still might possess low ecological validity. Future work should further explore the usage of our scale in realistic traffic scenarios, e.g., with participants in and outside the cars. SPAT was tested only in the United States sample. This sample was picked to prevent cultural biases and test the scale in a native English-speaking country. However, testing the performance of the scale in different samples might bring different results. Hence, it is important to point out that this scale was primarily prepared for English speakers from the United States and still needs to be validated for other languages and geographies.

2.2.5 Conclusion

We presented a new scale measuring road users' prosocial and aggressive behavior in urban traffic scenarios (SPAT). To create and validate the scale, we underwent a series of methodological steps, including workshops, group meetings, expert meetings, an online survey, and an outdoor experiment. As a result, SPAT contains semantically different items made of adjectives capturing the different factors contributing to the perception of prosocial and non-prosocial behavior in urban traffic. It can be used as a means to measure individuals' perceptions regarding the social behavior of other road users in different traffic situations. The factorial structure of SPAT indicated three dimensions comprising prosocial behavior perception in traffic. These were **socialness**, **coherence**, and **awareness** dimensions. The construct validity of SPAT was confirmed by confirmatory factor analysis, and external validity was demonstrated with an experimental study between drivers and a Wizard of Oz automated vehicle by utilizing a bottleneck scenario on a test track.

2.3 Chapter Summary

In this chapter, we presented different studies that we conducted to understand patterns and indications of social behavior in traffic. Firstly, we conducted a focus group with automotive experts regarding prosocial and aggressive behavior examples in traffic from the perspective of different types of road users. Then, we explored the types of social behavior that are expected from automated vehicles. The results of the focus group indicate various expressions of social behavior, i.e. being courteous or a clear indication of intention to name some of them generally. Moreover, not only did we ask experts in this domain, but also we observed natural driving interactions via video recordings and approached the topic with an ethnographic lens (see Section 2.1). This made us realize the use of social cues such as gestures in everyday traffic especially when rules become more vague or flexibly treated. Hence we emphasized further attention to the topic of explicit interaction in traffic when considering AV - human interaction. Finally, we revealed that the measurement of the social behavior of road users could be approached with different methods, yet these could not be used in testing situational differences in traffic including automated vehicles. Hence, we took the issue into our own hands by aiming to create a measurement tool that could be used in assessing how social or aggressive a road user is perceived in different situations, including non-human road users such as AVs (see Section 2.2). In conclusion, we contributed to the literature by revealing key dimensions of social behavior in traffic, emphasizing explicit interaction between humans in relation to traffic scenario ambiguity, and lastly, creating and validating a measurement tool for social behavior perception in traffic.

3 Influence of Automated Vehicles on Social Behavior of Road Users

After revealing the key features of human-to-human social interaction in traffic, the next step in the present thesis has been investigating the potential social behavior change of humans around automated vehicles. Recent studies on AV-pedestrian interaction draw on game theory, to argue that AVs' inability to adapt their behavior from a passive, conflict-avoiding stance, would incentive pedestrians to step in front of them [FCM+18, RT18a]. Testing a sequential game of chicken, Fox et al. [FCM+18] for example show that assuming a zero-probability of collision between an AV and a human-driven vehicle (HDV), based on the assumed conflict-avoidant programming, the expected cost of collision for the human driver likewise nears zero, which would result in the rational incentive to abuse AV for human drivers. Applying this model to the AV-pedestrian interaction, and assuming the payoff structure to consist of the trade-off between time-savings and risk of personal injury, while keeping the probability of crash at 0, we would receive the same result, even if the expected cost of a crash would be significantly higher for the pedestrian. Formally, this can be expressed by the expected utility theorem, which assumes that an individual's rational decision, given a set of possible choices, is a function of the expected utility of the different choice options, based on the probability distribution of the decisions' outcomes. The decision to abuse an AV thus occurs if the expected utility of this choice is larger than, or equal to the expected utility of alternative actions:

$$ExpectedUtility_{humanabuses} = Utility_{abuse} * Probability_{AV\,stops} > ExpectedUtility_{alternativeactions}$$

To illustrate this, we use the following hypothetical payoff matrix for the interaction between an AV and a pedestrian. We assume that for each player, the utility to yield possesses a utility of -1 (lost time) while walking/driving possesses a utility of 1 (gained time). When both players choose to walk/drive, the result is a crash, which is significantly more costly to both players, than the other choice outcomes.

		Pedestrian	
		$Wait$	$Walk$
$AutonomousVehicle$	$Yield$	$(-1, -1)$	$(-1, 1)$
	$Drive$	$(1, -1)$	$(-100, -1000)$

We can then calculate the expected utility for a pedestrian to either walk or wait:

$$EU_{Walk} = U_{Walk/AVyield} * p_{AVyield} + U_{Walk/AVdrive} * (1 - p_{AVdrive})$$

$$EU_{Wait} = U_{Wait/AVyield} * p_{AVyield} + U_{Wait/AVdrive} * (1 - p_{AVdrive})$$

Because $U_{Wait/AVyield} = U_{Wait/AVdrive}$,

which holds true for all possible payoffs, since the cost to wait is independent of the choice of the vehicle,

$$EU_{Wait} = U_{Wait/AVyield} = U_{Wait/AVdrive}.$$

Given that $U_{Wait/AVyield} = U_{Wait/AVdrive}$,

the decision to cross then depends on the probability that the car will yield, which is a function of the utilities for the car yielding or driving when the pedestrian crosses. In this example

$$EU_{Walk} > EU_{Wait} \text{ if } EU_{Walk} > U_{Wait/AVyield} = U_{Wait/AVdrive} = \text{-}1,$$

which is true if $p_{AVyield} > 99,8\%$.

Given this minimalist payoff structure, the introduction of conflict-avoidant AVs would indeed create the rational incentive for bullying AV, as highlighted in previous studies (e.g. [FCM+18, MB18]). However, the utilities of traffic interaction in real life do not solely consist of the trade-off between time savings and risk of personal injury, which makes this model too narrow to reflect real-life behavior. For instance, traffic interaction (in most instances) is regulated by formal rules and social norms. Hence, this chapter concerns the influence of automated vehicles on social behavior in traffic by employing a pedestrian simulator study in Virtual Reality (VR) and tests for various legal and social control on deviant behavior. The parts of this chapter have been published in the paper by Sahin, Hemesath, and Boll [SHB22]. It is worth noting that this topic is also explored in the following Chapter 4 in Sections 4.2 and 4.3.

3.1   Gamifying Jaywalking to Investigate Deviant Behavior Towards Automated Vehicles

This study investigates how different forms of social control moderate pedestrians' decision to jaywalk in front of AVs and HDVs. Utilizing jaywalking behavior of pedestrians to study deviant behavior in the context of AVs has several benefits: 1) pedestrians benefit the most from a conflict-avoidant AV, drastically reducing their vulnerability in accident-prone situations, thereby increasing their utility to exploit them; 2) deviant behavior of pedestrians is commonplace in urban traffic situations, making it the most probable cause of interference for AVs; and 3) compared to other road users, the behavioral movement of pedestrians is significantly less predefined by the physical traffic environment, offering more frequent opportunities to act in line with self-interest.

3.1.1   Motivation and Related Work

One of the favorable measures for understanding interaction dynamics between AVs and pedestrians has been the crossing decisions of participants alongside acceptance and trust. Faas et al. [FMKB20] emphasized the realistic walking behavior in related crossing paradigms, rather than using a button or a safety slider for a better matching experience to realism. As a feasible solution, VR has been widely used in pedestrian - AV interaction research, since it allows for reproducible and controllable environments in immersive settings [KF21, JCT+19, HWB19a, LGR19, MSS+19, DCDNV+19a]. VR has also been effectively used in experimental paradigms where time pressure was tested in crossing tasks [MCSH15, SRB19]. Moreover, Bhagavathula et al. [BWOG18] reported that pedestrian behavior was similar in VR compared to reality, in terms of perceived safety and risk.

In order to reveal pedestrian crossing decisions in detail, Kalatian and Farooq [KF21] conducted a large ($N = 180$) VR study. Their deep learning model emphasized the effect of AVs alongside street width, traffic density, and limited sight on elongated waiting times of pedestrians before crossing. In the VR CAVE study of Dommès et al. [DML+21], authors tested for crossing behavior of pedestrians in front of conflict-avoidant AVs and conventional vehicles in a mixed traffic environment. They reported that participants were more hesitant to cross in front of AVs in some conditions, however, they also argued that participants mainly relied on locomotion cues of vehicles independent of their automation status. Jayaraman et al. [JCT+19] conducted a gamified VR study to investigate pedestrian trust in AVs in situations where AVs' locomotion cues signalized aggressive, normal, and defensive behavior. Moreover, they have controlled the traffic environment by testing pedestrian trust in unsignalized and signalized crossings with a traffic light. Their results indicated an increase in trust when AVs exhibited defensive behavior and when pedestrians were on signalized crossings. The work of Jayaraman et al. explores the aspects that can establish more pedestrian trust in AVs, with the general aim of encouraging pedestrians to cross in front of AVs without hesitation. However, the long-term effects of trustworthy and defensive AV behavior on individuals' interaction with them are yet to be explored [DML+21].

One of the overlooked factors in AV-VRU research has been social norms and social factors [CWR19], alongside scalability problems [CWR20, DVC+21]. Pedestrians were found to be more likely to cross the road if other pedestrians around them had started to cross [FKK10]. In a very recent study, Colley et al. [CBR22a] tested the effects of pedestrian group behavior and a single pedestrian behavior on their participants' crossing decisions in front of AVs, and they found similar results to Faria et al. [FKK10]. However, there is still a large gap in exploring the social norms in AV-pedestrian research and carrying one-to-one interaction paradigms a step further.

In our study, we build on rational-choice theory, which assumes that individuals use their self-interests to make choices, and model deviance as a function of an individual's cost-benefit calculation [Bec68]. In this context, deviant behavior occurs, if the anticipated net gains from the specific action outweigh the anticipated losses associated with that action. This means, that exploiting the conflict-avoidant nature of AVs might only serve the self-interest of individuals, as it outweighs the costs of breaking social rules. Specifically, we focus on three different types of social control: (1) the "broken-window thesis" of a negative bystander effect [WK82], which should incentivize deviant behavior, (2) social conformity, moderating deviant behavior by conforming with societal expectations when in the presence of others, and (3) formal norm-enforcement and sanctioning by authority.Broken Windows Thesis suggests that visible signs of disorder and neglect in a community, such as broken windows, graffiti, or litter, can lead to an increase in crime and antisocial behavior [WK82]. In the context of deviant behavior toward automated vehicles (AVs), social control can manifest both negative and positive influences. Negative social control, suggests that visible signs of disorder or neglect, such as frequent jaywalking around AVs, may encourage others to engage in similar deviant acts, creating a negative bystander effect. In contrast, positive social control, such as social conformity, promotes adherence to societal expectations, as individuals observing others following traffic norms are more likely to mirror that respectful behavior, especially in public or observed settings.

Our research questions are formulated below:

- Are there differences between the crossing behavior of individuals when they encounter automated or conventional vehicles right after a traffic gap?

- Do positive, negative, and legal representations of social control cues affect the crossing behavior of individuals?

- Do different levels of task urgency related to time pressure affect the crossing behavior of individuals?

Our study timely concerns with newly emerging considerations in pedestrian - AV research. Firstly, we introduced a mixed traffic environment where both AVs and HDVs existed in the experimental scene. Secondly, we went out of widely studied one-to-one interaction paradigms between AVs and pedestrians and contributed to limited scalability research in this area. Third, we explored potential social control mechanisms that can reduce or enhance deviant behavior of pedestrians from three different dimensions, namely legal norm cues, and positive and negative norm cues. To our knowledge, such social control mechanisms were not taken as a major focus in existing research, except for a negative example of a crossing pedestrian or idle pedestrian groups. Moreover, we tested legal norm cues under a study where the legal sanctioning was ambiguous, as opposed to studies that utilized definitive traffic lights or traffic signs. Fourth, we further tested for the effect of vehicle type and social control on deviant behavior when controlling for the risk of accidents for conventional vehicles. This allowed us to test whether significant differences between human-driven vehicles and autonomous vehicles existed, that resulted from the autonomous nature of AV and not their conflict-avoidant stance. Last but not least, our research contributes to the small sample of gamification literature in pedestrian - AV interactions, which supports a better-blinded method for repetitive within-subject designs.

The Cost of Norm-Violation

Formally, traffic is regulated by traffic code, and to step in front of an AV would in many instances be considered a traffic violation, subject to fines and penalties. Similarly, even the AV/HDV interaction at an unmarked intersection used in the previous example, would in most jurisdictions fall under the "priority to the right" rule. Informally, traffic is further regulated by social norms (which include the norm of compliance with formal norms). Social norms generate a sense of pre-dictability under uncertainty. In other words: social norms can be understood as equilibria of strategies to solve repetitive games, reducing the cost of uncertainty, by believing that others will act in accordance with the norm. Frequent norm violations thus carry the risk of norm erosion, meaning that an established norm ceases to exist if individuals too frequently deviate from said norm. The resulting norm-erosion in return increases interaction costs, by creating uncertainty with regard to the behavioral choices of other individuals in future interactions, which is not limited to the individual committing the norm-violation, but for society. If drawing on the previous example, HDVs frequently violate the "priority to the right"-rule in the context of AVs, future interactions at unmarked intersections would be more time-consuming, as they would require individual negotiation be-tween traffic participants since the trust in norm compliance would be low, as the norm of "priority to the right" eroded.

Abusing or bullying a self-driving car, here in the form of jaywalking in front of it, is thus a form of human behavior commonly referred to as deviant behavior. Deviance describes actions or types of behavior that violate formal (i.e., laws, traffic code) or informal (i.e., social norms) rules [GBY10]. In other words, de-viance refers to behavior that goes against what is deemed acceptable by society. Building on a rational-choice approach to deviance [Bec68], we understand the associated norm-violation as a function of an individual's cost-benefit calculation, and following the expected utility theorem expect deviant behavior to occur if the anticipated net gain from breaking the (formal or informal) rules outweighs the anticipated net gain from alternative actions. To be more specific, we build on the argument by Keuschnigg and Wolbring [KW15], that a rule is rationally anticipated to be broken, if the expected benefit of breaking this rule minus the cost of punishment (multiplied by the probability the rule-breaking will be sanc-tioned), is larger than the expected utility of alternative actions. The cost of norm violation then results from the incentive of other individuals to sanction norm violations (to prevent norm erosion) and the cost of punishment, a mechanism often referred to as social control. From the other perspective, norm-compliance might also positively increase the utility of alternative actions (e.g. by intrinsic rewards). Adding the effect of social control to the utility function of jaywalking behavior, a person would then jaywalk if: $EU_J > EU_W$, thus if:

$$[U_{JS}*p_S+U_{JD}*(1-p_S)]^{\smile}U_{punishment}*p_{sanctioning} > [U_{WS}*p_S+U_{WD}*(1-p_S)]+U_{reward}*p_{reward}$$

Note: J = jaywalking, S = vehicle stops, W = pedestrian waits, D = vehicle drives

The decision to jaywalk would thus be influenced by three different components:

- The individual gross utilities for the different choice options

- The probabilities for the individual choice outcomes to occur

- The cost of punishment and the probability of sanctioning

Given that the moderating effect of norm compliance influences the net gains of the behavioral choice, all else being equal, its effect should be stronger in situations where the net gains are lower, that is the expected utilities between the different choice options are more similar, compared to a more limited effect when the utility trade-offs between the choice options are higher. Hence, we would expect that an increase in utility for the deviant choice of jaywalking would increase the expected utility to jaywalking, and therefore increase deviant behavior. We therefore expect that:

H_1 : *All else being equal, a higher utility payoff for the deviant behavioral choice will increase deviant behavior.*

Since the expected utility of the deviant behavioral choice is dependent on the probability of occurrence of the different choice outcomes, we likewise expect that passively programmed AVs should increase deviant behavior, given that the probability the car will yield is programmed to be 100%: :

H_2 : *All else being equal, individuals will jaywalk more frequently when interacting with an AV.*

The second hypothesis already implies that we do not expect social control (the cost of norm-violation) to fundamentally alter the utility differences between interactions with AV and HDV, that is, social control to formally interact with vehicle type. This would be the case, if the effect of social control would be substantially different for the individual vehicle types, or specific social norms would exist, that only apply to a specific type of vehicle. However, we are neither aware of empirical evidence that demonstrates that the cost of norm-compliance significantly differs between HDV and AV, nor specific social norms that only apply to one type of vehicle. On the contrary, our main argument in this study is that social control applies to both HDV and AV and reduces the overall occurrence of deviant behavior, disregarding the vehicle type. To understand the extent of this moderating effect, it is important to differentiate between different forms of social control.

Social Control as a Moderator of Deviant Behavior

The influence of others on deviant behavior was formalized by Hirschi [Hir69] in the theory of social control. Hirschi views social sanctioning, which he explicitly differentiates from formal sanctioning, as an even higher deterrent of deviant behavior than formal rules [HG94]. Norm-compliance in return results from individuals' motivation to conform with social norms. Social control, more generally, then refers to the rewards and sanctions that result from conforming with or deviating from, social norms (formal or informal) [Ros96, Ros09]. In line with this theory, research on red-light violations of pedestrians [PMPDA+18, RM22], for example, found individuals to cross with a higher frequency if they are alone, compared to situations where multiple individuals are waiting for the green-light. Recent evidence suggests that this effect is further moderated by social proximity, that is, it increases when individuals are surrounded by people they feel closer to, or who belong to their social group.

H_{3a} *(norm-conformity): The presence of other pedestrians will decrease deviant behavior.*

However, the presence of others can also have the opposite effect on deviant behavior. The observation of deviant behavior by other individuals incentivizes norm violations [KLS08]. Formally, other individuals violating norms might serve as a cue that norms are not enforced in this area, or norm-erosion occurs, which decreases the marginal cost for non-compliance. This effect exists, even if the behavior of others has not been observed directly, but the inference of low levels of norm-compliance is made by social cues, such as littering, graffiti, or broken windows [WK82].

H_{3b} *(negative bystander / broken windows): Cues signaling norm-violations by others will increase deviant behavior.*

While Hirschi [Hir69] argues that social sanctioning serves as a higher deterrent to deviant behavior than formal norms, evidence on traffic violations suggests that cues signaling the enforcement of formal norms have a strong negative effect on deviant behavior. Given the moderating effect of social proximity on norm-compliance, this might be explained by the larger social distance between individuals on public roads, which limits the effect of social sanctioning (e.g. a nasty look by a bystander is less costly than reproach by family members), while cues of formal norm-enforcement and sanctioning make the cost of norm-violation more salient for individuals.

H_{3c} *(formal norm-enforcement): Cues signaling sanctioning of formal norms will have a negative effect on deviant behavior.*

3.1.2   Apparatus and Method

In this section, firstly, we present the details of the pedestrian simulator we created for the study. The following sections include method details such as study design, participant profile, procedure, and analytical approach.

Virtual Reality Environment

To conduct this experiment, we designed a virtual street environment in Unity 3D (version 2020.3.0f1). VR served as a flexible and safe test bed for running our study. The environment was limited by tunnels on both sides of the road and surrounded by hills. Urban buildings were placed on both sides of the street. Since we used game elements in our experiment, we did not focus on making the virtual environment realistic and utilized low polygon mesh elements (see Figures 3.1 and 3.2). The placement of traffic signs, pedestrian crossings, and traffic lights were abstained intentionally so that participants could only use the information of vehicle movements and communication cues on their crossing decisions. The size of the street including pavement was 12 meters. Participants emerged a few steps away from the sidewalk while traffic was flowing on the road. The unidirectional traffic coming from the left side of the participant consisted of fully automated vehicles and conventional vehicles. Vehicles had a 50 km/h start speed and exponential deceleration behavior with a starting value of 1.98 km/h. Vehicles stopped at a sufficient distance to provide a traffic gap for participants to cross. Virtual human characters emerged on the left side of the participant when they accompanied the scene. This allowed both oncoming vehicles and virtual road users to be in the participants' field of view.

The task of the participants was to score points by delivering pizza to a virtual character waiting on the opposite side of the road (see Figure 3.2A). If participants failed to deliver the pizza for reasons such as getting caught by the police, they did not receive any points. Otherwise, they either received 1 base point for delivering the pizza or 2 points for delivering the pizza within the bonus timer. The traffic pattern consisted of two waves of vehicles, passing the scene from the left to the right. Between the first and second wave of vehicles, a gap of around 3 seconds opened up. Participants were then faced with the choice to either jaywalk in this situation or wait until the second wave of cars passed.

Experimental Design

Our experiment consisted of three factors (Vehicle type, Task Urgency, and Social Control) with different factor levels, resulting in a 2x2x4 full-factorial design, where all experimental conditions varied randomly within subjects. This design provided control for individual differences; it allowed us to examine the effect of multiple independent variables and their interactions at a time; and it was more efficient in the sense that smaller sample sizes could be sufficient for statistical power. The experimental treatments consisted of the combinations of the different factorial levels, that we operationalized by manipulating specific elements of the individual scenes:

Vehicle Type

To understand the differences in crossing behavior between self-driving and conventional vehicles, we manipulated the first vehicle of the second wave of cars to be either an AV or an HDV. To increase the realism of the situation, and to understand whether the crossing decisions are dependent on a lack of communication between pedestrian and vehicle, we operationalized the HDV condition in two ways, equal amounts of conditions with successful communication between the driver and the pedestrian when participants tried to negotiate for the right of way, and conditions with conventional vehicles that did not respond to negotiation request.

AVs always yielded to participants as soon as they stepped on the road, so we could simulate their defensive design principles. For sending feedback to participants, AVs switched on a light blue light when they started decelerating [Wer18] (see Figure 3.1A). Conventional vehicles stopped for the participant, if the participant performed a hand gesture coupled with a button press on the VR controller and the vehicle was a part of the successful communication subset. This gesture represented the explicit communication between vulnerable road users and drivers. For sending deceleration feedback, HDVs flashed their headlights to participants (see Figure 3.1C). In the failed communication subset, HDVs neither stopped nor indicated other forms of cues to participants. Participants were unaware of the types of conventional vehicles, and they were only informed that human drivers may or may not respond to them.

Social Control

To understand the effect of different forms of social control on crossing behavior, next to the baseline condition of no social control, we tested for the effect of social conformity, cues indicating formal norm enforcement, and the effect of a negative bystander. To represent different social controls, we placed virtual human characters on the left side of the participant (see Figures 3.2B, C, and D). To represent a positive norm of social conformity, a mother and a child waited before crossing until all vehicles passed. A mother and her child were chosen for this condition, as the social norm of rule-compliance should be stronger when acting as a possible role model for the child. The negative bystander / broken windows condition was operationalized by a walking person who stopped the oncoming vehicle wave after the small traffic gap was used. Formal norm enforcement and possible sanctioning were operationalized by the presence of a police officer. Participants were informed that police may or may not see them. If police saw them attempting to cross by obstructing the traffic flow, participants were stopped, hence they received 0 points from that trial. This game mechanism represented a subtle cost of legal punishment. Since crossing the road in our

Figure 3.1: Vehicle Type and Task Urgency factor levels in the experiment. **A**: Decelerating AV casts blue light cues. **B**: Urgent task indicator with a running man on a red background. **C**: Decelerating HDV flashes headlights. **D**: Non-urgent task indicator with a resting man on a green background.

scenario wasn't illegal, we avoided any direct punishment implications. To reduce the bias of police behavior, we sat up equal amounts of catching and non-catching police conditions in the design.

Task Urgency

To understand the effect of different payoffs on jaywalking behavior, we tested for the effect of different task urgency, and respectively different payouts for jaywalking. This factor consisted of two levels, which were Urgent and Non-Urgent. Urgency levels were cued with symbols before each trial started (see Figure 3.1B and D). In the scenario, participants received 1 base point for a successful pizza delivery, however, they had the possibility to double their earnings when completing the task in a set time frame. Scenarios were therefore presented with a timer indicating the remaining time for earning an extra bonus point. In non-urgent trials, the bonus timer started counting back from 23 seconds, which was

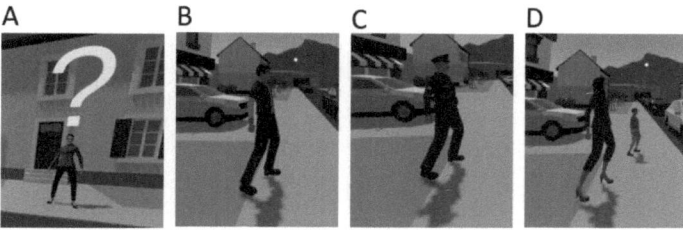

Figure 3.2: Non-Player Characters. **A**: Target customer waiting for pizza delivery. **B**: A walking person who crosses the road represents negative social control. **C**: Police officer representing legal control. **D**: Mother and child represent positive social control of abiding by the rules.

enough for waiting until all vehicles passed, and it was safe to cross. In this condition individuals therefore received 2 points (base + bonus), disregarding their crossing decision. In urgent trials, the bonus timer started counting back from 13 seconds, meaning that participants had to jaywalk in front of a vehicle in order to complete the task with 2 points.

Collected Measures

As dependent variables we collected both, the crossing decision of individuals, and the associated crossing onsets. Crossing onsets captured the time passed from the moment a trial started until a participant stepped on the road (in seconds). The crossing decision was observed by the researchers and was crosschecked with the collected crossing onsets, which were filtered by a series of criteria: First, participants have crossed if the crossing onsets are smaller than the time needed for the last car of the second wave of cars to pass an invisible line. Or second, if the last car could not reach the invisible line before the participant either successfully reached the other side, or because a crash occurred.

We implemented a second choice task for human-driven vehicles, to test for the effect of vehicle type and social control under equal risk of collision between human-driven and automated vehicles, we then split the dependent variable of crossing onsets into two: For the general differences we only used those observations, where the crossing decision was made within 1 second after the first wave of cars passed (7.75 seconds), which equals around 1 second before the second wave of cars arrived. This point is likewise below the reaction time of the risk-controlled, yielding signaling its intention to stop. For those observations we could logically assume that the crossing decisions for scenarios with an HDV were made, disregarding the behavior of the other vehicle and under unknown probabilities of a collision. To compare the crossing decision under equal risk for crash, we used all observations where the participant crossed later than the initial time frame, crossed or didn't cross when interacting with an AV, or elected to not cross when faced with an HDV where successful negotiation could have been possible (which was unknown to the participant, but signalized that no attempt to stop the car was made). As independent variables, we used the experimental treatment conditions and coded them into three factors (Vehicle Type, Task Urgency, Social Control).

After having finished the VR experiment, participants filled out an online survey in LimeSurvey (version 3.27.26) [S+12] consisting of the igroup Presence Questionnaire (IPQ) [SFR01], a demographics form [DSC+17], the Pedestrian Receptivity Questionnaire for Fully Autonomous Vehicles (PRQF) [DSC+17], the Pedestrian Behavior Questionnaire (PBQ - Short Version) [DSC+17], and the Social Value Orientation (SVO) [MAH11] scale. Within the scope of this study, we have only used these measures to draw a clearer participant profile, and we didn't evaluate them further in statistical analysis. Lastly, we presented five open questions regarding the effects of manipulated factors in the experiment.

Participants

36 Participants (21 females, age: $M = 25.22, \pm SD = 5.15$) were recruited via the online notice board of the university, and via printed "Pizza Delivery Game" advertisements on bus stops. Participants were informed they would be reimbursed with 8–10 Euros, depending on the final game score. However, all participants eventually received a compensation of 10 Euros for their participation, which was revealed at the end of the experiment. The Ethics Committee of the University of Oldenburg gave ethical approval for the experiment according to the Declaration of Helsinki.

The majority of our participants reside in big cities with an overall population density of at least 193 people per square km. Most of them were high school graduates ($N = 14$) or graduate students ($N = 10$). 32 participants would fall into the prosocial category on the Social Value Orientation angle ($M = 32.69, \pm SD = 8.77$) [MAH11]. Their (PRQF) [DSC+17] grand scores had a mean more on the positive side of the scale ($M = 66.63, \pm SD = 10.88$), indicative of greater receptivity for AVs. The average PBQ - Short Version [DSC+17] grand score of the participants was 43.08, on the negative side of the scale, indicating safer pedestrian behavior ($\pm SD = 6.80$). Inspection of Igroup Presence Questionnaire (IPQ) [SFR01] revealed high general presence ($M = 4.52, \pm SD = 1.20$), high spatial presence ($M = 4.29, \pm SD = 0.97$) and above average involvement $M = 3.77, \pm SD = 1.12$) in our VR experiment, however, experienced realism was rated on the negative side of the scale ($M = 2.60, \pm SD = 0.74$) (see Figure 3.3).

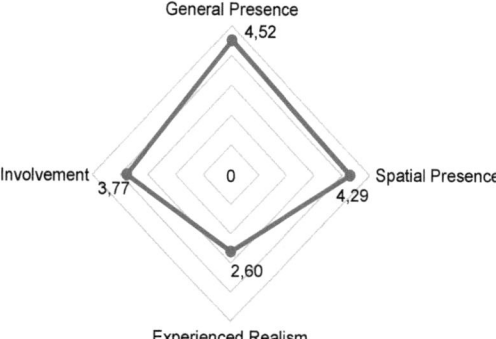

Figure 3.3: iGroup Presence Questionnaire evaluation with means of the subscales involvement, experienced realism, spatial presence, and general presence.

Experimental Procedure

Participants were invited to a large meeting room. This provided enough space for walking a street-long distance of 12 meters. First, participants gave their written consent and received specific information about the study and the associated task. Secondly, they were introduced to the Oculus Quest 2 VR headset and controllers (Facebook Technologies, LLC). Then, they were instructed about the virtual guardian walls that indicate safe zones in the real environment. The virtual environment was re-positioned in a way that participants could walk straight to the virtual customer within the safe zone.

Before the experiment started, each participant conducted five test trials in order to familiarize with the environment as in Jayaraman et al. [JCT+19], and Kalatian and Farooq [KF21]. In the first one, participants experienced crashing and dying, where they received the information of dying with a text on a black background. They were also falsely informed that if they died in the experiment, the experiment would be over without earning extra incentive. We gave this information to increase the cost of dying in the game. In the second trial, participants tried to stop the conventional cars by communicating with a gesture combined with a button press on the controller. The third test trial showed them that conventional vehicles do not always take their requests into consideration, and they keep on driving. In this trial, they also saw a very large traffic gap where the road was free of vehicles. They were reminded that this gap existed in each trial. The last two test trials were dedicated to police conditions where a policeman is either aware or not aware of the participant. In these last two trials, participants also practiced crossing in front of an AV. After making sure participants did not have any questions, 30 pseudo-randomized experimental trials began. Participants repetitively started walking from the same point until they reached the avatar on the other side by paying attention to the oncoming traffic and other factors. Upon reaching the other side, they walked back while oncoming traffic was ceased. Then, the next trial began. They could take breaks in between the trials. Lastly, participants filled out online survey questions at the end. The VR experiment was arranged to take on average 30 minutes, since fatigue may increase after 30 minutes [KF21]. The survey took 30-40 minutes to complete.

Analytical Approach

Before conducting the analysis, we ran a series of validity checks and excluded observations that were either implausible or instances where participants did not start crossing due to rare bugs. These include instances where respondents were free-falling from the environment, or the trial time was elapsed. Unusual crossing onsets that were smaller than 1 second and bigger than 20 seconds (4/864) were ignored, resulting in a final sample size of N = 36 with 860 observations.

To understand the effect of the experimental treatments on crossing behavior, we calculated a generalized linear mixed-effects model (GLMM) [NW72], including the experimental factors as fixed effects, and treating within-subject variance as random effects. The crossing behavior of individuals served as a binomial dependent variable in the analysis, which we regressed on dummy variables for the experimental factors. We tested for both, the main effects of the three experimental factors, and the interaction effects between vehicle type and both social control and task urgency. The statistical analysis was performed in RStudio (version 1.4.1106) [RSt20], using the glmer function of the Lme4 package (version 1.1-27.1) [BMBW15]. The distribution of residuals in our models was cross-checked with check_distribution function of R performance package (version 0.8.0) [LBSP+21]. Model fittings were tested via base anova function of R with Chi-squared tests and compare_performance function in performance package. We also report the predicted marginal effects of each condition with crossing probabilities, which were calculated using the ggeffects package (version 1.1.1.1) [Lüd18]. They are reported in percentages after the multiplication of 100. Marginal effects indicate the average treatment effect of our experimental factors (or interaction of factors), holding the other factors constant at their proportions.

3.1.3 Results

In this part, we report the results of the experiment, both for the baseline experiment under unknown risk of a crash with an HDV and a second analysis using a subset of risk-controlled crossing decisions, where participants were able to stop the HDV. The part with general crossing predictions includes crossing attempts in front of HDVs where participants didn't try to negotiate with the driver. The part with risk-controlled crossing predictions excludes these trials and demonstrates the results of participants when they negotiated with HDVs and when they tried to stop the vehicles by communicating with the drivers with a gesture. We have made this two-level analysis, to observe the overall effect of vehicle types on our study and the pure effect of vehicle automation on crossing behavior when the risk of crashing is eliminated for HDVs.

For reporting the main effects, we elected to present both, the average marginal effect of the experimental factors, that is the effect of the factor levels of interest in reference to the baseline level, while holding the other factors constant at their proportions, and the marginal means, that is the average crossing-probability of participants when holding the other factors constant at their proportions. While the average marginal effect helps to illustrate the causal effect in reference to the reference level, the marginal means illustrate the overall descriptive means for the different treatment conditions. We chose to report marginal effects, since they are more intuitively understandable than odds-ratios, reporting changes in, or the overall means of crossing decisions for the different treatment conditions in percentages.

Overall, participants chose to deviantly cross in 62,1 % of the trials, while in 37,9 % of the cases they decided to wait. The crossing decisions were most common when confronted with an AV, where they chose to cross in 71,4 % of the trials, whereas when confronted with an HDV, only 57,4 % elected to cross. The crossing decision when faced with an HDV was equally distributed between observations where participants didn't know about the probability the car would stop (27,7 %) and trials where participants successfully signaled the car to stop (29,7 %).

General Crossing Predictions

The results of the Generalized Linear Mixed Effects Model to model individuals' general crossing decisions are provided in Table 3.1, and the predicted marginal effects and marginal means for the different treatments are illustrated in Figure 3.4. We used distinctive models to calculate the marginal effects. While models 1, 2, and 3 show the results for the main effects of Vehicle Type, Task Urgency, and Social Control respectively, models 4 and 5 indicate the interaction between Vehicle Type x Task Urgency and Vehicle Type x Social Control (see Table 3.1).

All else being equal and keeping the effect of the other factors constant at their proportions, we find the presence of AV to significantly increase the crossing probability by 43 % in comparison to HDV ($\beta = 2.03$, $z(860) = 12.01$, $Pr(> |z|)$ $< .001$) (see Figure 3.4 top left). Overall, this meant for our participants that the average probability to cross increased from 26 % when interacting with a human-driven vehicle to around 73 % when interacting with an AV (see Figure 3.4 top right). Similarly, in reference to non-urgent scenarios, urgent scenarios significantly increased the average probability to cross by 13 % ($\beta = 0.56$, $z(860)$

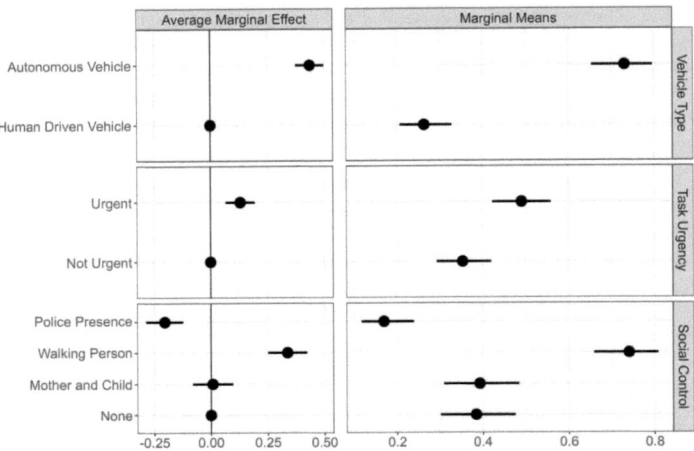

Figure 3.4: Average Marginal Effects and Marginal Means for General Crossings. The left plot shows the average marginal effects (AME) of our three experimental factors in reference to their baseline factor levels. The vertical line represents the effect of the reference level. The right column reports the marginal means (MM) for the different factor levels on crossing probabilities, holding the other factors constant at their proportions. Points indicate AME/MM, horizontal lines the 95% CIs. Effects based on results of GLMM.

$= 3.95$, $Pr(> |z|) < .001$) (see Figure 3.4 middle left). The average probability of crossing in urgent scenarios was 49 %, while it was 35 % in non-urgent scenarios (see Figure 3.4 middle right). Lastly, when contrasted to the baseline social control condition of being alone, the presence of a police significantly reduced the crossing probability by 20 % ($\beta = $ -1.11, $z(860) = $ -4.77, $Pr(> |z|) < .001$); the presence of a walking person significantly increased crossing probability by 33 % ($\beta = 1.52$, $z(860) = 7.06$, $Pr(> |z|) < .001$); and the bystanders mother and child did not change the probability of crossing ($\beta = 0.03$, $z(860) = 0.17$, $Pr(> |z|) = 0.86$) (see Figure 3.4 bottom left). Our participants' crossing probability was predicted as 16 % in the presence of police. Moreover, an increase of 74 % was observed when accompanied by a walking person who attempted to cross the road. With mother and child condition the crossing probability was at 39 %. Finally, when the participants were alone in the scene their crossing probability was 38 % (see Figure 3.4 bottom right).

Table 3.1: General results for the effect of vehicle type, task urgency, and social control on crossing decisions

Predictors	M1 Odds Ratios	M2 Odds Ratios	M3 Odds Ratios	M4 Odds Ratios	M5 Odds Ratios
(Intercept)	0.36 ***	0.55 ***	0.62 *	0.25 ***	0.23 ***
Autonomous Vehicle	7.61 ***			7.94 ***	14.68 ***
Urgent		1.76 ***		2.01 ***	
Walking Person			4.58 ***		6.85 ***
Police Presence			0.33 ***		0.31 **
Mother and Child			1.04		1.06
Autonomous Vehicle * Urgent				1.04	
Autonomous Vehicle * Walking Person					2233228.92
Autonomous Vehicle * Police Presence					0.56
Autonomous Vehicle * Mother and Child					1.02
Random Effects					
σ^2	3.29	3.29	3.29	3.29	3.29
τ_{00}	0.57	0.35	0.54	0.61	1.08
ICC	0.15	0.10	0.14	0.16	0.25
N	36	36	36	36	36
Observations	860	860	860	860	860
Marginal r^2 / Conditional r^2	0.192 / 0.312	0.022 / 0.117	0.187 / 0.301	0.220 / 0.342	0.865 / 0.898

*** $p < .001$, ** $p < .01$, * $p < .05$

Note: Results of Generalized Mixed Effect Regression Models. Odds ratios and Random Effects are reported for models 1 - 5. M1: Vehicle Type, M2: Task Urgency, M3: Social Control, M4: Vehicle Type x Task Urgency, M5: Vehicle Type x Social Control.

Risk Controlled Crossing Predictions

Since participants were unaware of the probability a human-driven vehicle would stop for the initial crossing decision, the strong effect of AV on the crossing decision might likewise be caused by their passive programming, as well as their autonomous nature. To test whether the decision to cross is influenced by their autonomous nature, and whether the effect of social control changes under equal risk distributions between AV and HDV, we conducted a second analysis, excluding those observations where the risk of crash with an HDV was unknown.

The results of the Generalized Linear Mixed Effects Model to model individuals' risk-controlled crossing decisions are provided in Table 3.2, and the average marginal effects and marginal means for the different treatments are illustrated in Figure 3.5. Similar to table 3.1, models 1, 2, and 3 show the results for the main effects of Vehicle Type, Task Urgency, and Social Control. Models 4 and 5 indicate the interaction between Vehicle Type x Task Urgency and Vehicle Type x Social Control (see Table 3.2).

All else being equal and holding the effect of other factors constant at their proportions, we see no effect of AV compared to HDV when we controlled for the risk ($\beta = -0.03$, $z(524) = -0.15$, $Pr(> |z|) = 0.87$) (see Figure 3.5 top left). While the crossing probability in front of AVs was 71 %, the crossing probability in front of HDVs was observed to be 72 % (see Figure 3.5 top right). The effect of urgency remains significant when crossings are controlled for the risk. Compared to non-urgent scenarios, urgent scenarios increased crossing probabilities by 10 % ($\beta = 0.55$, $z(524) = 2.78$, $Pr(> |z|) < .01$) (see Figure 3.5 middle left). Their effect on

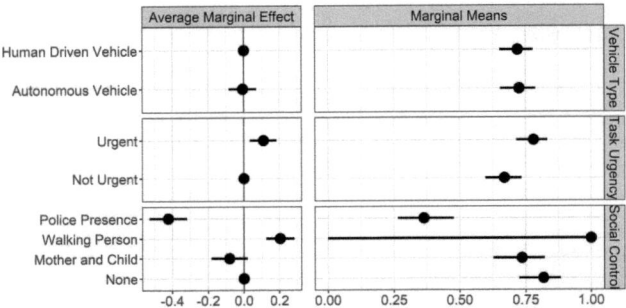

Figure 3.5: Average Marginal Effects and Marginal Means for Risk Controlled Crossings. The left plot shows the average marginal effects (AME) of our three experimental factors in reference to their baseline factor levels. The vertical line represents the effect of the reference level. The right column reports the marginal means (MM) for the different factor levels on crossing probabilities, holding the other factors constant at their proportions. Points indicate AME/MM, horizontal lines the 95% CIs. Effects based on results of GLMM.

crossing probabilities was observed as 78 % for urgent and 66 % for non-urgent scenarios (see Figure 3.5 middle right). Compared to baseline social control condition, while police presence significantly decreased crossing probabilities by 42 % (β = -2.05, $z(524)$ = -6.97, $Pr(> |z|) < .001$), walking person increased it by 20 %, which was not significant (β = 18.18, $z(524)$ = 0.020, $Pr(> |z|) = 0.98$). Mother and child lead to a decrease of 8 %, which remained insignificant (β = -0.47, $z(524)$ = -1.56, $Pr(> |z|) = 0.11$) (see Figure 3.5 bottom left). The effect of social control levels on crossing probability, when they are kept constant at their proportions, is observed to be 36 % for police presence, 100 % for the walking person, 73 % for mother and child, and lastly, 81 % when participants were alone in the scene (see Figure 3.5 bottom right).

Exploring Interactions

Given the lack of empirical evidence on a potential interaction effect between social control and vehicle type, that is whether social control might have a different effect on AV than HDV, we further explored potential interactions with GLMM models 4 and 5 for general crossings in Table 3.1 and risk-controlled crossing in Table 3.2. The average marginal effects for the interactions, AMEs of Social Control, and Task Urgency conditioned on Vehicle Type are illustrated in Figure 3.6.

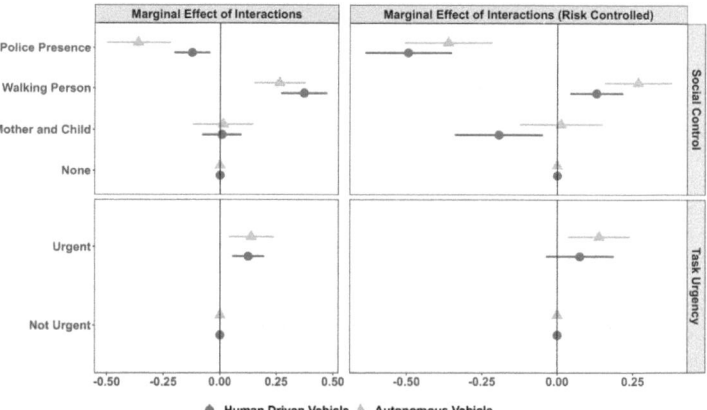

Figure 3.6: Effect of Social Control and Task Urgency conditioned by Vehicle Type. The figure illustrates the average marginal effects on crossing probabilities of Social Control and Task Urgency, conditioned on Vehicle Type, both for the baseline crossing decision under uncertainty of HDV behavior (left side), and for interactions where participants were faced with equal risk of collision between AV and HDV (right side). Purple points represent HDV, and orange triangles represent AV. Horizontal lines show 95% CIs. Vertical lines represent the average crossing probability of reference level.

Table 3.2: Risk controlled results for the effect of vehicle Type, task Urgency, and social control on crossing decisions

Predictors	M1 Odds Ratios	M2 Odds Ratios	M3 Odds Ratios	M4 Odds Ratios	M5 Odds Ratios
(Intercept)	2.65 ***	2.03 ***	4.50 ***	2.25 ***	8.13 ***
Autonomous Vehicle	0.97			0.82	0.38 *
Urgent		1.75 **		1.47	
Walking Person			79112259.30		44516415.95
Police Presence			0.13 ***		0.07 ***
Mother and Child			0.62		0.28 *
Autonomous Vehicle * Urgent				1.38	
Autonomous Vehicle * Walking Person					2.64
Autonomous Vehicle * Police Presence					2.57
Autonomous Vehicle * Mother and Child					3.81 *
Random Effectss					
σ^2	3.29	3.29	3.29	3.29	3.29
τ_{00}	0.28	0.29	0.79	0.30	0.83
ICC	0.08	0.08	0.19	0.08	0.20
N	36	36	36	36	36
Observations	524	524	524	524	524
Marginal r^2 / Conditional r^2	0.000 / 0.079	0.021 / 0.102	0.944 / 0.955	0.023 / 0.105	0.944 / 0.955

*** $p < .001$, ** $p < .01$, * $p < .05$

Note: Odds ratios and Random Effects are reported for models 1 - 5. M1: Vehicle Type, M2: Task Urgency, M3: Social Control, M4: Vehicle Type x Task Urgency, M5: Vehicle Type x Social Control.

When general crossings are considered, compared to being alone, the presence of police decreased crossing in front of AVs by 36 % and HDVs by 12 %. This interaction was not significant ($\beta = -0.58$, $z(860) = -1.07$, $Pr(> |z|) = 0.28$). The walking person increased crossing probability in front of AVs by 26 % and HDVs by 37 %. However, this interaction was also insignificant ($\beta = 14.61$, $z(860) = 0.03$, $Pr(> |z|) = 0.97$). Mother and child had an effect of increasing crossing probability in front of AVs by 0 % and HDVs by 1 %, which was an insignificant result ($\beta = 0.02$, $z(860) = 0.04$, $Pr(> |z|) < 0.96$) (see Figure 3.6 top left).

When we controlled for risk and checked the interaction of vehicle type x social control, compared to being alone, police presence decreased the crossing probability in front of AVs by 36 % and HDVs by 49 %, however, this interaction was not significant ($\beta = 0.94$, $z(524) = 1.54$, $Pr(> |z|) = 0.12$). The walking person increased the crossing probability in front of AVs by 26 % and HDVs by 12 %. The interaction was not significant ($\beta = 0.97$, $z(524) = 0.001$, $Pr(> |z|) = 0.99$) Mother and child increased crossing probability in front of AVs by 1 % and decreased the crossing probability in front of HDVs by 19 % and this interaction was significant ($\beta = 1.33$, $z(524) = 2.09$, $Pr(> |z|) < .05$) (see Figure 3.6 top right).

The interaction of vehicle type with task urgency did not yield significant results both in general and in risk-controlled results. Considering general crossings and compared to non-urgent situations, in urgent scenarios participants' crossing probability in front of AVs increased by 12 % and in front of HDVs by 13 % ($\beta = 0.03$, $z(860) = 0.10$, $Pr(> |z|) = 0.91$) (see Figure 3.6 bottom left). When controlled for risk for the same interactions, participants' crossing probability in front of AVs increased by 13 % and HDVs by 7 % ($\beta = 0.32$, $z(524) = 0.79$, $Pr(> |z|) = 0.42$) (see Figure 3.6 bottom right).

3.1.4 Discussion and Conclusion

To answer the question of whether individuals will bully or abuse AVs for individual gain, we have run a 2-step analysis on the results section where we tested crossing decisions when the anticipated risk for AV was low and the anticipated risk for HDV (human-driven vehicle) was higher in the first step. This step mimicked the expected future mixed traffic environment with the imbalanced costs of exploiting a human-driven vehicle and an AV. Our results indicated a higher deviant behavior towards AVs when the risk distribution was not balanced. These results support the findings of Moore et al. [MCSS20], where they observed deviant behavior towards self-driving vehicles in their field observation. Moreover, our results are also corroborated by remarks from our respondents. When we asked whether different vehicle types influenced their crossing behavior, more than half of the answers indicated an existing effect. Participants stated that they crossed the street *"without hesitation"* in the presence of AVs, relied on the passive stance of AVs, and were more willing to cross in front of AVs. One respondent explained in AV conditions that he crossed even without waiting for the blue deceleration signal of AVs. These results are in the direction of "Overtrust" towards AVs problem Holländer et al. [HWB19a] argued. However, in the second step of the analysis, when we balanced the risk distribution by only including HDV trials where HDVs could yield if participants negotiated with them, our data could tell if there were remaining differences in crossing behavior stemming from the sole effect of automation attributes of vehicles. As we ran the analysis, we observed that the existing difference between crossing predictions among HDVs and AVs simultaneously disappeared when the crash risk of HDVs disappeared. These results emphasize the importance of risk avoidance in participants' crossing decisions more than the automation status of vehicles, which is in line with the remarks of Dommès et al. [DML⁺21], that pedestrians rely mainly on vehicle dynamics and locomotion cues before taking a crossing decision. We therefore, can only confirm H_2 in so far that, when the collision risk is introduced in HDVs while AVs stay risk-free, deviant behavior towards AVs increases as Millard-Ball [MB18] anticipated with his game theory derived remarks.

Kalatian and Farooq [KF21] observed in their VR study-derived models that, pedestrians' waiting time before the crossing was longer in mixed traffic and in only AV scenarios, than in only human-driven vehicle scenarios. Their study did not report trials where vehicles did not stop, hence the risk distribution among vehicle type levels seemed equal. When we compare their results with our risk-controlled crossings, we fail to observe a similar effect in the crossing behavior of pedestrians, in terms of crossing predictions. This could be due to our strategy of priming participants before the experiment by informing them about the different characteristics of AVs and HDVs; that AVs would always yield to them in order to prevent a collision and HDVs may or may not yield to them. We have done this so that we could approximate pedestrian behavior once they are accustomed to conflict-avoidant AVs after long-term exposure in the future. Hence, the difference between our results and Kalatian and Farooq [KF21] might indicate differences in novel and primed mental models of pedestrians when they encounter AVs. Furthermore, Kalatian and Farooq [KF21] reported that some teenage participants performed deviant behavior against virtual vehicles, once they realized that vehicles react according to their crossing behavior. Participants then would play with them by moving back and forth on the street. Authors pointed out future implications of deviant behavior towards AVs in their work and their statements are in line with our general crossing results and the study of Moore et al. [MCSS20] in this regard.

Moreover, Colley et al. [CBR22a] tested pedestrian behavior in the presence of constant oncoming AVs which would not yield for participants. Their results showed that after a couple of passing AVs, pedestrians relied on the prior information of an emergency braking system of AVs and preferred crossing for saving time. However, they have only tested this condition for AVs. In our experiment, we utilized always-yielding AVs, yielding and non-yielding HDVs. To draw a clearer picture on whether pedestrians treat AVs and HDVs differently, a follow-up study including non-yielding HDVs and non-yielding AVs can support our risk-controlled results from another perspective.

The gamification of our experiment further enabled us to manipulate conditions that directly affect individual gains in the form of earning points and extra reimbursement in Euros. Task urgency was directly linked to maximizing the incentivize participants would gain. Generally, we found urgent scenarios to predict higher chances of crossing instead of waiting, confirming that participants showed more deviant behavior under time pressure, in line with studies of Morrongiello et al. [MCSH15], and Schneider et al. [SRB19], as well as our theoretical expectations formulated in H_1.

Results of our analysis also indicate that different forms of social control, indeed, influence individuals' decision to jaywalk. We find the mere presence of cues signaling formal norm-enforcement (police presence) to deter individuals from crossing, hence confirming H_{3c}. This finding is likewise corroborated by participants' responses: participants state that police played a role in the majority of their decisions. In this condition, our approach and application of formal traffic norm cues differs from the work of Jayaraman et al. [JCT+19] in essence. While Jayaraman and colleagues utilized signalized and non-signalized pedestrian crossings as a factor for investigating the effect of formal traffic rules on pedestrians' crossing decisions, we have placed the police officer character as a mere cue for the presence of legal authority. Moreover, this character didn't have a definite effect on traffic rules as in the case of a traffic light that Jayaraman et al.

used. In our experiment, jaywalking was not illegal and police presence didn't directly signify a punishment if participants jaywalked. Moreover, 50 % of the time police was not effective in the trials. Another difference between our approach and Jayaraman et al. is that we tested for deviant behavior of pedestrians in the presence of legal authority, while they tested for pedestrian trust in automated vehicles in the presence or absence of a formal traffic sign. Our results are also in line with Camara and Fox [CF20]. They suggested that rare large penalties could be replaced with milder and more frequent negative utilities, hence preventing pedestrians from acting deviant. In our study, the mere cue of legal norms without certainty of sanctioning seemed to deter our participants from crossing.

Looking at the effect of negative social cues, that is the effect of cues signaling low levels of social conformity, we see a strong increase in deviant behavior with a crossing probability up to 100 %. These results match with the results of Colley et al. [CBR22a] and the reporting of Faria et al. [FKK10], where they observed an increase in crossing behavior probability when other pedestrians started to cross. While this finding indicates the negative effect of cues signaling low levels of norm compliance on the deviant behavior of participants, this strong effect might also result from our experimental design. Compared to a mere cue, our implementation of the negative bystander effect stopped the oncoming traffic, thereby transforming the individual decision to jaywalk into a decision to free-ride. Moreover, Mahadevan et al. [MSS+19] reported an insignificant effect of crossing group behavior on participants' crossing decisions on their pedestrian simulator, which is opposite to our findings. Hence, we cautiously confirm our hypothesis H_{3b} and overall, negative social cues worth deeper research.

In our experiment, positive social cues represented the social sanctioning in the forms of a mother and a child character. We did not observe a difference in crossing behavior predictions in this condition when compared to being alone in the scene, as a result, failed to confirm H_{3a}. However, when we explicitly asked participants how their behavior would differ in real traffic situations, the majority stated that they would generally abide by the rules in the presence of children and police. Overall, this seems indicative that even though participants were in a low-fidelity virtual environment with a delivery task assigned to them, they were affected by the social control of bystanders, however, social sanctioning might play a bigger role in real-life interactions, than observed in the virtual environment.

When we explored the potential interaction effects of vehicle type by task urgency or social control on crossing predictions, we only found a significant difference between AVs and HDVs in mother and child condition compared to being alone. This effect existed only in risk-controlled trials, meaning that when the risk of collision is balanced, having the mother and the child in the scene decreased the crossing probability in front of HDVs while it didn't change the crossing probability in front of AVs. A potential explanation might be that, when mother and child existed in the scene participants were more risk-avoidant and cautious about crossing in front of human-driven vehicles, while they still relied on the defensive nature of AVs, and they didn't alter their behavior in the presence of the mother and the child. On the whole, to our knowledge, no study regarding pedestrian - AV interaction considered the effect of social norms by focusing on the effect of bystanders as we utilized.

Limitations and Future Directions

We used a gamification approach to eliminate task fatigue in the experiment and to make the participants more involved with the task. The majority of our participants seemed to enjoy the idea of earning points. Furthermore, the point system helped us to establish costs and benefits more realistically, than leaving these concepts to participants' imagination in our VR study. We have observed that gamification fits well with repetitive tasks since it places these tasks conceptually in a meaningful context. However, since we used gamification, we took the liberty of keeping the environment in low fidelity. The effect of this decision was reflected in the experienced realism ratings of participants in IPQ results. Benefiting from a more realistic environment in the next iteration can improve experienced realism, hence an overall more immersive experience, which might provide more fine-grained results.

Since we primed our participants that AVs would always be conflict-avoidant and yield to them, we did not include non-yielding AVs in our design. A future study where we introduce non-yielding AVs can help us position our current results regarding risk control in a more validated place.

We had a rather young sample with individuals from similar educational backgrounds. Deb et al. [DSC+17] reported on their PRQF scale validation study that younger people were more receptive towards AVs. We could confirm this finding with our young sample. However, a more diversified sample could draw a more realistic picture of the existing traffic dynamics. Another limitation of the study is the unbalanced gender distribution, as the high number of female participants—generally more prosocial—may have skewed the results. Moreover, we arranged the traffic flow unidirectional in our experiment, for the sake of keeping the task less complicated and making sure that participants would not miss the target vehicle. However, this can be enhanced with some alterations in the study design. Furthermore, we have given participants the repetitive task of crossing the same street. Even though we have emphasized the pizza delivery task in our instructions and in our game concept, benefiting from different virtual streets could have blinded our manipulations even better.

In reality, the presence of actual cars might intensify the impact of social control mechanisms. For instance, the negative bystander effect could be more pronounced with real-world cues like visible wear on vehicles or disregard for traffic rules, reinforcing deviant behavior. Conversely, social conformity might be stronger in real-life settings where participants observe real people adhering to norms around AVs, making them more likely to conform due to the tangible social pressure and accountability. Additionally, real AVs would provide direct feedback on the effects of deviance or conformity, possibly affecting individual cost-benefit calculations more strongly than in a VR simulation.

3.2   Chapter Summary

In summary, it seems that AVs of the future will be the inferior counterpart of interaction with humans if they remain risk-aversive and if there is an imbalanced distribution of crash risk among human-driven and automated vehicles. When the costs of deviant behavior are balanced while crossing in front of these vehicles, the sole effect of automation attributes does not influence the crossing behavior, which supports the idea that, in essence, people would treat the AVs the same as HDVs if they behave similarly. While the defensive nature of AVs is essential for the safety of future mixed traffic and for the acceptance of AVs, this might incentivize individuals to exploit them in the long term. Lastly, our exploration of social norm dynamics reveals that social control, especially legal cues carries the potential to be the regulator of humans' deviant behavior.

4 Facilitating Social Behavior Through External Interaction

Even though humans may not alter their behavior around AVs and treat them as manually driven cars, the current communication situation still has room for improvement. Although traffic rules seem to play a big role in regulating traffic interactions, it is not the ultimate solution, and depending on the location, they are treated more flexibly than intended. Hence, it becomes useful to look for ways to improve the interaction between AVs and humans in traffic, even if there seems to be a small change in human behavior around them. This does not keep us from going beyond and striving to make traffic interactions smoother. In this chapter, we present the work in which we explore ways to improve communication and interaction between AVs and humans through external communication cues, by exploring their timing and intended message to convey. The parts in this chapter were published in papers Şahin et al. [ŞDMB21], Şahin İppoliti et al. [ŞİDD+23] and Sahin Ippoliti et al. [SITKB23].

4.1 Correct Timing of External Communication

The current section presents an online game intended to reveal the optimal timings for cueing a deceleration intention of an AV for pedestrians to understand its intentions efficiently.

4.1.1 Motivation and Related Work

eHMIs have been explored in recent years to compensate the lack of communication between drivers and other traffic participants. With regard to making decisions to cross a street, Dey et al. [DHB+20] and Ackermans et al. [ADR+20] found that participants' willingness to cross remained higher when eHMIs were placed on the vehicle in comparison to the baseline condition where no eHMIs were introduced. Petzoldt et al. [PSB18b] experimented with front-breaking lights on vehicles.

A study by De Clercq et al. [DCDNV+19a] investigated participants' feeling of safety by presenting yielding state eHMIs before the deceleration point, after the deceleration point, and on the deceleration point. They confirmed that eHMI timing had an effect on participants' feelings of safety. Dietrich et al. [DTB20] designed a study where they measured the crossing initiation time of the participants in front of an AV. They changed the deceleration style and eHMI presence in their experiment. They found that participants started crossing earlier when eHMIs existed and larger breaking distances yielded shorter crossing times.

Though existing works show that deceleration distance and signaling yielding intent has an effect on the crossing behavior and perceived safety, it remains unclear when the automated vehicle's intent to yield should be presented by the eHMI and how this is connected to the deceleration of the vehicle. We conduct a study using an online video-game setting. Our results suggest that the most efficient timing strategy to signal a yielding intent is either simultaneously with the deceleration maneuver or before the deceleration maneuver.

4.1.2 Apparatus and Method

We based our eHMI timings on the implicit cue of the deceleration maneuver. In this sense, we arranged our late and early timings with equal distances to the deceleration point. We also added a synced eHMI timing with the deceleration maneuver.

Our hypotheses for the study are:

- H1: Participants will cross the street earlier when they see a yielding intent signal in comparison to yielding vehicles without a signal.

- H2: Participants will cross the street earlier if automated vehicles signal their yielding intent earlier.

- H3: Participants will perceive yielding intent cues that were signaled earlier more positively regarding measures such as trust and perceived safety.

We created an online game that presents a first-person view in 3D to participants, where they could participate remotely.

Dependent variables

Crossing onset: This measure was collected by starting a timer from the moment the vehicle appeared until the participant initialized crossing by stepping on the street.

User Experience: Participants scored 4 different 11-point Likert scale statements after each trial. These were: 1- *"It was easy to recognize the intent of the vehicle"*, 2- *"It would be easy to see that the vehicle will yield without the display"*, 3- *"I trusted the vehicle"*, and 4- *"I felt safe when crossing the street"*. The second statement was only presented after yielding AV conditions.

Apparatus

The experimental environment was developed as a web application using Unity3D (version 2017.4). The street design and 3D models of Gruenefeld et al. [GWL+19]

IVs	Levels					
Vehicle Type	Automated Vehicle				Conventional Vehicle	
Vehicle Behavior	Yielding			Non-yielding	Yielding	Non-yielding
eHMI	60m	45m	30m	Off	NA	
	🚗x5	🚗x5	🚗x5	🚗x5	🚗x3	🚗x3

Figure 4.1: Independent variables and their levels in the experiment. We used a within-group design. Three independent variables were introduced: Vehicle type with two levels as automated vehicles (AV) and conventional vehicles (CV), Vehicle behavior with two levels as yielding and non-yielding, yielding intent eHMI signaling distances as 60 m, 45 m, and 30 m. Conditions with eHMIs were presented 5 times, while the rest of the conditions were presented 3 times.

were used in the study (see Figure 4.2). The virtual 3D environment consisted of a street with buildings in an urban setting. The task of the participants was to cross the road while a single vehicle was approaching from their left. Yielding vehicles emerge 65 m away from the participant with a velocity of 50 km/h (13.89 m/s). They start to decelerate at a 45 m distance. They come to a stop at 5 m from the participant with a deceleration rate of 2.4 m/s^2. Non-yielding vehicles drive past the participant with a constant speed. The task of the participant is to cross the road by starting from the green box and reaching the red box.

Figure 4.2: Top View of Experimental Setup.

Participants used a mouse and keyboard for navigating in the game.

Figure 4.3: Visualization of the AV with an eHMI. Left: eHMI is off, the vehicle is cruising. Right: eHMI is on, vehicle will yield for the participant. Conventional vehicles did not have any light cues. Participants were introduced to different vehicle types in the game before the experiment.

Participants

20 participants (6f, age 19-59, $M = 27.5$, $SD = 10.75$) completed the experiment. Participation was voluntary, and the selection criteria were based on living in Germany and speaking German.

Procedure

After participants were introduced to the experiment, an online consent form appeared. Following a short demographic form, instructions were given. Participant data were anonymized.

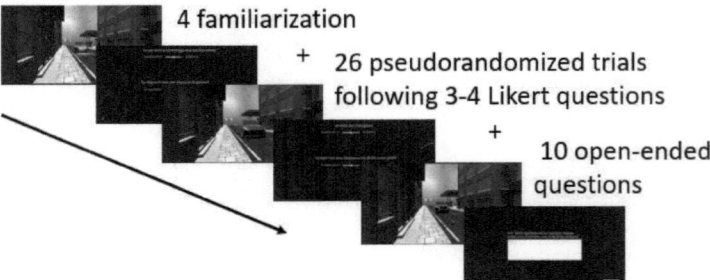

Figure 4.4: Experimental procedure. Participants started with familiarization with the environment and vehicles. Afterward, they completed 26 crossing tasks.

Statistical Analysis

Statistical analysis was performed via the statistics programs JASP (version 0.14.0.0) [JAS20] and RStudio (version 4.0.3) [T+15].

The distribution of data was tested using a Shapiro-Wilk test. The homogeneity of variance was tested with Levene's test. Since the criteria were not fulfilled for ANOVA due to non-normal distributions, the data was transformed using $\log_{10}(x + 1)$ as the transformation function in RStudio. Transformed, normally distributed and homogeneity of variance ensured data sets were used. For statistical analysis of the crossing onsets of factors "Vehicle type" and "Vehicle behavior", a 2 x 2 Repeated Measures ANOVA was performed in JASP. To analyze the possible differences among different eHMI conditions (60 m, 45 m, 30 m) and the baseline yielding CV condition, One-Way Repeated Measures ANOVA with four levels was conducted. Likert scale questions in between trials were tested with Friedman's ANOVA in RStudio.

4.1.3 Results

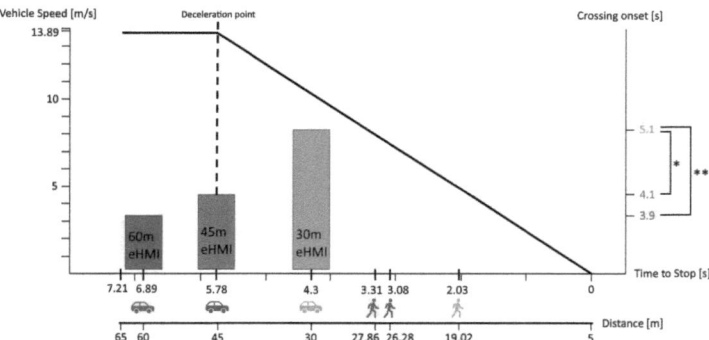

Figure 4.5: Vehicle movement graph with participant crossing onsets and distances. X Axis on the left (Vehicle Speed) indicates vehicle speed in m/s. The other x axis on the right (Crossing Onset) shows crossing onset in seconds for each yielding AV condition. * p < .05, ** p < .01. The first Y axis (Time to Stop) demonstrates yielding intent signaling and crossing initiations in seconds before the vehicle comes to a stop. The second y axis (Distance) indicates distances in meters where yielding intent was signaled for each yielding AV condition and how much distance existed between the participants and vehicles when participants started crossing.

For each yielding vehicle condition, the vehicle emerged from 65-meter distance from the participant with 50 km/h or 13.89 m/s speed. At this moment, the time until stopping was 7.21 seconds. The vehicle started decelerating at 45 meters when the time to stop was 5.78 seconds. The vehicle came to a stop at 5 meters from the participant. It can be observed from vehicle and human icons that participants started crossing around the same time for 60 m and 45 m eHMI conditions even though there were equal distances among all yielding intent eHMI conditions. In this sense, signaling yielding intent before the deceleration maneuver was not more efficient than signaling it simultaneously with the deceleration maneuver.

Crossing Onset

The initial inspection of crossing onset differences between factors "Vehicle type" (AV, CV) and "Vehicle behavior" (yielding, non-yielding) yielded a significant main effect of Vehicle behavior ($F(1, 19) = 6.95$, $p = .016$, $\eta_G^2 = .268$). Bonferroni corrected Post hoc test resulted in significant earlier crossing onsets for yielding vehicles ($p_{\text{bonf}} = .016$). Further, a non-significant effect of Vehicle type ($F(1, 19) = 4.08$, $p = .057$, $\eta_G^2 = .177$) and a significant interaction effect of Vehicle behavior x Vehicle type ($F(1, 19) = 11.16$, $p = .003$, $\eta_G^2 = .370$) was found. Bonferroni corrected Post hoc tests indicated that yielding AVs lead to significantly earlier crossing onsets than all the other conditions ($.001 < p_{\text{bonf}} < .013$). The rest of the comparisons did not yield any significant differences ($p_{\text{bonf}} = 1$) (see Figure 4.6).

To explore the crossing onset differences between yielding AVs signaling their yielding intent from 60 m, 45 m, and 30 m and yielding CV condition, a One-Way ANOVA with four levels was performed. Results indicated significant differences among these conditions ($F(1.98, 19) = 10.97$, $p < .001$, $\eta_G^2 = .366$). Bonferroni corrected Post hoc tests yielded a statistically significant difference between 30 m and 45 m eHMI ($p_{\text{bonf}} = 0.034$), 30 m and 60 m eHMI ($p_{\text{bonf}} = 0.002$), 45 m eHMI and yielding CV ($p_{\text{bonf}} < 0.001$) and lastly, 60 m eHMI and yielding CV conditions ($p_{\text{bonf}} < 0.001$) (see Figure 4.7).

User Experience

Friedman's ANOVA was used to analyze the answers to the 11-point Likert scale statements. The first statement was *"It was easy to recognize the intent of the vehicle"*. Participants generally answered this question with high scores ($6.84 < M < 8.17$, $2.10 < SD < 2.80$) and no significant differences among yielding vehicle conditions (30 m eHMI, 45 m eHMI, 60 m eHMI, yielding CV) were present ($\chi^2(3) = 6.70$, $p = .081$).

The second statement *"It would be easy to see that the vehicle will yield without the display"* resulted in no significant differences among the yielding AV conditions (30 m eHMI, 45 m eHMI, 60 m eHMI) ($\chi^2(2) = .88$, $p = .641$). Participants generally answered this question with low scores ($3.35 < M < 3.86$, $2.85 < SD < 3.30$).

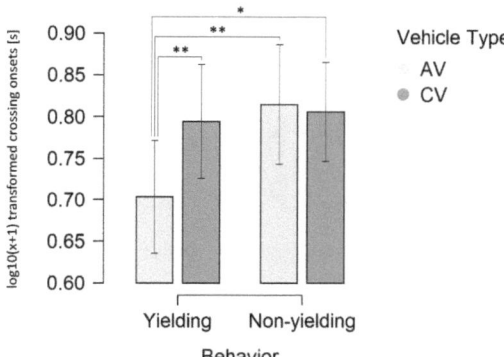

Figure 4.6: Average crossing onsets for yielding and non-yielding vehicles. The time on the y-axis represents $\log_{10}(x + 1)$ transformed crossing onsets in seconds after a vehicle appeared in the scene. The x-axis represents vehicle groups with different behavior. Standard errors are represented by the error bars attached to each column. * p < .05, ** p < .01.

The third statement *"I trusted the vehicle"* was rated differently by participants. Friedman's ANOVA for 4 yielding vehicle conditions (30 m eHMI, 45 m eHMI, 60 m eHMI, yielding CV) resulted in significant differences ($\chi^2(3) = 14.19$, $p = 0.002$). Post hoc tests indicated a significant difference between the yielding AV conditions (30 m eHMI, 45 m eHMI, 60 m eHMI) and the yielding CV condition ($p < 0.05$).

The analysis of the fourth statement *"I felt safe when crossing the street"* indicated no significant differences between the 4 yielding vehicle types (30 m eHMI, 45 m eHMI, 60 m eHMI, yielding CV) ($\chi^2(3) = 5.03$, $p = .169$). The mean ratings seemed high for all conditions ($6.49 < M < 8.07$, $2.49 < SD < 2.89$).

4.1.4 Discussion

As hypothesized in H1, seeing a yielding intent presented on the eHMI resulted in earlier crossing initiations by pedestrians in comparison to not seeing them. Hence, we could confirm H1, that explicit communication of AVs encourages pedestrians to initiate their crossings sooner as De Clercq et al. [DCDNV+19a],

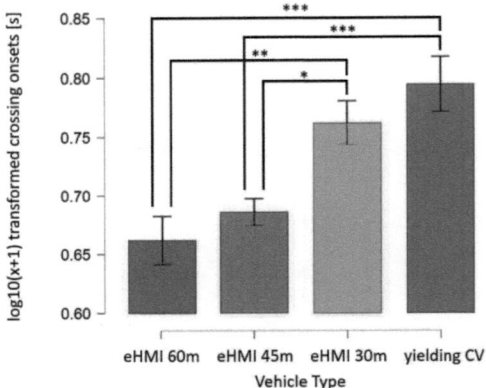

Figure 4.7: Average crossing onsets for yielding vehicles. The time on the y-axis represents $\log_{10}(x + 1)$ transformed crossing onsets in seconds after a vehicle appeared in the scene. The x-axis represents yielding vehicle groups. Standard errors are represented by the error bars attached to each column. * $p < .05$, ** $p < .01$, *** $p < .001$.

Dietrich et al. [DTB20], and Holländer et al. [HCM+19] suggested. However, our results also indicated that a late yielding intent cue did not significantly shorten the crossing onsets. When we signaled the yielding intent from a 30 m distance, participants initiated their crossing similar to the trials, in which we did not present an eHMI. It seems that, by the time the late yielding intent cue was presented to participants, they had already decided to cross or not to cross by checking the deceleration maneuver of the vehicle.

Early yielding intent eHMIs, which were presented before the actual deceleration maneuver of the vehicle, enabled the shortest crossing onsets. Participants started crossing the street significantly earlier in early eHMI condition when compared to late eHMI condition Hence, we could also confirm H2 partially in our study, where we expected shorter crossing onsets in earlier signaled eHMI conditions. However, participants did not start crossing significantly earlier when yielding intent eHMI was presented from a 60 m distance when compared to 45 m distance, which is the distance of the actual deceleration maneuver started. If distance only played a role in participants' crossing initiations, a significant difference would have been observed between these two conditions as well.

Participants might have mainly relied on vehicle locomotion in their decisions and used eHMIs as a reassuring secondary source of information. Participant 9 expressed this as *"You have more of a feeling of being noticed by the cars even as a pedestrian. However, the important decision criterion remains breaking*

itself." As Dey et al. [DMB+20a] suggested, our results and participants' answers
support the notion that yielding intent is communicated more effectively when it
is presented in coordination with the motion dynamics of the vehicle.

In our hypothesis H3, we expected earlier signaled yielding intent cues to foster
higher trust on participants. Our results failed to confirm this, however, participants in the present study reported trusting the vehicles significantly more when
eHMIs were present compared to when eHMIs were not present, in line with
previous work [KML+20, HCM+19, FKSB21].

In our study, we kept the deceleration point constant while changing the eHMI
signaling distances. This enabled us to compare the sole effect of eHMI timing.
Our study differs from Dietrich et al. [DTB20] in this sense since they have
changed the deceleration distances.

Limitations and Future Work

Since our study was conducted remotely, there could have been noise or distracting factors that we could not control. We expect larger differences in reality
where distance and speed can be perceived more correctly. Our findings are limited to a vehicle that drives at a constant speed of 50 km/h and it always starts
decelerating from 45m distance to the participant.

Future work could replicate the present study in VR for a more high-fidelity environment or it could be replicated on a test track with a Wizard of Oz technique
[RLS+15].

4.1.5   Conclusion

The present study investigated the effects of signaling yielding intent with eHMIs
at different times relative to vehicles' deceleration maneuvers with a remote video
game experiment. While the earlier presentation of yielding intent before the deceleration maneuver did not significantly improve crossing onsets when compared
to signaling it simultaneously with the deceleration maneuver, the later presentation of yielding intent did not perform better than not presenting it at all. Our
results suggest that the most efficient timing strategy to signal a yielding intent is
either simultaneously with the deceleration maneuver or before the deceleration
maneuver.

4.2   Fostering Prosocial Behavior Towards Automated Vehicles with External Communication

This section presents a video vignette survey which we explored sympathy eliciting external human-machine interfaces to increase the social driving behavior of

individuals in different common traffic situations requiring deviation from formal rules to help another traffic participant.

4.2.1 Motivation and Related Work

With this work, we contribute to AV-human interaction research by exploring sympathy-eliciting eHMIs with individuals and testing their effects on prosocial driving decisions of participants in a video-vignette-based online survey (N = 90). We hypothesized that these eHMIs invoke sympathy in participants and manipulate their driving or yielding choices. Our results provide supporting evidence that indications of urgency and the amount of waiting time in traffic increase the predictions of yielding the right of way to others. Moreover, we expected that the number of vehicles that are positively affected by the prosocial decisions of participants would be an influential factor in driving decisions. We observed that multiple beneficiaries increased yielding predictions. Lastly, we tested the effect of different traffic scenarios on driving choices. Consequently, we observed an effect of traffic scenarios on yielding predictions when other factors such as vehicle type and the number of beneficiaries are also considered.

Our results demonstrate the effects of automated vehicles with sympathy-eliciting cues such as waiting time and urgency on the prosocial driving choices of individuals. Furthermore, the number of beneficiaries and different traffic situations influence this effect. Our results can aid car manufacturers and HCI researchers when designing communication interfaces for automated vehicles and pave the way for more cooperative traffic interactions in future mixed traffic.

AV-Human Interaction

The current focus of AV research is to create safe vehicles for humans, which humans could rely on the fact that AVs will not violate traffic rules, and they will not put any humans in danger. As Sikkenk and Terken [ST15] pointed out, this leads to a very uniform and defensive driving style of AVs, which may not be ideal in all traffic situations and for passengers that AVs carry. The long-term effects of such exposure to safe and defensive intelligent vehicles on road users' behavior are yet to be discovered [CBR22a, FKB20]. The essential safety features of AVs could affect their fluidity in traffic and potentially undermine their usability in the future. The term "Freezing Robot problem", coined by Trautman and Krause [TK10], describes such situations where intelligent systems not being able to move due to everything else moving around them. Furthermore, considering the game of chicken [RC66] situations where one of the parts needs to "chicken out" in order to solve a crossing problem with the least damage, individuals' repeated exposure to the defensive behavior of AVs might change the dynamics always in the favor of humans since the cost of taking precedence when encountering an AV significantly decreases for humans [FCM+18, CRM+18, CCB+20]. In other

words, conflict-avoidant AVs are assumed to increase humans' rational incentive
to exploit their defensive nature, which was supported by the study results of
Faas et al. [FKB20] and Colley et al. [CBR22a], where they observed a quick
adaptation of individuals crossing in front of yielding AVs. In a large survey
conducted across China and South Korea, Liu et al. [LDWDY20] found that
individuals had an increased intention to bully AVs compared to human drivers,
and they drew attention to potential hindrances of the deployment of AVs due to
the aggressive behavior of human drivers. Our work [SHB22] looked for traces of
deviant pedestrian behavior in their encounters with defensive AVs. Their results
indicated an increased probability of deviant behavior toward AVs, while this
effect occurred due to the reduced perception of risk when crossing in front of
AVs. Considering the aspects of prosocial behavior in traffic while designing AVs
can solve various negative behaviors towards AVs ranging from playful curiosity
to aggression, which was further reported in previous works [SCY+10, MCSS20,
MNF+19].

To our knowledge, there are a limited number of studies placing prosocial behavior under focus in AV-human interaction research. For instance, Sadeghian
et al. [SHE20b] explored the prosocial communication aspects among AVs and
pedestrians in different traffic situations in an online video vignette study. They
pointed out the need for a prosocial approach while designing AVs to foster cooperative behavior beyond technical considerations. They explored how the yielding signal of an AV influenced the perception of traffic climate as an indicator of
prosociality in different traffic scenarios. To investigate factors such as weather
conditions and the vulnerability of road users on the willingness to give right
of way, Sikkenk and Terken [ST15] conducted a study where their participants
decided whether to yield their right of way or continue driving. They sought to
answer whether AVs should be given the ability to choose polite behavior where
it is possible, or whether they should insist on their right of way regardless of the
situation. Our workshop regarding prosocial behavior in mixed traffic explored
the key features of prosocial interaction in different traffic environments such as
motorways and residential areas. The results indicated safety, courtesy, compliance with traffic rules, and communication and cooperation as the frequent
facilitators of prosocial behavior in traffic [SMS+21]. Furthermore, it was expressed by the participants that similar behavior was expected from AVs in the
future. In their intercultural study comparing China and Germany, Lanzer et
al. [LBY+20] explored the effects of polite and dominant communication strategies of autonomous delivery vehicles on individuals' compliance to the request
AV showed. They reported the positive effect of polite strategies on the yielding
compliance of individuals. In our study, we tested for eHMIs that can implicitly
enhance the sympathy in individuals towards AVs, hence leading to one's giving
up on their right of way where there is an opportunity for politeness.

4.2.2   Apparatus and Method

In this section, we present not only the details of an online video vignette survey but also touch upon the design rationale of the stimulus used in the study.

Rationale for Choice of Stimulus

Our research followed the Human-centered Design process [Coo00] by benefiting from early feedback from individuals to reveal eHMI designs inducing sympathy, which are utilized in the follow-up online study. In these sessions, we informed each attendee ($N = 16$, age range $= 23$ - 54, $M = 28.7$, $\pm SD = 6.9$, 12 females, 1 diverse, 4 males) about automated vehicles, and we introduced existing ideas followed by exploring new ideas regarding prosocial behavior in traffic. Consequently, participants elaborated eHMI messages and design ideas to convey cues eliciting sympathetic behavior in other road users. These sessions consisted of two parts, the first part started with the elicitation of potential factors promoting prosocial driving behavior. Attendees were asked to remember the last time they had observed examples of prosocial behavior in traffic. In the second part, the focus was shifted to automated driving and eHMIs. Attendees were instructed to create one eHMI design per each aspect explored in the first part (see Figure 4.8 for some examples). We considered these insights by taking existing research, visibility of the messages on full-screen videos, formal regulations regarding liability, and the use of certain cues in traffic into account.

As a result, a car signals that it has an urgency for helping individuals in need (*urgency*), which is a familiar concept to allow social expression in Schroeter et al. [SRF12], a car that carries prosocial driving qualities and deserves reciprocal cooperative behavior (*driving prosocial*), and a car waiting for a long time in traffic indicating how long it had been immobile (*waiting*) emerged as facilitators of prosocial behavior in traffic.

- Urgency

For conveying a sense of urgency attendees suggested familiar urgency cues such as SOS signal, blue and red lights, and a cross. Yet, some of these signals such as blue light are restricted only to the use of emergency vehicles according to German traffic regulations (§ 38 StVO). Moreover, signaling a cross could have confused individuals about the AV being an ambulance. Hence, we utilized a signal displaying an exclamation mark alternating with a hand receiving a heart to subtly signal a sense of urgency (see Figure 4.9).

- Driving prosocial

An interesting factor was brought up and favored by some of the attendees. If they know a driver is a good driver who takes care of traffic rules and, who is

Figure 4.8: A selection of design solutions from our participants. Top-rated
sympathy-eliciting factors "Urgency", "Prosocial" and "Waiting" were expressed via
different designs such as SOS signals or thumbs-up icons. For ease of comparison,
we have exhibited them on the same car template.

calm and polite, then they would like to return a favor to him/her. Indicating a
prosocial driving vehicle revealed concepts such as a star rating system [Mor20] or
different forms of scoring. We opted for a design without numbers, as indicating
a low score on a vehicle would be against the idea of praising the good drivers,
hence not acceptable by society. Moreover, digits could have been mixed up with
the chronometer concept in the current study. Since the thumbs-up icon has the
meaning of approval and only indicates a positive message, we utilized this sign
as in Wang et al. [WTHR16] for hinting at the prosocial driving qualities of an
AV, with the prerequisite that individuals would be familiarized with the concept
first.

- Waiting time

Indicating a long waiting time was mostly associated with timers shown. We
have adopted this trend and used a chronometer showing how long an AV had
been waiting stative on a traffic scenario. We abstained from using color changes
for waiting time as the use of green and red could have confused individuals
regarding whether the color is aimed at them as a traffic light or is an indication
of the vehicle's state [DHP+20].

Participants

93 participants volunteered without incentivization. 3 participants were excluded
from the analysis due to inconsistent answers and technical problems. 90 partic-

ipants between the ages of 18 and 64 ($M = 27.9$, $\pm SD = 9.98$) were included in the final dataset. All participants were required to be 18 years or older and to hold a driving license allowing them to drive passenger cars. They were recruited via reddit.com, Facebook groups, and on the online notice board of the university. The ethics committee of the university approved the studies according to the Declaration of Helsinki.

Study design

Three favorable ideas, namely urgency AV, waiting (time) AV, and prosocial (driving) AV were utilized as the factor levels for "vehicle type" with their chosen eHMI designs. To control the effect of automation itself as a cue, an AV without eHMI -baseline AV-, and a conventional human-driven vehicle -HDV- with a gender-neutral driver sitting behind the steering wheel was added as the fourth and the fifth level (all factor levels in Figure 4.9). Factor "vehicle type" investigated the potential behavioral influence of vehicle automation and sympathy-eliciting eHMIs on individuals' driving choices. As the second factor, the existence of multiple drivers behind the recipient vehicle was investigated to explore whether multiple beneficiaries affect the driving decisions of the participants (see Figure 4.9). This factor included the levels "single car" and "multiple cars". Lastly, the factor "traffic scenario" aimed to detect potential differences in driving choices in different traffic scenarios (see Figure 4.9). The first of these scenarios contained a recipient vehicle on the opposite lane, indicating to turn into a side road from the busy main road ("cross"). The second scenario demonstrated a recipient vehicle coming from a side road wishing to merge into the busy main road ("merge"). In the last scenario, the recipient vehicle on the opposite lane had roadwork in front of it, hence it indicated changing the lane for passing the obstacle ("roadwork"). In short, we had a 5x2x3 factorial within subjects design. The dependent variable in the present study was a binary answer on driving behavior, namely "yield" or "go first". With the combination of factor levels, we created 30 video snippets which lasted 15 to 17 seconds each, depending on the traffic scenario.

Video vignettes were prepared in Unity 3D (version 2019.4.10) (Unity.com). 3D videos consisted of urban road scenarios where the upper speed limit of 50 km/h was clearly indicated with a signpost. Higher speed limits were considered less ideal for planned scenarios since braking and yielding could be perceived as dangerous acts by our participants. The videos started on a moving vehicle and continued until the vehicle arrived at a point where participants needed to make a decision: to proceed or yield (see Figure 4.10). Participants viewed the traffic from the driver's perspective on full-screen and the last frame was visible when they were making a decision. A full set of 30 vignettes and five training videos can be viewed in supplementary materials. Information regarding the automation level of the car participants perceive themselves in was not given. High traffic density was implemented in order to contain the rationale of yielding

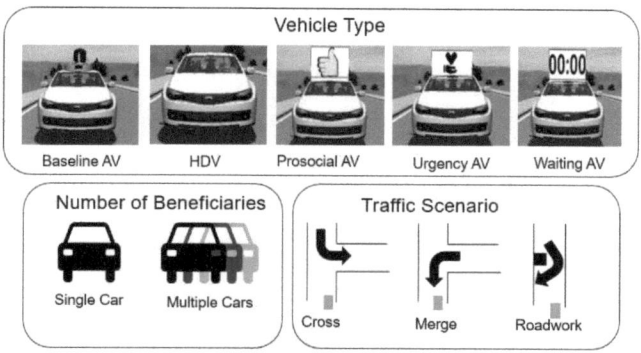

Figure 4.9: Visual demonstration of experimental factors and levels. Factor Vehicle
Type at the top included an AV with sensors, an HDV, and AVs with prosocial eHMI
demonstrated with a green thumbs-up, Urgency eHMI with a novel care urgency
icon, and waiting eHMI with a chronometer. Factor Number of Beneficiaries at the
bottom left included a single car and multiple cars. At the multiple cars level, a
queue behind the single car was formed. The traffic scenario factor at the bottom
right contained a crossing from a priority road to a side road, merging from a side
road to a priority road, and passing around roadwork.

to a "recipient vehicle" for the purpose of helping. Otherwise, one could consider
the yielding action not as helpful but as an unnecessary act if there is a large
traffic gap behind their vehicle. In our videos, there were cars behind, in front,
beyond, and on the side of the participant's perspective. Hence, the only way
a recipient vehicle could continue to drive was when a car on the priority road
yielded to them. In our scenarios, this decision only belonged to our participants
and their main task was whether to yield or to continue driving.

Procedure

Participants were provided with a survey link to the SoSci Survey tool [Lei14]
after they agreed to participate. Firstly, they approved the online consent form
to proceed further. Then, their demographics were asked. Afterward, 5 training
videos introducing different vehicle types on the survey were presented. Each
video explained what type of cars participants may see and what would their
communication interface indicate if they possessed one. In other words, we did
not test for the intuitiveness of the designs but rather informed participants
regarding the exact message the AV carries via eHMIs. Then, the experimental
part started with the task of the participants watching 30 pseudo-randomized
video vignettes of traffic situations and choosing whether they would proceed
without stopping or yielding their priority after videos ended at a decision-making

Figure 4.10: Three different scenario snippets from participants' perspective. Top: an AV with urgency eHMI signals a left turn to a side road, with a queue of cars behind it (scenario "cross"). Middle: An AV with waiting eHMI signals a left turn to a priority road, with no queue behind it (scenario "merge"). Bottom: An AV with a prosocial eHMI waiting for a traffic gap to pass the roadwork, with a queue of cars behind it (scenario "roadwork").

point. Randomization enabled eliminating the learning effects on collected data.
Participants chose their decisions for each video while they could still see the
last frame after the video ended. Furthermore, they optionally explained the
grounding reason for their decision with a text box. All videos were viewed in
full-screen and on average participants needed 27 minutes to complete the survey.

Statistical Analysis

All steps were performed in RStudio (version 1.4.1106) [RSt20]. To analyze the
yielding and taking priority behavior, we calculated a generalized linear mixed-
effects model (GLMM) [NW72], by using the glmer function of the Lme4 package (version 1.1-27.1) [BMBW15] with logic link option. While experimental
factors were added as fixed effects, within-subject variance was added as a random effects factor. To compare best fitting models, we used forward stepwise
method and detected best performing model with compare_performance function in performance package and base ANOVA function in R with Chi-squared
tests [LBSP+21]. Furthermore, we reported the predicted marginal effects of each
condition with crossing probabilities, which were calculated using the ggeffects
package (version 1.1.1.1) [Lüd18].

4.2.3   Results

In this section we demonstrated figures in average marginal effects as an indicator
of the change of observed behavior in comparison to the reference level in each
factor, that are HDV in vehicle type, Single car in Number of Beneficiaries and
Cross scenario in Traffic scenario. Moreover, we presented marginal means which
indicate average probability of yielding the right of way while holding the other
factors constant at their proportions. This enabled us to present more intuitive
results. Furthermore, we reported odds ratios of each condition in the model
comparison table (Table 4.1). Our best fitting model indicated significant main
effects of Vehicle Type, Number of beneficiaries and Traffic scenario; interaction
effects of Number of Beneficiaries x Vehicle Type, and Number of Beneficiaries x
Traffic Scenario. Overall, participants chose to drive on 61 % of the time, while
choosing to yield 39 % of the time.

Main Effects

The presence of Baseline AV did not significantly alter crossing probabilities (β
$= 0.07$, $z(2700) = 0.27$, $Pr(> |z|) = 0.78$) (see Figure 4.11). An AV indicating
prosocial driving qualities significantly increased yielding probabilities ($\beta = 0.81$,
$z(2700) = 3.18$, $Pr(> |z|) < .01$). Furthermore, Urgency indicating AV signifi-
cantly increased yielding probabilities ($\beta = 3.18$, $z(2700) = 12.51$, $Pr(> |z|) <$
$.001$). Similarly, waiting time indicating AV significantly increased yielding prob-
abilities ($\beta = 1.56$, $z(2700) = 6.34$, $Pr(> |z|) < .001$). No significant differences

Table 4.1: GLMM results of vehicle type, number of beneficiaries and traffic Scenario on driving behavior

Predictors	M1 Odds Ratios	M2 Odds Ratios	M3 Odds Ratios	M4 Odds Ratios	M5 Odds Ratios
(Intercept)	0.25 ***	0.11 ***	0.14 ***	0.11 ***	0.08 ***
Baseline AV	0.90	0.89	0.89	0.89	1.08
Prosocial AV	1.59 **	1.67 ***	1.67 ***	1.68 ***	2.26 **
Urgency AV	10.46 ***	13.10 ***	13.38 ***	13.50 ***	24.11 ***
Waiting AV	2.53 ***	2.78 ***	2.81 ***	2.82 ***	4.80 ***
Multiple Cars		3.83 ***	3.87 ***	6.01 ***	10.52 ***
Merge			0.63 ***	0.85	0.85
Roadwork			0.71 **	1.05	1.05
Multiple Cars * Merge				0.56 *	0.58 *
Multiple Cars * Roadwork				0.48 **	0.49 **
Baseline AV * Multiple Cars					0.74
Prosocial AV * Multiple Cars					0.63
Urgency AV * Multiple Cars					0.33 ***
Waiting AV * Multiple Cars					0.41 **
Random Effects					
σ^2	3.29	3.29	3.29	3.29	3.29
τ_{00}	1.96	2.38	2.42	2.46	2.38
ICC	0.37	0.42	0.42	0.43	0.42
N	90	90	90	90	90
Observations	2700	2700	2700	2700	2700
Marginal r^2 / Conditional r^2	0.131 / 0.456	0.198 / 0.535	0.204 / 0.542	0.206 / 0.546	0.214 / 0.544

*** $p < .001$, ** $p < .01$, * $p < .05$

Note: *Results of Generalized Mixed Effect Regression Models. Odds ratios and Random Effects are reported for models 1 - 5. M1: Vehicle Type, M2: M1 + Number of Beneficiaries, M3: M2 + Traffic Scenario, M4: M3 + Traffic Scenario x Number of Beneficiaries, M5: M4 + Vehicle Type x Number of Beneficiaries.*

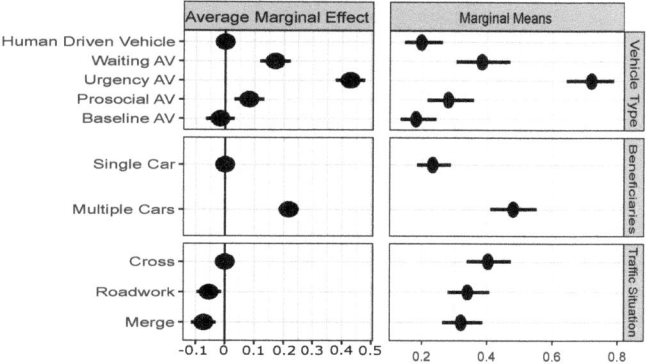

Figure 4.11: Average Marginal Effects and Marginal Means for Main effects of
Vehicle Type, Number of Beneficiaries and Traffic Scenario. Left plot shows the
average marginal effects(AME) of our three experimental factors in reference to their
baseline factor levels. The vertical line represents the effect of the reference level.
The right column reports the marginal means (MM) for the different factor levels
on yielding probabilities, holding the other factors constant at their proportions.
Points indicate AME/MM, horizontal lines the 95% CIs. Effects based on results of
GLMM.

among crossing probabilities in merging scenario (β = -0.16, $z(2700)$ = 0.91,
$Pr(> |z|)$ = 0.36) and roadwork scenario (β = 0.04, $z(2700)$ = 0.27, $Pr(> |z|)$
= 0.78) were found under main effects, however multiple interaction effects with
other factors were revealed.

Interaction Effects

When multiple cars were present behind the recipient car, yielding probabilities
decreased in Merge traffic scenario (β = -0.54, $z(2700)$ = -2.35, $Pr(> |z|) < .05$)
(see Figure 4.12). Similarly, yielding probabilities decreased significantly in the
presence of multiple cars in Roadwork scenario (β = -0.72, $z(2700)$ = -2.97, $Pr(> |z|) < .01$). The presence of multiple vehicles did not affect yielding probabilities
in Baseline AV (β = -0.30, $z(2700)$ = -0.87, $Pr(> |z|)$ = 0.38) and Prosocial
AV condition (β = -0.45, $z(2700)$ = -1.39, $Pr(> |z|)$ = 0.16). However, when
multiple cars existed behind the oncoming car, yielding probabilities significantly
decreased in Urgency AV (β = -1.10, $z(2700)$ = -3.31, $Pr(> |z|) < .001$) and in
Waiting AV conditions (β = -0.90, $z(2700)$ = -2.83, $Pr(> |z|) < .01$).

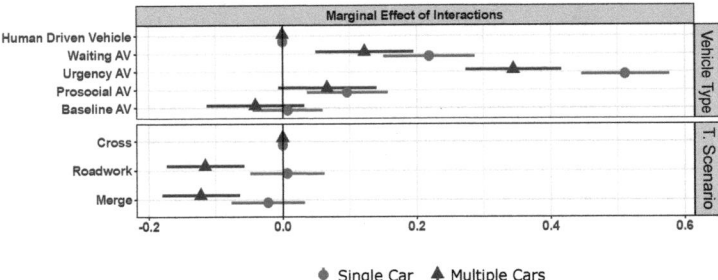

Figure 4.12: Effect of Vehicle Types and Traffic Scenario conditioned by Number of Beneficiaries. The figure illustrates the average marginal effects on yielding probabilities of Vehicle Type and Traffic Scenario, conditioned on Number of beneficiaries. The red point represents single car, while the blue arrow indicates multiple cars. Horizontal lines show 95% CIs. Vertical lines represent the average crossing probability of reference level.

4.2.4 Discussion

This section elaborates on the results regarding driving choices we presented in the previous section.

Individuals Treat Automated Vehicles Similar to Human-Controlled Vehicles

Our study concluded that assumed differences in people's yielding or driving behavior did not exist among human-controlled and baseline automated vehicles equipped with sensors. These results indicate a different outcome than the survey results of Liu et al. [LDWDY20], where they reported individuals' greater intention to bully AVs. However, such behavioral change is presumed to be formed after a longitudinal exposure to defensive AV behavior on the streets. Our study design was primarily formed to find potential solutions to a future problem; thus investigating a longitudinal behavioral change was not our key focus, even though our participants were repeatedly exposed to AVs through repeated measures design. Faas et al. [FKB20] conducted a longitudinal experiment where they tested for temporal behavior change of individuals crossing in front of AVs. They reported increased trust and decreased crossing time in time. Furthermore, Colley et al. [CBR22a] indicated similar habituation of pedestrians crossing behavior in front of AVs after repeated exposure. These results encourage further studies regarding longitudinal behavior change in AV-human interaction.

Sympathy-Eliciting eHMIs Foster Prosocial Behavior

Although we did not observe a fundamental difference between human-controlled
and baseline automated vehicles, we find that sympathy-eliciting eHMIs, especially urgency and waiting time indications significantly increased individuals'
yielding behavior predictions. Hence, we could argue that such cues may facilitate prosocial behavior in traffic, regardless of being utilized by AVs or human-
controlled vehicles. Furthermore, they could be utilized not only in high-level
AVs but also in other levels where the driver still sits behind the steering wheel.

Among all eHMIs we have looked into, urgency indication increased yielding
predictions exceptionally. It is likely that participants may have connected urgency indicating eHMI with emergency vehicles and gave trained answers similar
to their behavior in the presence of daily instances, even though we abstained
from using existing medical urgency signals such as a red cross. These results are
also in line with the empathy-altruism hypothesis by Batson [Bat10]. Since the
urgency signal indicated greater distress of the recipient, participants might have
acted more with sympathy in their encounter with AVs indicating urgency. We
further revealed that individuals' yielding decision was more emphasized when
urgency indicating vehicle was alone in the scenario, potentially due to reduced
time costs of waiting. This concept was highly similar to participant ideation
workshop results of Schroeter et al. [SRF12], where they suggested allowing social expressions by conveying messages such as being "in a hurry" or "driving
kids to school". These results point out a need for expressing such cues even in
today's traffic. As presented by Wang et al. [WTHR16], driving a car leads to
the depersonalization of individuals, which could result in road rage instead of
sympathy e.g. to a mother who is driving her children to the hospital to see their
dying father [Byr00]. Care urgency signaling may have contributed to breaking
the depersonalization of AVs in our survey.

Similar to urgency, waiting indication with eHMIs reminded participants of
everyday traffic situations where they could sympathize with the frustration of
minutes-long waiting. This familiarity may have moved participants to act more
prosocially in the presence of waiting timers. Similar to urgency indicating AV,
it seems that individuals felt more encouraged to yield their right of way when
this vehicle was alone in the scene, compared to a human-driven vehicle. These
results may indicate that such cues work the best when helping a recipient costs
the least while maximizing the benefit of the recipient.

Despite being a novel concept, prosocial eHMI was suggested as a desirable
option to perform a reciprocal reaction towards prosocial vehicles. This desire
for reciprocity seems to be in line with the results of Knobel et al. [KHM+13],
in which they reported the frequent answers of their participants while explaining prosocial behavior. Moreover, the thumbs-up icon was used by Wang et al.
[WTHR16] for drivers to receive feedback regarding their driving behavior and
send feedback to other drivers. Yet, in our study, the use of the thumbs-up sign

might have led to unintended interpretations of the cue despite its being introduced to its design and intended message before the survey. Even though we sought to convey the general message of cooperative driving in this concept, in some cases the eHMI was taken as a cue that the AV was being courteous to participants personally because of the green thumbs-up icon. This could explain why their yielding choices in this condition were decreased compared to other eHMI concepts. These results might point out bigger issues in AV-human interaction research such as the frame of reference [DHP+20], that general messages might be interpreted by individuals as personal messages.

Increasing the Number of Recipients Amplifies Prosocial Driving Decisions

An increasing number of vehicles waiting for a traffic gap usually affects participants' decisions toward prosocial behavior. When a queue formed behind the recipient vehicle, participants conceived the situation with a longer period of waiting time due to traffic dynamics. They inferred that if a queue is formed, cars must have been waiting without anybody yielding for them. Thus, the majority of participants seemed to be more willing to help in the presence of a long queue, with some exceptions concerning one's own waiting time in case of yielding their right of way to multiple cars. This could be explained by the arousal: cost–reward model by Piliavin et al. [P+81]. The cost of multiple vehicles not receiving help could have been evaluated as higher than the participants' own cost of waiting. Similarly, the cost of a single vehicle not receiving help could have been perceived by participants as less important than their cost of yielding the right of way, since the possibility of a single car finding a traffic gap is higher than a long queue of vehicles. However, it is important to point out one more aspect: in our survey, participants did not experience the real cost of waiting after making their decision. Introducing real waiting time after their yielding action may have pointed out different results.

The Role of Different Traffic Situations on Prosocial Behavior is Implicit

In all the scenarios, participants were on a priority road where they did not have to stop for other vehicles due to traffic regulations. This enabled us to collect yielding behavior only for the purpose of helping other cars as a prosocial act. Two of these scenarios included the same crossroad, with the recipient vehicle coming from different directions. In one of them, the recipient vehicle signaled to join the opposite lane of the priority road where the participant was situated, while the other scenario indicated a turn of the recipient vehicle to the side road from the opposite lane. The third scenario demonstrated a roadblock situation where the ego perspective car still had priority. These scenarios might have been too similar in nature to detect the situational effects on driving decisions since in all of them the ego perspective car had the priority. Alternatively, a game of chicken [FCM+18] scenario can be used for controlling priority rules in the future.

Yet, we observed an interaction effect of the number of beneficiaries and traffic scenarios on yielding choice predictions. When a single-car existed in these situations, the behavior of the participants did not differ. However, when multiple cars existed, yielding predictions decreased in merge and roadwork scenarios. compared to the cross scenario. This effect might be due to familiarity with such experiences in such situations on priority roads. Participants might have considered a traffic jam on the other side of the priority lane as less costly to solve than helping out a line of cars waiting for their time to merge into the priority road, or a line of cars waiting behind a roadwork. In the cross scenario, participants may have considered that the queue of cars following the recipient car may not be making a left turn, but continuing straight. This could have let them help many people by yielding for the recipient car, without inflating their waiting costs.

Investigating Prosocial Behavior in Traffic is a Worthy Effort

Prosocial behavior in traffic is multifaceted, and it is usually not clear-cut whether a person is acting prosocially in traffic. While the intentions of a traffic participant can be prosocial, the outcome may not follow a similar fashion. Thus, conducting behavioral studies on such a multilayered topic require a closer look at collected behavioral data. We obtained categorical answers from participants regarding their behavioral choices as "yield" or "go first" in three different traffic congestion scenarios and asked them to justify their choices with a short explanation. On the one hand, the majority of yielding choice explanations indicated traces of prosocial behavior. Individuals took into consideration the recipient vehicle and other cars' urgency or waiting time in traffic and established empathy with them (e.g.: "Everyone stands (waits) in such places (crossroads) at one time or another, so you know how annoying it can be"). These results supported the empathy-altruism hypothesis [Bat10]. On the other hand, we observed that there were still considerations regarding prosocial behavior while choosing to drive, such as being afraid of obstructing the traffic flow in one's own lane or being concerned about rear-end-collisions, similar to situational factors for not acting considerate in Knobel et al. [KHM+13]. We presented scenarios deliberately in a traffic jam on the priority lane, for a perception of slow-moving traffic and the least chances of a traffic gap opening for the recipient's car to drive after the participant's car moves. Taking speed and gap sizes under special consideration while creating video vignettes did mostly well in order to provide optimal scenarios for detecting prosocial behavior.

However, participants stated that in some scenarios the speed was perceived as too high, as a result, a potential collision risk was the reason for continuing to drive. Moreover, one may argue that strictly following priority rules and by abiding traffic rules are also components of prosocial behavior in traffic as in PADI [HHV+14]. However, we could distinguish that the majority of driving choices were mentioned solely as the incentive of following traffic rules while yielding explanations were more diverse in the sense that they emphasized the benefits of other traffic participants.

Even though we did not find any behavioral differences regarding drivers' yielding or non-yielding choices towards human-controlled or automated vehicles only with sensors, the future might bring a different outcome, when human traffic participants are repeatedly exposed to conflict-avoidant behavior of AVs.

Overall, it is a timeless effort to find ways to foster prosocial behavior in traffic for the benefit of society. According to the Global Status Report on Road Safety shared by the World Health Organization [VPV+09] approximately 1.3 million people lose their lives in traffic. This indicates room for improvement in today's traffic. Eckoldt et al. [EHL+16] emphasize that considerate driving is the key to safe traffic; thus, fostering considerate driving in new ways is a valuable attempt.

Our results have shed light on contributing factors to prosocial decisions in traffic such as the number of traffic participants benefiting one's prosocial action. Moreover, we have revealed that sympathy-eliciting cues could act as a catalyst for prosocial behavior. Indicating personal urgency played a major role in participants' yielding behavior. Emphasizing waiting time with an eHMI made our participants more aware of the struggle of the recipient vehicle or its users. These insights could be facilitated by stakeholders to promote a more cooperative traffic environment of today and in the future.

Limitations and Future Directions

Our research had limitations regarding the study design. Since we ran an online study, participant distractions could not be controlled. We excluded participants who gave inconsistent answers. Furthermore, our eHMI designs were deliberately low-fidelity and bigger than they could have been in reality. While using large and simple designs was favorable in video views shown on a computer screen, this may have decreased the realness of video vignettes. Hence, our results may not be representatives of future physical prototypes of eHMIs, and they may not be generalizable to all driving contexts. Yet, participant answers support that video vignettes, which were also utilized in the study of Sadeghian et al. [SHE20b], were effective in making the online survey more realistic than simple descriptions. Moreover, participants were able to imagine the potential results of their actions on the traffic scene after they had made their choices and consequently chose behavioral options by speculating on these potential outcomes. A future study might benefit from carrying this survey in virtual reality with more real-sized and realistic prototypes and a more immersive environment. Moreover, the real consequence of waiting after decision points can be introduced in order to proximate the decision costs to reality.

In our study, we did not focus on individual differences in the driving style of the participants. We only focused on cues that could potentially affect the yielding choices of drivers, other concepts such as locomotion intention cues were outside the scope of this study. However, future studies could investigate the effects of different cues on prosocial behavior.

4.2.5 Conclusion

In summary, this study contributes insights into the behavior of human drivers toward AVs in the far future when AVs co-exist in traffic. A potential behavioral difference towards AVs compared to human-controlled vehicles was assumed, but not found. Our online video vignette survey (N = 90) indicated the positive effects of sympathy-eliciting external human-machine interfaces such as urgency and waiting time indications on individuals' prosocial driving choices. Moreover, other factors such as the number of recipients and traffic scenarios were tested for their effects. While an increased number of recipients led to higher yielding the right-of-way predictions, different traffic scenarios did not influence participants' behavioral choices directly, however, it contributed to their choices when taken together with the number of beneficiaries receiving the prosocial act. Our results shed light on the factors influencing prosocial driving decisions in traffic and how to foster prosocial behavior via external communication cues.

4.3 Balancing the Game of Chicken with AVs via External Communication

Imagine yourself driving your regular car and approaching a narrow passage where two cars are parked on both sides of the road. On the opposite side, a passenger-less self-driving vehicle is approaching the narrowing almost at the same time as you are. Who is going to take priority, and why? Even when fully automated vehicles will become available, there will be a longer phase of "mixed traffic", where both automated and manually driven vehicles are present. Game of chicken scenarios with AVs as in this example pose a crucial consideration for the usability of the services of AVs, such as, how their intention will be understood by humans, and if humans change their social behavior around them. In ambiguous scenarios, humans rely on informal communication originating from vehicle locomotion cues such as acceleration, and from humans, such as gestures and eye contact. While previous simulation studies suggest that vehicle locomotion cues may suffice to resolve the conflicts in bottleneck scenarios [MLKB22], an explicit indication of locomotion intention helps to resolve the conflicts more efficiently [RB21]. We validated these insights on a controlled test track study by using the Wizard of Oz (ghost driver) method [RLS+15]. In our study, we tested explicit locomotion intention cues conveyed with an external display in a realistic bottleneck scenario. Thereby, we hypothesized that in this ambiguous driving scenario, indicating locomotion intention cues with an external interface will alter (1) the driving choices of participants, (2) social perception of AV, and (3) trust in AV compared to non-indication of locomotion intention cues.

4.3.1 Motivation and Related Work

This section presents general AV-human interaction dynamics and conflicts, and the assistive role of external communication interfaces with an emphasis on bottleneck scenarios. It also reviews social interaction dynamics and the role of trust in AV-human interaction.

AV-Human Interaction in Ambiguous Scenarios

Markkula et al. [MMN+20] define interactions as a space-sharing conflict in traffic or an "event with a collision course where interactive behavior is a precondition to avoid an accident". Some interactions can be resolved seamlessly by following predetermined traffic rules, while others, where the rules or the intentions of other road user(s) are unclear, require special communication between road users [EAKA19]. In such ambiguous situations, communication between both road users is particularly important. For example, Risto et al. [REV+17] showed that pedestrians rely particularly on communication with drivers when crossing roads. If communication is missing or misunderstood, it can lead to the participants feeling uncomfortable in the crossing situation, or in the worst case, conflicts. This raises the question: how do road users decide who goes first and how is this communicated? There is evidence that when the situation is ambiguous and the intention of the vehicle is not clear, pedestrians resort to explicit communication to seek confirmation [DT17]. In the case of road users interacting with AVs in such ambiguous situations where the intention of the vehicle is not clear from its kinematics alone, the lack of explicit, driver-centric communication poses a problem. To solve the communication problem of missing driver-centric communication in AVs, eHMIs (External Human-Machine Interfaces) have been proposed. In their real-world AV-pedestrian interaction experiment, Dey et al. [DMB+20b] showed that when the intention of the vehicle is clear from its movement/kinematics alone, pedestrians do not need an eHMI, but it can disambiguate situations where the intention of the vehicle is unclear from vehicle kinematics.

Bottleneck/Game of Chicken Scenarios and eHMI

One of the classic scenarios of ambiguity, when AVs interact with HDVs, arises when there is a deadlock or bottleneck situation without any clear rules that dictate the right of way, and there is a clear need for initiating a communication within a comfortable window of time for a seamless interaction [RB20]. Previous work has shown that vehicle kinematics still have a significant role to play here in communicating intent – lateral movement within the road (driving close to the edge of the road vs. occupying more road space by driving in the center) offers a very clear indication of intent as opposed to longitudinal movements (speed) [RDB21b, MLKB22]. Furthermore, drivers of HDVs expect AVs to yield, and complying AVs were perceived as more trustworthy [MKKB22], although novel behaviors from AVs can confuse drivers [CFR22]. That said, eHMIs are shown to increase perceived safety and reduce mental workload [CFR22], while also facilitating shorter passing time and reducing crashes [RPSB19, RAB20a]. A recent simulation study also corroborated these insights and found that an ideal way for AVs to communicate intent in bottleneck situations is by a combination of eHMI and employing lateral movements [RB21]. Prior research has also shown that eHMIs are not universally beneficial and that they can have adverse effects in terms of overtrust [HWB19a] and violation of safety arising from confusion or ambiguity [FMX+19]. However, the substantial corpus of research showcasing the potential advantages of eHMIs outweigh the drawbacks, and we argue that this warrants a real-world investigation to evaluate its ecological validity, especially in this context of bottleneck negotiation.

From the social interaction perspective, these bottleneck or the game of chicken [RC66] scenarios in which one of the road users makes the decisive move to insist on the right of way or to "chicken out", humans may adapt their behavior in favor of themselves if AVs are strictly defensive and conflict-avoidant [MB18, FCM+18, CCB+20]. This supposition is supported by insights from recent studies: in a large survey conducted across China and South Korea, Liu et al. [LDWDY20] found that individuals had an increased intention to bully AVs compared to human drivers, and they drew attention to potential hindrances of the deployment of AVs due to the aggressive or antagonistic behavior of humans, a phenomenon also corroborated in a study conducted in the United States [MCSS20]. While past research has investigated the function of eHMIs in terms of courteous behavior and polite strategies [LBY+20] and prosocial behavior by means of perceived traffic climate [SHE20b], the potential of eHMIs for improving cooperative and positive behavior in traffic remains unexplored.

While keeping these social dynamics in mind, previous research has established that trust in automation is the key factor for interacting with them and resolving conflicts. Trust in automation can be defined as "the attitude that an agent will help achieve an individual's goals in a situation characterized by uncertainty and vulnerability" [LS04]. Due to a series of trust-related accidents with Tesla Autopilot, the psychological construct of trust has become one of the key issues that need to be resolved to allow a successful implementation of AVs on a large scale [FWR+19]. Drivers and other traffic participants can either appropriately trust, distrust, or overtrust an automation system. Distrust occurs when humans' trust falls below a system's actual capabilities, whereas overtrust means that one excessively trusts automation even in situations the automation cannot handle. The goal of trust research is to "calibrate" users' subjective trust to a level where it matches a system's objective capabilities. Trust was widely addressed in studies on driver-vehicle interaction in the last years and remains an essential requirement in AV-human interaction [HLVK16, GKH+15, WSS+21, HWB+19b]. For measuring trust in AVs in different situations Holthausen et al. [HWWR20] created Situational Trust Scale (STS-AD), measuring different affectors of situational trust such as perceived risks and benefits.

4.3.2 Apparatus and Method

The following section presents details regarding study planning and execution, as well as analysis methods.

Study Design

The study tested one independent variable, which was the type of communication cue on the AV in three different levels. The first condition was acceleration intention. This condition was demonstrated similarly to Mirnig et al. [MGF+22], with a white bar extending sideways repetitively on an LED matrix attached to the radiator grill of AV. The second condition, -deceleration intention- was demonstrated with two white bars moving and merging in the center of the matrix (see Figure 4.13). Both of these designs were based on literature [MGF+22], expert opinions, and a short round of interviews with individuals, as well as field testing for visibility (see Appendix 5.6 for design evolution). Since peripheral vision is more specialized in detecting movement, we opted for animation patterns [GC21]. As closer objects are perceived as bigger and distant objects are smaller, we extended the light animation to imitate a growing and approaching object in acceleration intention while using a shrinking animation pattern in deceleration intention [BWHB18]. Lastly, in the baseline condition, the display did not show anything. Each condition was presented to each participant three times in a pseudo-randomized order.

Dependent variables were (1) binomial driving choices of participants as waited or passed first, (2) SPAT (see Section 2.2), and STS-AD [HWWR20]. SPAT has 7-point semantic differential items made of adjectives in opposite poles. The middle point indicates neutral evaluation. Higher composite average scores indicate that the road user is evaluated as more prosocial by participants. STS-AD composes 6 items measuring situational trust score on a 7-point Likert scale form (1 = fully disagree, 7 = fully agree).

Furthermore, to be informed about the general sample profile, Prosocial and Aggressive Driving Inventory (PADI) [HHV+14] and Prosocial Tendencies Measure Revised PTM-R [CHCR03, RUM+17] were used. PADI has 29 statements which are constructed as 6-point Likert scale items, 1 indicating never acting as described in the statement, and 6 indicating always acting as described in the statement. PTM-R has 15 items with five points, 1 indicating stated behavior "does not describe me at all" and 5 indicating "describes me greatly".

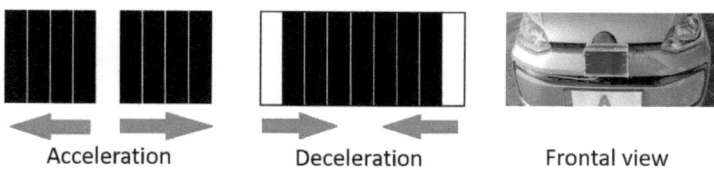

| Acceleration | Deceleration | Frontal view |

Figure 4.13: From left to right: Acceleration intention eHMI with a white bar extending sideways repetitively; deceleration intention eHMI with two white bars extending and merging in the center repetitively; frontal view of AV and eHMI attachment on radiator grill. In no eHMI condition, the display was off.

Apparatus

A 64 x 32 flexible RGB LED matrix[1] with an Adafruit RGB matrix HAT [Ada23] was used for eHMI. The matrix was programmed on a Raspberry Pi 4 Computer (Model B 2GB RAM) with Python Version 3.9. The connection to the Raspberry Pi was built with PuTTy [chi23], and Thonny [Tho23] was used for programming with Python. The matrix was programmed with the rpi-rgb-led-matrix library [Zel23]. To make the matrix work without an internet connection, a Python autostart script was written, which starts the LED-image-viewer directly after the Raspberry Pi is booted. To remotely switch between different displays, i.e. acceleration or deceleration, a simple PowerPoint Presenter with a USB receiver was used. The AV used in the study was a manually driven Volkswagen e-UP. The driver was hidden under a car seat costume similar to Rothenbücher et al. [RLS+15]. Stickers indicating automated driving were placed on the sides and the hood of the car (see Figure 4.16). A dysfunctional Microsoft Xbox 360 Kinect was placed on the roof to simulate a sensor attachment. A custom-made LED matrix with a plexiglass casing was attached with a thin rope and cable binders to the radiator grills (see Figure 4.13). Lastly, branding and license plates were covered.

Participants

24 participants (8 female, 16 male, age range 20 - 67, $M = 30.21$, $SD = 13.44$ years) took part in the study. Selection criteria were being over 18 years old, holding a driver's license ($M = 15.96$ years, $SD = 13.22$), owning a car, and having a normal or corrected-to-normal vision. Their average prosocial ($M = 4.9$ $SD = 0.45$) and aggressive driving scores ($M = 2.32$ $SD = 0.41$) indicated an overall positive and non-aggressive driving style. Their average composite PTM-R results ($M = 2.79$ $SD = 0.48$) signify neutral to a small prosocial tendency in the overall sample. Participation was compensated with 12 euros per hour and 30 cents in travel costs per kilometer. They were reached online and with printed

---

[1] https://www.adafruit.com/product/3826,[Online; accessed 15-March-2023]

flyers. The ethics committee approved the study according to the Declaration of Helsinki.

Procedure

Figure 4.14: Driving paths of AV (blue) and participants (red). Flags indicate trial starting positions. White cars pinpoint the narrow passage where implicit negotiation happens.

All participants were sent an online pre-questionnaire form that could be filled up voluntarily. On the experiment day, participants were invited to the test area with their own cars. AV was parked away from the reception area with the ghost driver inside. Upon arrival, the experimenter provided a consent form, study information, and demographics document in the reception area. Afterward, the experimenter drove with the participant through the driving path and explained the tasks. (see Figure 4.14). Locomotion intention eHMIs and their meanings were also introduced. In the meantime, the ghost driver drove to the starting position of AV. Then, the experimenter positioned herself near the narrow passage and started trials by counting until 3 over walkie-talkies, where both the participant and ghost driver could hear simultaneously (see Figure 4.15). The ghost driver adapted her driving speed according to the participants' driving speed, to approach the narrow passage at the same time. Yet, the ghost driver left enough distance and time to enable the participant to make the decisive move to resolve the conflict. In line with Rettenmaier et al. [RDB21b], implicit locomotion cues of AV were matched with locomotion intention eHMI conditions. In other words, in acceleration eHMI condition, the ghost driver approached the narrow area more assertively with constant speed, while in deceleration eHMI condition she drove with a more defensive style. Lastly, in the neutral condition, a neutral driving style was adopted. The baseline speed was 10-12 km/h unless the participant was a very slow or fast driver. Consequently, the participant either slowed down and stopped, or continued driving and took priority to pass the narrow area. Both parts followed their paths and reached their starting points. Then, the experimenter asked how the driving or waiting decision was formed and to which aspects the participant paid attention. Afterwards, the participant filled out the intermediate questionnaires. After 9 repetitions, the participant drove back to the reception area filled out post-questionnaires, and answered to post-interview questions. On average, each trial including intermediate questionnaires took 3.5 minutes, while the entire study took 90 minutes per participant.

Figure 4.15: Participant POV, driving towards narrow passage.

Figure 4.16: Front view of the AV used in the study.

Analytical Approach

The interviews were analyzed employing an inductive category development [M+04, Tho06] to identify the frequency and distribution of specific words or phrases in the transcripts. We adopted this approach in exchange for Thematic Analysis, as our interviews did not include many statements with underlying feelings and emotions, but rather rich with recurrent words and phrases. Since each question had a specific theme such as usefulness or attention, they were treated as primary codes. Then, the answers were inspected, and similar themes were coded and summarized with code categories, which enabled statements with similar meanings to be grouped into joint code categories. For instance, attention was a predefined code since the question "What did you pay attention to?" would give attention-related answers. "AV reached the gap first" or "AV was too far" would be two different codes under attention-related answers, which eventually be merged under "distance". For the answers given after each trial, the number of occurrences of the same code over 72 trials was reported. Pre-questionnaire (N = 28) and post-questionnaire (N=24) answers were reported per participant. Participants could contribute to multiple codes if they answered with multiple themes. The codes were created and discussed together. All qualitative analysis steps were performed in the software MAXQDA Version 2022 [MAX23].

Quantitative analysis steps were performed in RStudio (version 2023.03.0+386) [RSt20]. To analyze the driving choices of participants, a generalized linear mixed-effects model (GLMM) [NW72] was calculated, by using the glmer function of the Lme4 package (version 1.1-27.1) [BMBW15]. Since the decisions of the participants were binomial, binomial family with logit link option to the regression model was added. The analyses of STS-AD and SPAT were done with two separate linear mixed-effects models (LMM), by using lmer function. In all models, eHMI conditions were added as fixed effects. Within-subject variance, sex, and age-related variability were added as random effects factors.

4.3.3 Results

This section presents quantitative and qualitative results regarding experimental conditions only (acceleration and deceleration intention, and baseline eHMI). In the discussion section, further insights gained from qualitative results are shared.

Effects of Locomotion Intention on Driving Choices, SPAT, and STS-AD

Cumulative driving choices and average SPAT and STS-AD scores are given in Table 4.2.

Table 4.2: Driving choices and descriptive statistics of SPAT and STS-AD evaluations

	Acceleration	Deceleration	Baseline
Number of times Passed/Waited	19/53	64/8	32/40
Aver. Social Perception (SD)	5.21 (0.69)	5.43 (0.74)	4.9 (0.91)
Aver. Trust (SD)	5.39 (0.82)	5.44 (0.82)	5.14 (0.90)

Indicating deceleration intention significantly increased waiting probabilities of participants ($\beta = 2.34$, $z(216) = 5.22$, $Pr(> |z|) < .001$). Indicating acceleration intention significantly decreased waiting probabilities compared to the baseline level of no indication of locomotion intention ($\beta = -0.81$, $z(216) = -2.26$, $Pr(> |z|) < .05$). Furthermore, the indication of deceleration intention significantly increased the probability of AV being perceived as prosocial ($\beta = 9.87$, $t(199.76) = 3.47$, $Pr(> |t|) < .001$). Indication of acceleration intention did not predict an increase in prosocial perception ($\beta = 5.23$, $t(199.76) = 1.84$, $Pr(> |t|) = .06$). Finally, the indication of deceleration ($\beta = 2.05$, $t(190.03) = 1.81$, $Pr(> |t|) = .07$) or acceleration did not predict any changes in situational trust scores compared to the baseline condition ($\beta = 1.61$, $t(190.03) = 1.42$, $Pr(> |t|) = .15$).

Qualitative Feedback: The Effects of Locomotion Intention on Driving Choices

In 53 out of 72 trials (74%), participants decided to wait when faced with an acceleration intention eHMI. Of all the reasons given, half of the answers (26/48) indicated that acceleration intention eHMI affected their decision to wait. Some others (7/24) stated that they did not pay attention to the display in every trial, with four of them only not paying attention to the display at the beginning and three others sometimes not paying attention to the display. Overall, some (7/48)

Table 4.3: GLMM and LMM results of eHMI conditions on driving choices, situational social perception (SPAT), and situational trust (STS-AD)

Predictors	M1 Odds Ratios	M2 Estimates	M3 Estimates
(Intercept)	0.72	37.29 ***	20.22 ***
Acceleration Intention	0.44 *	5.24	1.61
Deceleration Intention	10.41 ***	9.88 ***	2.06
Random Effects			
σ^2	3.29	290.68	46.29
τ_0 ID	0.02	0.00	0.01
τ_0 Age	0.03	31.15	3.13
τ_0 Sex	0.14	0.00	1.58
ICC	0.05		0.09
N ID	24	24	24
N Age	17	17	17
N Sex	2	2	2
Observations	216	216	216
Marginal r^2 / Conditional r^2	0.342 / 0.376	0.053 / NA	0.015 / 0.106

*** $p < .001$, ** $p < .01$, * $p < .05$
Note: GLMM Odds ratios and Random Effects are reported for model 1. LMM Estimates and Random Effects are reported for model 2. M1: eHMI on driving choices, M2: eHMI on situational prosocial perception (SPAT), M3: eHMI on situational trust (STS-AD).

of the answers included feelings, meaning that participants perceived the car was driving more assertively than usual. Other answers included lateral position (2/48), speed (2/48) of the car, and distance (4/48) from parked cars.

Answers explaining the reason participants chose to drive first in the acceleration intention condition were diverse. In some cases (8/23), participants wanted to test the capabilities of the AV. In doing so, participants were pleased that the AV prioritized safety and waited until the participant safely passed the narrowing. However, not all of them wanted to test the AV, but they paid attention to the speed (9/23), and distance (2/23) of the AV and decided to take priority accordingly. They either felt reaching the narrow area faster or the AV hesitated to take priority. There were other reasons, such as S15, misinterpreting the display or two other participants already planning to take priority before the trial, regardless of the AV's intention.

With the deceleration intention display, 89% of the time (64/72) participants chose to pass first. In half of the reasons given (35/70), the deceleration intention display was the reason for deciding to take priority. In 5 trials the participants were insecure because the display did not harmonize with the intention, i.e. the AV drove too fast, although indicated to decelerate. Yet, despite the uncertainty, participants still chose to trust the display and passed. However, the display was not the only source for deciding to take priority. 22 out of 70 reasons given were related to AV's locomotion cues such as position, distance, and especially speed. S19, for example, stated that she was paying attention to the display and acted accordingly, but she had nevertheless waited until the car stopped before passing. The reasons for participants not driving despite deceleration intention eHMI varied. Two participants intentionally tested the AV by giving priority to it, and they observed how the car reacted. Two participants did not drive in order to be cautious, since it was their first trial. One participant misinterpreted the eHMI sign and another participant felt that the display did not match the car's driving behavior, so they preferred to wait. For one participant, the AV was too close to parked cars, so she was unsure if her car could fit through, hence she let the AV drive.

For no eHMI (i.e., baseline condition), driving or waiting decisions were fairly balanced. Participants decided to pass in 56% of the trials (32/72) and waited in 44% of the trials (40/72). Participants stated paying the most attention to speed, lateral position, and distance (17/32 when waiting and 25/35 when passing). Thus, many of them chose to drive when the AV slowed down or stopped, and waited when they felt the AV would not stop. The other important decision factor was assessing who reached the narrowing first. Participants were more likely to let the AV pass if they perceived the AV reaching the parked cars first. Similarly, they insisted on their priority if they arrived first. Another aspect was the lateral position of AV. If the AV was driving in the middle of the road, the participants assumed that it would drive through. If it drove more on the right, the participants thought that it would wait. Some participants assumed that the AV would behave defensively if it did not have a display on, which is why they passed. Lastly, 8 out of 32 of the reasons for waiting and 3 out of 35 of the reasons for passing included statements regarding uncertainty because the display was off.

4.3.4   Discussion

The following section elaborates on experimental results and brings up new insights gained from qualitative interview results regarding participants' expectations from AVs.

Explicit Locomotion Intention Acts as a Mediator for Resolving Traffic Conflicts

Our results indicated a significant regulatory effect of acceleration and deceleration intention displays on participants' decision-making processes. Furthermore, participants stated explicitly that they took the information on the display into account while making their decision, together with actual locomotion cues and lateral positioning [MKKB22, MLKB22, RDB21b] of the AV on the road, which was also expressed in previous research [DT17, SDR17]. Overall, we could validate the findings of Rettenmaier and Bengler [RB21] from their driving simulation study in a realistic setting, that AV should indicate its intention implicitly and explicitly to solve conflicts in ambiguous scenarios more easily.

Locomotion Intention Can Support Social-embeddedness of AVs

We found that when AV indicated deceleration intention with its display and with more defensive locomotion maneuvers, individuals' likelihood to perceive it as more prosocial increased compared to baseline (AV not indicating any intentions coupled with a neutral driving style). This emphasizes the preference of humans regarding the defensive behavior of AVs with clear intentions in ambiguous driving scenarios, which was further emphasized in the qualitative feedback our participants gave. This desire also corroborates with the findings of Miller et al. [MLKB22], where they run a similar bottleneck scenario with an AV on a driving simulator. Moreover, the perception of social behavior was indifferent when AV signaled acceleration intention or did not indicate any explicit intention with its display. Even though the clear acceleration intention may have made participants content, the AV asking for priority might have neutralized their perception and resulted in similar evaluations to the baseline condition. On the deceleration intention condition, however, we might have observed a highlighted effect of both aspects of clear indication and yielding behavior, which resulted in a significant prosocial perception of AV when compared to the baseline condition. Moreover, during the interviews, participants responded positively regarding the displays, and viewed them as helpful, in line with previous studies [DMB+20b, CFR22]. Overall, these results indicate that, for AVs to be perceived as social, they do not have to equip anthropomorphic features [CTSI17, LGR19], and emphasized locomotion intention cues might partially substitute the missing validation cues of human-human interaction. The high focus on safety, predictability, and rule compliance in interview answers suggests that AVs are perceived as more positive and social if they have reliable functionality.

Situational Trust in Automation Requires a Wider Perspective

The average situational trust scores of our participants did not indicate any change in their trust across locomotion intention conditions. One potential reason could be that the items in STS-AD were primarily tailored for AV drivers, not for the other drivers interacting with an AV externally. Hence, we believe that the average of the entire item set may not have been sensitive enough to reveal changes in trust in different conditions in our experiment. Extending the perspective of the driver in STS-AD items (from inside to outside) could be a new way to utilize the scale for a wider range of situations. Furthermore, existing studies have mostly investigated trust in the context of eHMIs from the perspective of pedestrians, with mixed results. A study by Liu et al. [LHW21] suggests that pedestrians trust AVs similar to manual vehicles in crossing situations. Similar results were obtained in an experiment by Bonneviot et al. [BCB21], who showed that a communication HMI can increase pedestrians' subjective trust similar to encounters with human drivers. Since pedestrians are more vulnerable than drivers, and given the low speeds as present in our experiment, maybe the situations were not risky enough to require higher trust levels. Furthermore, in our experiment, the eHMI status always matched the behavior of the AV, while in related experiments with pedestrians, trust often varied after experiencing automation failures [HWB19a, FKSB21]. Future experiments may investigate this issue in the context of vehicle-to-vehicle interactions as well. Lastly, to get additional feedback in the post-interviews, participants were asked about their general trust in AV during the experiment. Some participants (9/24) trusted the AV from the beginning, considering that a safety-critical situation cannot occur during a controlled test. The other participants (9/24) reported that although they felt insecure, cautious, or unsafe at the beginning, they felt secure and confident as they proceeded and as they got used to encountering the AV.

Mixed Traffic with AVs: Expectations and Challenges

When participants were asked in pre-questionnaires regarding their expectations from AVs and how they envision future mixed traffic, the most important themes seemed to be rule compliance (23/28), predictable behavior (8/28), and safety (11/28). Furthermore, participants wanted AVs to behave thoughtfully (4/28), reliably (3/28), and defensively (3/28) [MKKB22]. Participants mentioned that AVs would be more efficient (7/28) in urgent situations such as forming an emergency lane (3/28). However, concerns and negative effects were also raised. For example, P05 was concerned that the car might fail to detect people and thus increase the accident rate. Others described AVs as untrustworthy, confusing, and uncertain. P04 stated the reason as the fear of giving up on control, which makes individuals feel insecure. P05 justified his fear by stating his worry about AV overlooking them. The general opinion seemed to be that AVs should be subordinate to humans and not insist on their right of way. In this way, accidents could be avoided and safety could be ensured. Moreover, AVs are expected to strictly follow traffic rules. However, strict adherence to traffic rules might inhibit AVs from reacting to ambiguous situations, especially caused by rule-braking human drivers.

When participants were asked how AVs should react in ambiguous situations where the right of way is not clear in post-interviews, participants proposed either a defensive (11/24) or reactive (13/24) approach. Participants who argued for defensive behavior stated that an AV should always be passive in potential conflicts and give the right of way to humans, similar to the direction of answers reported by Miller et al. [MKKB22]. Some of the participants who advocated strict adherence to traffic rules nevertheless mentioned a few exceptions such as safety-critical situations where deviation from rules would be necessary. Participants arguing for a reactive approach exposed their wish to have communication with AV, through signaling with flashing lights or displays. They further expressed that AVs should adapt to humans by analyzing their behavior, speed, and position to decide whether they should wait or take priority, as strict enforcement of driving rules would otherwise be too unfamiliar or annoying. Two participants specifically stated that AVs should have defensive behavior, while P09 argued that AVs should not only follow traffic rules but also insist on their rights, as this would make them less likely to be taken advantage of. Three participants argued that a distinction should be made between traffic with only autonomous vehicles and mixed traffic, as humans can disrupt the traffic flow through unexpected behavior. Thus, it was suggested that in pure traffic with only AVs, vehicles should be strictly rule-abiding, while in mixed traffic, AVs should act more human-like and sometimes deviate from the rules to resolve conflicts. Two other participants suggested special lanes for AVs similar to bus lanes, where they could have additional regulations while still being a part of urban traffic.

During the experiment, some participants wanted to test the capabilities of the AV and forced the ghost driver to make a decision. In one instance, both AV and the participant kept driving very slowly to see who would break the ambiguity and make the decision first. The other two times the ghost driver had to reverse since she was already in the narrow area, yet the participants wanted to see what would happen if they changed their minds and insisted on taking priority. Other times they chose to drive on even if AV indicated acceleration, to see if it was reactive. These instances emphasize similar playful reactions of individuals in Moore et al. [MCSS20]. It seems that when encountering a new technology, some individuals will likely act unexpectedly and potentially undermine the usability of AVs.

Methodological Implications, Limitations and Future Directions

We conducted a realistic field experiment on a bottleneck scenario naturally formed by two parked cars. Our participants drove their own cars or their family cars so that they would feel the most comfortable while driving. This aspect gave us the most naturalistic results we could obtain from a controlled test track study. We did not reveal to our participants that AV was manually driven until the end of the experiment. This resulted in a successful manipulation of the perception regarding the automation status of the car, which we validated with post-interviews. None of our participants suspected that AV was manually driven and only a few considered the possibility of AV being remotely controlled, or someone might be sitting in the back seat. Conducting this study on a test track in a realistic condition extends the existing research with results that have higher external validity in terms of perception of auditory, visual, and vestibular/motion cues [KTVDH96]. Furthermore, the perception of risks in field studies is generally higher than in driving simulators [Eva91]. However, it is important to point out several limitations. Due to the lack of access to AVs, and the safety-critical nature of the tested scenarios, it was ethically impossible to conduct such an experiment in an uncontrolled environment. Nevertheless, as our study mainly explored the effect of an eHMI in such a scenario , it still maintains a high relative validity of the effects observed in comparison to previous studies conducted in driving simulators. Furthermore, the controlled design of the study ensures internal validity of the effects observed [KTVDH96]. As this study –to our knowledge– is the first one testing the eHMIs in real-life bottleneck scenarios, further research is required to understand whether the presence of other variables will have an effect on the results observed. Moreover, The US National Highway Traffic Safety Administration (NHTSA) Standing General Order on Crash Reporting (SGO)[2] indicate that the most crashes occur with passenger cars. Although we set up our study with passenger cars, there is a wide range of other scenarios to be investigated beyond bottleneck situations.

Regarding the communication interface, we utilized an LED matrix where many signals could be easily shown. After pilot tests, we noted that the most visible cues were vertical bars in white. Our participants reported in the interviews that the display was visible (19/24). Most of them understood the communication cue on the display with ease (19/24). S07 found the acceleration display more understandable than the deceleration display, which is why he suggested only using an acceleration indicator. Almost all the participants found the display helpful (23/24), because it helped to compensate for the missing driver-driver communication, and provided additional feedback and guidance. Only S23 found the display more annoying and distracting than helpful. Data collection took an entire month, under adverse and good weather conditions including fog, snow storms, strong winds, heavy rain, and bright sun. The display was robust and visible through all conditions. On sunny days when the sunlight directly reflected on the display the visibility decreased, however, it was still sufficient at closer distances. Under a snowstorm, we had to clean the snow on the eHMI after every trial. We did not run the experiments at sunset, as the visibility under the car seat costume decreased significantly.

Participants were asked if they had any suggestions for improvement. Five people wished that AV would indicate their intention with flashing lights. Some participants suggested using turn signals since the AV didn't use them in the experiment to limit confounding variables. Two participants wished that the AV would brake faster or keep more distance from the narrowing. For the improvements regarding the communication interface, some participants wished for colors (11/24), in particular red and green. There was no consensus regarding the meaning of the colors among participants. Some suggested that it should be about AVs' intention, while others suggested that it should indicate what others should do as in traffic lights, which further validates the frame of reference problem in the use of traffic light colors [DHP+20]. We were able to prevent different perceptions of the cues by introducing the interface before the experiment, yet in the wild, the introduction of abstract cues may create confusion among road users. This calls for further realistic and longitudinal studies to grasp the long-term impact of eHMIs on road users. In our study, 90-minute exposure could only serve as an introduction to these novel interfaces. Participants further wanted the display to be larger (7/24), and indicate other signs including vertical arrows, a circular sun, a traffic light, and a human face (7/24). S22 liked the idea of displaying

---

[2] https://www.nhtsa.gov/laws-regulations/standing-general-order-crash-reporting#
ads,[Online; accessed 19-June-2023]

human needs on a display, such as a pregnant woman or being late. Last but not least, four participants suggested changing the position of the display, ideally more around the eye level. S13 suggested digitizing the license plate as well and alternating it with the display whenever it would be needed.

Our eHMIs signaled locomotion intention explicitly, however, they were not dynamic. This means that they were not adaptive to the actual speed changes of the car. Participants encountered one design per condition and the eHMI they saw in each condition strictly indicated the intention of the AV in the bottleneck situation. Yet, the display was on from the beginning, until the end of the trial. The display could have been more adaptive and situation-specific, where it could be turned off once the ambiguity was resolved. Furthermore, we had only 24 participants due to short-notice dropouts. However, their backgrounds, ages, and driving experience were diverse. As the next steps, not only driving decisions but also the actual driving behavior of participants and the driving behavior of ghost driver could be analyzed and another perspective on driver behavior could be presented. Furthermore, quantitative validation of where participants paid attention during the encounter could be achieved with mobile eye trackers. Lastly, STS-AD can be adapted for measuring the situational trust of drivers outside the AV.

4.3.5 Conclusion

We conducted a realistic test track study in an ambiguous bottleneck scenario where participants drove their own cars. They had to decide whether to give or yield the crossing priority to a self-driving vehicle, which was manually driven by a human under a car seat costume in reality. AV was equipped with an external display indicating the locomotion intention of the car explicitly with vertical bars. We used mixed methods to evaluate the effects of yielding intention and acceleration intention compared to the baseline condition. Our results revealed that deceleration intention significantly decreased yielding probabilities and significantly increased prosocial perception of the AV, and it was desired as the default behavior of AV in ambiguous scenarios by our participants. Furthermore, acceleration intention significantly increased yielding probabilities but did not have any effect on prosocial perception compared to the baseline condition. Situational trust was not affected by different conditions in our study. Participants reported using explicit locomotion intention cues together with implicit locomotion cues such as lateral movement, speed, and distance of the AV. Lastly, they found explicit locomotion intention cues, understandable, visible, and helpful.

4.4 Chapter Summary

This chapter presented the necessary considerations when designing an external communication interface in terms of their optimal timing and more notably, the message of the communication cues to foster a more balanced social interaction among humans and AVs in urban traffic. Firstly, we have shown with an online gaming study that the yielding intention of the vehicle, which is deemed as one of the crucial messages an AV can indicate, works the best in preparing pedestrians to react when presented before or during the actual deceleration of the AV (see Section 4.1). This study helped us to decide when to present similar communication cues in the following test track study where we presented acceleration and deceleration cues on a Wizard of Oz automated vehicle. Not only did we focus on emphasizing locomotion cues such as acceleration and deceleration via eHMI, but also we explored some novel ideas where eHMIs could be used to foster prosocial driving behavior towards AVs in Section 4.2. The video vignette survey showed the potency of increasing social behavior of drivers when AVs indicate either a sense of urgency, prolonged waiting times, or indications of overall prosocial driving of the AV. Furthermore, it helped to reveal an understanding of whether humans change their social behavior around automated vehicles, which has also been the main goal of Chapter 3. The results indicated that humans did not act differently when facing an AV equipped only with sensors than when they saw a human-driven vehicle with a human avatar inside. Hence, we could confirm the findings in Section 3.1 that humans do not have preconceived attitudes towards AVs or their automated status while using sympathy eliciting eHMIs could still foster courteous behavior in traffic regardless of the automation status of the AV. Lastly and most importantly, we confirmed the use of empathized locomotion cues through eHMIs to help perceive AVs as more social through a study we conducted at a controlled test track, which could serve to support the argument that emphasizing locomotion cues and making the intention of AV clearer could be sufficient to perceive them as more social traffic participants, hen helping to preserve more balanced mixed traffic environment (see Section 4.3).

5 Discussion and Conclusion

The present chapter discusses each research focus with respect to their appearances in Chapters 2, 3 and 4, as well as highlighting future directions, a summary of research contributions, finalizing with closing remarks.

5.1 Essence of Social Behavior in Traffic

Our goal to reveal the elements of social behavior in traffic through different studies has unraveled key findings in this topic. At the beginning of our research, we asked ourselves:

RQ1: How can we define and measure social behavior in traffic to explore its role for road users?

Acting in a way that is coherent with traffic rules is the beginning of seeking clarity of intentions in traffic. In social situations, understanding someone's intentions helps us interpret their actions and respond appropriately. Similarly, in traffic, being able to anticipate the intentions of others is essential for humans. Hence, the general finding of our results from different studies (Study in Section 2.2, Focus group in Chapter 2) reveals that humans seek predictability through rule compliance and a clear indication of movement trajectories. This comes as one of the most essential pillars of social behavior in traffic. However, it does not end here. Rule compliance and predictability do not encapsulate the social behavior in traffic entirely. Instead, we see that humans seek deviance from rules to resolve conflicts smoothly as well. This comes in handy mostly in unexpected situations such as a roadblock or emergency requiring situations. As stated in previous works, prosocial behavior cannot be isolated from its social context [DPSP17], some situations may require rule deviation to perform an act of prosocial behavior in traffic. Hence, every social judgment is situation-dependent. As a counter-effect, even if behavior and intention are prosocial, the outcome may be negative on the traffic flow depending on the situation. Lastly, awareness level seems to play a role in perceiving whether an act is social or not in traffic. If a person is intentionally acting prosocial or aggressive, their behavior is perceived as more prosocial or more aggressive by others. Overall, the situation plays a big proportion in evaluating the social behavior of road users including AVs. This is why we find it challenging to list specific types of behavior or intention as prosocial and rather emphasize the situation specificity. To measure a situation-specific perception of social behavior, we created SPAT (see section 2.2) by using semantic differentials, which can be used in versatile ways to tackle each unique traffic situation or road user perspective.

Naturally, social expressions such as courteous behavior in expressing gratitude or acknowledgment seem to play a role in defining social behavior in traffic.

As Brown et al. [BBV23] stated, traffic is a "long-established social domain". However much traffic is strictly regulated, humans still seek the expression of prosocial behavior by thanking each other via smiles or waves. Consistent answers we receive from our participants through different forms of studies (see Chapter 2) have shown us that using eye contact, gestures, and verbal communication creates a more prosocial traffic environment, and individuals appreciate it. While the current trends in research [DT17, LMG+21] emphasize that the use of such human-to-human cues is less in proportion compared to rule compliance and predictability, we revealed with our studies that it is still an essential part of the social fabric of traffic. It helps individuals to understand the intentions of others more clearly. Looking in depth at the situations with different levels of ambiguity, we could follow this trend better. Hence, even though courteous behavior seems to have less impact on traffic consisting of iron cages that limit humans' communication [Urr06], it still constitutes a dimension of social behavior that our results could not ignore. As stated in Lee et al. [LMG+21], having AVs acting according to social norms in traffic may increase individuals' acceptance and feeling of safety around them. If the norms indicate reliance on driver-specific explicit cues to disambiguate ambiguous situations, disregarding this aspect of the design of AVs might bring social challenges to urban roads with mixed traffic. In their video observation paper, Brown et al. [BBV23] give an example of a miscommunication between a family with children and an autonomous shared taxi in a residential area. AV waits for family to take priority, while the father of the family waves at AV to continue driving. As the family intends to move, AV starts moving as well. Reliance on kinematics fails both sides to understand each other's intentions. In this example, had the AV indicated a cue to substitute an explicit communication of yielding the right of way, the family could have understood and felt more confident in crossing in front of the AV. Or, if AV was able to understand and react to human gestures and grouping factors, then it could have started moving earlier and not let the chain of misunderstandings take place. These instances may seem anecdotal, yet, they occur daily, and they need to be investigated to establish the grounding research on socially embedded automated vehicles in urban roads. If we give explicit interaction less credit in resolving conflicts and establishing prosocial exchange in these situations, it could take more time to reach the goal of having a harmonious coexistence between AVs and humans. Hence, we find it useful and timely to address these seemingly infrequent problems, yet should not be disregarded in the current research domain.

5.2 Social Perception of Automated Vehicles

After building a better understanding of human-human social interactions in traffic, our next challenge has been understanding the influences of AVs on human behavior. Hence, we presented the next research question:

RQ2: What are the influences of automated vehicles on the prosocial and aggressive behavior of road users?

Two of our studies indicate that individuals do not treat AVs differently than human-driven vehicles (See Sections 3.1 and 4.2). However, individuals react to the conflict-avoidant behavior of AVs in a way that they use to their own advantage. Hence, our results supported the notion of the freezing robot problem that needs to be addressed for the future of automated vehicles [TK10], that if these vehicles continue to be overly cautious, they will be treated as passive beings by humans. However, considering both sides of the coin, i.e. users and bystanders of AVs, when designing these vehicles is crucial for their long-term social embeddedness.

From the bystander perspective, while creating a feeling of safety around these vehicles is important, one ought to be aware that humans are highly adaptive, and they will quickly realize their upper hand in any encounter or confrontation with AVs. Moreover, cultural biases might influence how people treat automated vehicles, including the propensity to treat them aggressively. Cultural factors such as attitudes towards technology, trust in authority, and perceptions of safety may play a role in shaping how individuals interact with automated vehicles in different parts of the world. In some extreme cases, this has even resulted in vandalism towards AVs as we observe from recent reports [Kor24]. However, legal norms seem to have the potential to deter bullying of automated vehicles (see Section 3.1). Their effectiveness hinges on robust enforcement mechanisms, public awareness, and international cooperation. By establishing clear rules and consequences for aggressive behavior towards automated vehicles, societies can foster an environment where these technologies can thrive and contribute to more efficient transportation systems. Striving for a more socially balanced urban mixed traffic will eventually provide better usability for these vehicles and create better user and bystander satisfaction. As a practical solution to this, eHMIs seem to help regulate the interaction between humans and AVs.

5.3   Enhancing Social Embeddedness of Automated Vehicles with Communication

After revealing the potential problems of overly cautious AVs in urban mixed traffic, we decided to address this challenge by adopting an established communication method in AV-human research. As introduced in the earlier chapters, eHMIs help individuals understand the intention of the vehicles better. This could lead to an overall better satisfaction of individuals when they are interacting with AVs in traffic. Hence, we addressed this opportunity to enhance interaction with our final research question:

RQ3: What kind of design solutions can we provide for supporting prosocial behavior between AVs and human road users?

Addressing the features of human-human interaction that have been lost in translation when designing for AV-human interactions, our results revealed that sympathy eliciting cues such as indicating elongated waiting time or degree of urgency or communicating the level of politeness of a car to others can increase prosocial behavior towards them (see Section 4.2). Furthermore, we explored alternative communication cues AVs can provide beyond sympathy eliciting cues or anthropomorphic cues that literature suggests. These are the explicit communication of vehicle locomotion intention, in line with guidelines of Rasouli and Tsotsos [RT19]. Such intention signaling was found to help resolve the right of way in ambiguous traffic situations such as bottleneck scenarios in our study (see Section 4.3). When AVs indicate their locomotion intention explicitly through eHMIs, drivers feel more certain regarding the future movements of the AV, and they react according to what AV intends to do. Furthermore, an AV indicating its intention -especially deceleration- was found to be perceived as more social compared to an AV not indicating anything explicitly. Hence, explicit communication of locomotion intention in AVs could serve as a potential solution to increase their predictability and social acceptability, by replacing overly-cautious AVs that are safe, yet socially awkward [BBV23]. Compared to anthropomorphism we believe these cues could be easier to adopt and be established under current regulations. Informed from our natural interaction observations (see Section 2.1), emphasizing locomotion intention can be an alternative to gesture used to disambiguate the traffic situations, since fundamentally, they serve the same purpose of making one's intention clear.

5.4 Future Directions

The current section presents some of the research directions that have not been covered in this thesis, yet could be explored in the future to help reveal interaction dynamics between AVs and other road users.

5.4.1 Individual Differences

Investigating individual differences may reveal important results for the future of prosocial driving toward AVs. For example, Sikkenk and Terken [ST15] controlled drivers' willingness to yield according to driving their style by using the multidimensional driving style inventory (MDSI) [TBAMG04] and they found that individuals with an angry or anxious driving style were less likely to yield. Other aspects worth considering are the overreliance, potential confusion, and cognitive overload of humans when they see an external communication cue [WD22].

These factors may undermine the use of such cues and create an opposite effect of prosocial behavior, which should be addressed in future works.

5.4.2 Scalability and Social Norms

One of the overlooked factors in AV-VRU research has been social norms and social factors [CWR19], alongside scalability problems [CWR20, DVC$^+$21]. Pedestrians were found to be more likely to cross the road if other pedestrians around them had started to cross [FKK10]. In a very recent study, Colley et al. [CBR22a] tested the effects of pedestrian group behavior and a single pedestrian behavior on their participants' crossing decisions in front of AVs, and they found similar results as Faria et al. [FKK10]. However, there is still a large gap in exploring the social norms in AV-pedestrian research and carrying one-to-one interaction paradigms a step further. Furthermore, AVs also need to be trained to analyze various situation-dependent social cues as much as possible in order to function better in the social fabric of traffic. Otherwise, they will continue receiving dislike by bystanders and other drivers, while the passengers will continue feeling awkward whenever these vehicles can't handle social cues beyond written formal traffic regulations.

5.4.3 Validation of SPAT

In the future, SPAT being used in different studies with various traffic situations and road user perspectives can continue to improve its validation (i.e. driving inside an AV, e-scooter riders, delivery robots, pedestrians). Thus, an additional elicitation round might be necessary for future work. However, with this work, we presented a first scale for assessing prosocial behavior in traffic as a basis for standardized traffic scales. Researchers in traffic psychology, social interaction in traffic, and the social interaction of automated vehicles can use SPAT to investigate the social behavior perception of road users.

5.4.4 Ethnographic Studies with AVs

Some recent work seems to have taken ethnographic studies with AVs under their focus by taking publicly available video footage [BLV23, BBV23]. Yet, a more structured ethnographic study with registered participants as well as long-term recordings of natural driving interactions via multiple video angles might help to reveal ongoing challenges humans have when interacting with AVs.

5.5   Summary of Research Contributions

Our contributions to existing research with this thesis are listed as follows:

We revealed gesture use in traffic with different levels of ambiguity.

We investigated how gestures are utilized in traffic situations, especially with varying degrees of ambiguity. This contribution aids in understanding and designing effective communication strategies for AVs to ensure clear communication between AVs and other road users, ultimately enhancing safety and efficiency on the roads.

We created a quantifiable metric to measure social behavior perception.

We developed a measurable scale to assess social behavior perception in traffic environments. This metric provides a standardized tool for evaluating the effectiveness of AVs' interactions with humans. The semantic differential items have shown themselves as suitable for evaluating various types of situations from various types of road user perspectives. Hence, we believe our situational social perception scale, SPAT, will be useful in evaluating social behavior in traffic without falling into the pitfalls of generalization. By using this metric, we can guide the design and testing of AV systems to ensure they are perceived positively by road users, promoting acceptance of AVs.

We revealed deviant behavior around overly cautious AVs.

We identified instances of deviant behavior triggered by overly cautious AVs. Understanding and addressing these challenges are crucial for fostering harmonious interactions between AVs and human drivers, contributing to smoother traffic flow and avoiding freezing robot problems [TK10] in the future.

We emphasized considering the needs of both users and bystanders in designing AV behavior and communication.

We emphasize the importance of considering the needs of both AV users and bystanders. This holistic approach to AV interactions prioritizes accessibility and social acceptance. By considering the broader societal impact of AV deployment, we highlight the importance of AVs that are not only technically proficient but also considerate of human factors.

We explored different external cues to successfully elicit prosocial interaction.

We investigated external cues that facilitate prosocial interaction between road users and AVs. By understanding and leveraging these cues, we can help design AVs that seamlessly integrate into social traffic environments, promoting cooperative behavior among all road users.

We revealed the effective use of locomotion intention to elevate the social perception of AVs, an easily transferrable alternative to anthropomorphism.

We demonstrated the effectiveness of conveying locomotion intention to enhance the social perception of AVs. This practical approach offers a way to improve communication between AVs and humans by addressing the same need when humans use implicit communication and explicit gestures, to make their intentions clear.

We validated existing simulator studies of bottleneck scenarios by adopting the Wizard of Oz method in a more ecologically valid study design.

We validated simulator studies of bottleneck scenarios using ecologically valid methods. This validation ensures that our research findings can more accurately reflect real-world conditions, enhancing the credibility of our research and contributing to the development of AVs by enhancing the findings of previous works.

5.6 Closing Remarks

In conclusion, this dissertation highlights the necessity of integrating social dynamics into the development and deployment of AVs. Through a comprehensive exploration of social behavior in traffic and the role of AVs as social agents, the thesis reveals crucial insights for diverse stakeholders. By unveiling key dimensions of prosocial behavior, analyzing communication cues, and investigating human responses to AVs, this thesis delineates pathways toward harmonious coexistence between humans and automated vehicles.

The findings emphasize the significance of considering social factors alongside technological advancements in AV design and implementation. Notably, the thesis illuminates the potential impact of AVs' driving styles on human behavior and the efficacy of external communication cues in promoting prosocial interactions. By offering actionable recommendations and novel metrics, it provides a roadmap for enhancing social integration and navigating the complexities of human-robot interaction on the road.

Moving forward, this work underscores the need for continued research, collaboration, and adaptation to address emerging challenges and opportunities in the realm of autonomous transportation. By fostering a deeper understanding of human-vehicle interaction and fostering dialogue among stakeholders, this thesis paves the way for a more inclusive and socially conscious approach to mobility in the era of self-driving cars.

Appendices

Presentation of SPAT

Please give your evaluations about the behavior of the other person as in the following example. If you think the behavior of the other person is good, then choose one of the points closer to good on the left side, depending on how good this behavior is for you.

Good ○ ● ○ ○ ○ ○ ○ Bad

Similarly, if you think the behavior is rather bad, then choose a point closer to bad on the right side, depending on how bad you perceive it.

Good ○ ○ ○ ○ ○ ○ ● Bad

If you think the behavior was rather neutral, then choose a point closer to the middle.

Good ○ ○ ○ ● ○ ○ ○ Bad

I think the other traffic participant / the behavior of other traffic participant was

Cooperative	○ ○ ○ ○ ○ ○ ○	Competitive
Helpful	○ ○ ○ ○ ○ ○ ○	Unhelpful
Considerate	○ ○ ○ ○ ○ ○ ○	Inconsiderate
Courteous	○ ○ ○ ○ ○ ○ ○	Impolite
Prosocial	○ ○ ○ ○ ○ ○ ○	Antisocial
Supportive	○ ○ ○ ○ ○ ○ ○	Unsupportive
Reckless	○ ○ ○ ○ ○ ○ ○	Cautious
Safe	○ ○ ○ ○ ○ ○ ○	Unsafe
Trustworthy	○ ○ ○ ○ ○ ○ ○	Untrustworthy
Rational	○ ○ ○ ○ ○ ○ ○	Irrational
Caring	○ ○ ○ ○ ○ ○ ○	Uncaring
Unexpected	○ ○ ○ ○ ○ ○ ○	Expected
Predictable	○ ○ ○ ○ ○ ○ ○	Unpredictable
Ungrateful	○ ○ ○ ○ ○ ○ ○	Thankful
Aware	○ ○ ○ ○ ○ ○ ○	Unaware
Inattentive	○ ○ ○ ○ ○ ○ ○	Attentive
Acknowledging	○ ○ ○ ○ ○ ○ ○	Ignoring

Figure 1: Presentation of SPAT

Path Diagrams of Confirmatory Factor Analysis on Other Scenarios

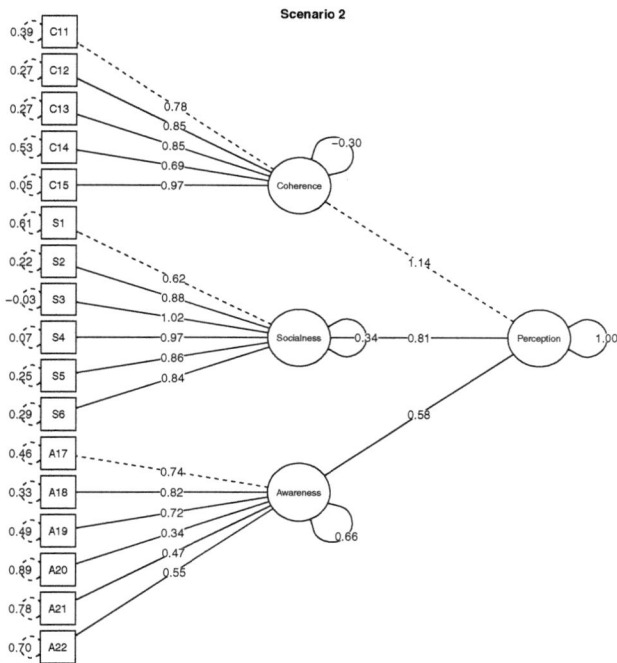

Figure 2: Path diagram of Scenario 2. Participant from the pedestrian's perspective encounters an aggressive driver. Items are presented as squares with their associated error variances and latent variables as circles with their associated variances and covariance (edge). The values on the arrows are the loadings.

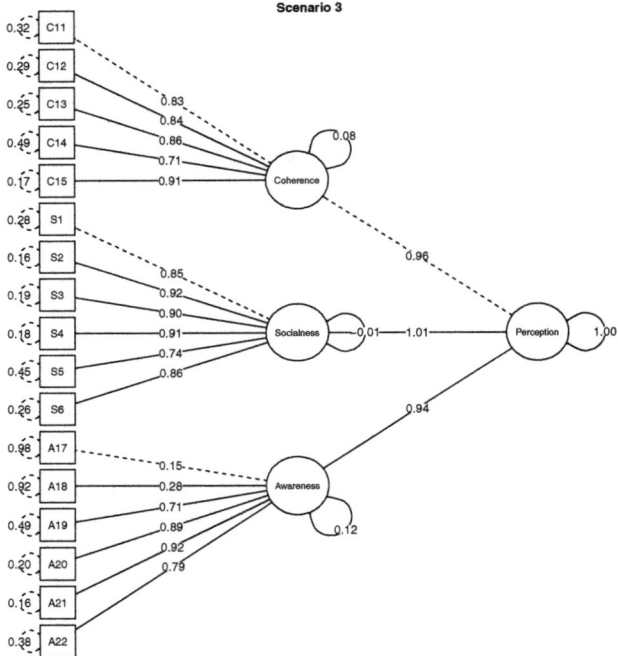

Figure 3: Path diagram of Scenario 3. Participant from the driver's perspective encounters a prosocial pedestrian. Items are presented as squares with their associated error variances and latent variables as circles with their associated variances and covariance (edge). The values on the arrows are the loadings.

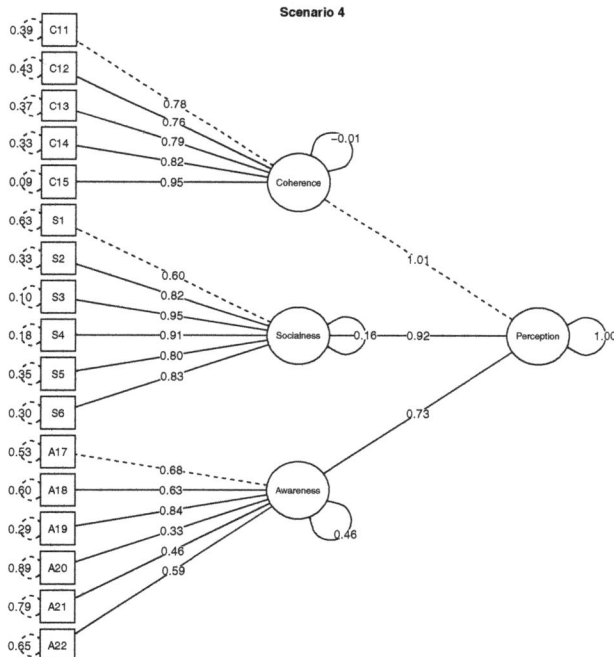

Figure 4: Path diagram of Scenario 4. Participant from the driver's perspective encounters an aggressive pedestrian. Items are presented as squares with their associated error variances and latent variables as circles with their associated variances and covariance (edge). The values on the arrows are the loadings.

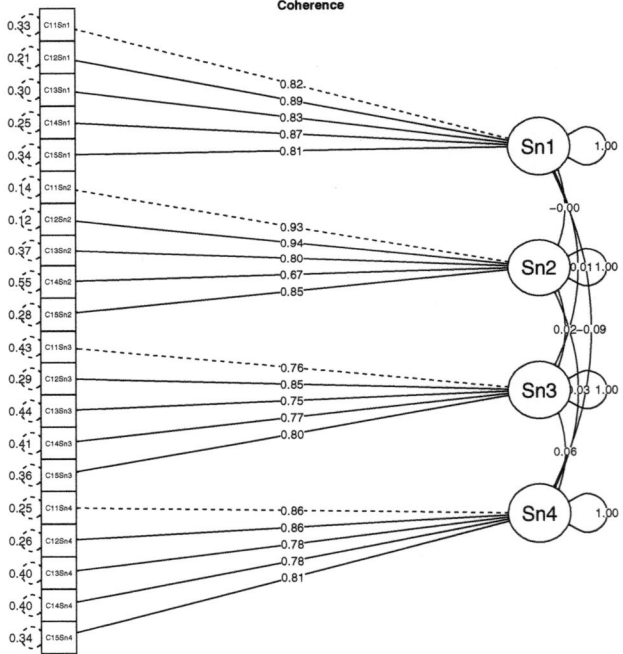

Figure 5: Path diagram of factor Coherence and correlations of each scenario. Items are presented as squares with their associated error variances and latent variables as circles with their associated variances and covariance (edge). The values on the arrows are the loadings. Notation example: C11Sn1 indicates item C11 from Scenario 1.

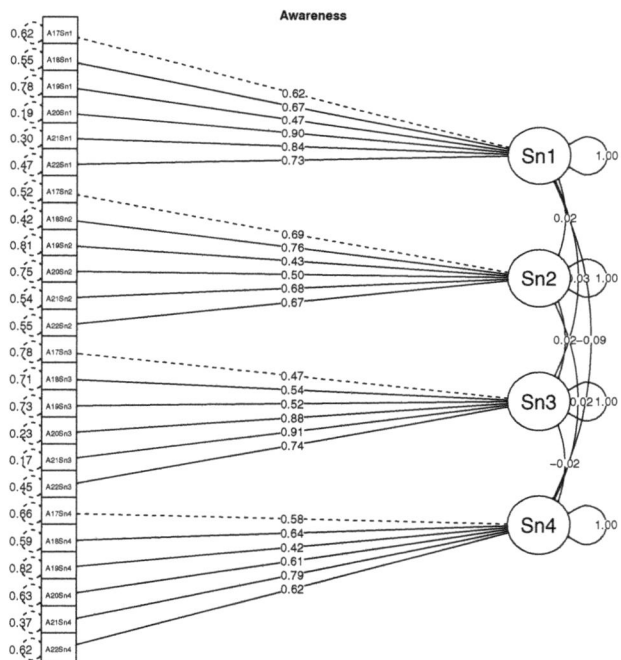

Figure 6: Path diagram of factor Awareness and correlations of each scenario. Items are presented as squares with their associated error variances and latent variables as circles with their associated variances and covariance (edge). The values on the arrows are the loadings. Notation example: A17Sn1 indicates item A17 from Scenario 1.

Non-Used eHMI designs in Test Track Study

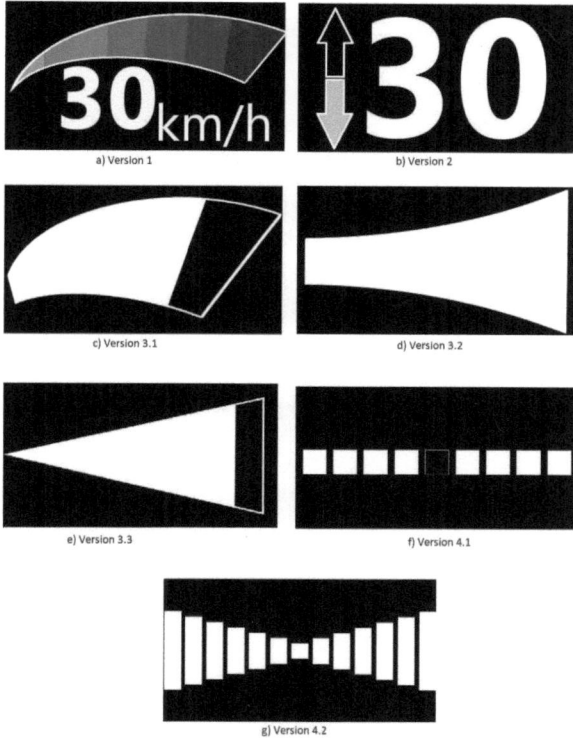

Figure 7: Some unused results of the iterative design process of eHMIs. Blue color did have ideal visibility in the field. Digits and animation combinations were found to be too crowded by pilot testers. Cone-shaped bars were interpreted as turn indicators. Thin light bars had less visibility than the full-screen use of long light bars we eventually selected for our study.

Figures

Tables

Bibliography

[AB14]   AGUINIS, Herman ; BRADLEY, Kyle J.: Best practice recommen-
              dations for designing and implementing experimental vignette
              methodology studies. In: *Organizational research methods* 17
              (2014), Nr. 4, S. 351–371

[ABBK18]   ACKERMANN, Claudia ; BEGGIATO, Matthias ; BLUHM, Luka-
              Franziska ; KREMS, Josef: Vehicle movement and its potential
              as implicit communication signal for pedestrians and automated
              vehicles. In: *Proceedings of the 6th Humanist Conference* Hu-
              manist Publications The Hague, 2018, S. 1–7

[ABSK19]   ACKERMANN, Claudia ; BEGGIATO, Matthias ; SCHUBERT, Sarah
              ; KREMS, Josef F.: An experimental study to investigate design
              and assessment criteria: What is important for communication
              between pedestrians and automated vehicles? In: *Applied er-
              gonomics* 75 (2019), S. 272–282

[Ada23]   ADAFRUIT: *Adafruit RGB Matrix HAT + RTC for Raspberry
              Pi - Mini Kit.* 2023. – https://www.adafruit.com/product/
              2345,[Online; accessed 15-March-2023]

[ADR+20]   ACKERMANS, Sander ; DEY, Debargha ; RUIJTEN, Peter ; CUI-
              JPERS, Raymond H. ; PFLEGING, Bastian: The Effects of Explicit
              Intention Communication, Conspicuous Sensors, and Pedestrian
              Attitude in Interactions with Automated Vehicles. In: *Proceed-
              ings of the 2020 CHI Conference on Human Factors in Comput-
              ing Systems*, 2020, S. 1–14

[AS10]   ATZMÜLLER, Christiane ; STEINER, Peter M.: Experimental
              vignette studies in survey research. In: *Methodology* 6 (2010), S.
              128–138. http://dx.doi.org/10.1027/1614-2241/a000014. –
              DOI 10.1027/1614–2241/a000014

[Bat10]   BATSON, C. D.: *Altruism in Humans.* USA : Oxford Uni-
              versity Press, 2010. http://dx.doi.org/10.1093/acprof:
              oso/9780195341065.001.0001. http://dx.doi.org/10.1093/
              acprof:oso/9780195341065.001.0001. – ISBN 9780195341065

[Bat12]   BATSON, C D.: *A history of prosocial behavior research.* East
              Sussex, United Kingdom, 2012

[BBV23]   BROWN, Barry ; BROTH, Mathias ; VINKHUYZEN, Erik: The
              Halting problem: Video analysis of self-driving cars in traffic. In:
              *Proceedings of the 2023 CHI Conference on Human Factors in
              Computing Systems*, 2023, S. 1–14

[BCB21]   BONNEVIOT, Flavie ; COEUGNET, Stéphanie ; BRANGIER, Eric:
            Pedestrians-Automated Vehicles Interaction: Toward a Specific
            Trust Model? In: *Proceedings of the 21st Congress of the Inter-
            national Ergonomics Association (IEA 2021) Volume III: Sector
            Based Ergonomics.* Virtual : Springer, 2021, S. 568–574

[Bec68]   BECKER, Gary S.: Crime and Punishment: An Economic Ap-
            proach. In: *Journal of Political Economy* 76 (1968), Nr. 2,
            169–217. http://www.jstor.org/stable/1830482. – ISSN
            00223808, 1537534X

[BLV23]   BROWN, Barry ; LAURIER, Eric ; VINKHUYZEN, Erik: Designing
            Motion: Lessons for Self-driving and Robotic Motion from Hu-
            man Traffic Interaction. In: *Proceedings of the ACM on Human-
            Computer Interaction* 7 (2023), Nr. GROUP, S. 1–21

[BMBW15]   BATES, Douglas ; MÄCHLER, Martin ; BOLKER, Ben ; WALKER,
            Steve: Fitting Linear Mixed-Effects Models Using lme4.
            In: *Journal of Statistical Software* 67 (2015), Nr. 1, S. 1–
            48. http://dx.doi.org/10.18637/jss.v067.i01. – DOI
            10.18637/jss.v067.i01

[BNF+18]   BOATENG, Godfred O. ; NEILANDS, Torsten B. ; FRONGILLO,
            Edward A. ; MELGAR-QUIÑONEZ, Hugo R. ; YOUNG, Sera L.:
            Best Practices for Developing and Validating Scales for Health,
            Social, and Behavioral Research: A Primer. In: *Frontiers in
            Public Health* 6 (2018). http://dx.doi.org/10.3389/fpubh.
            2018.00149. – DOI 10.3389/fpubh.2018.00149. – ISSN 2296–
            2565

[BRC08]   BARTNECK, Christoph ; REICHENBACH, Juliane ; CARPENTER,
            Julie: The carrot and the stick: The role of praise and pun-
            ishment in human–robot interaction. In: *Interaction Studies* 9
            (2008), Nr. 2, S. 179–203

[BS11]   BORTZ, Jürgen ; SCHUSTER, Christof: *Statistik für Human-
            und Sozialwissenschaftler: Limitierte Sonderausgabe.* Cham :
            Springer-Verlag, 2011

[BWHB18]   BOROJENI, Shadan S. ; WEBER, Lars ; HEUTEN, Wilko ; BOLL,
            Susanne: From reading to driving: priming mobile users for take-
            over situations in highly automated driving. In: *Proceedings of
            the 20th international conference on human-computer interac-
            tion with mobile devices and services.* Barcelona, Spain : ACM
            SIGCHI, 2018, S. 1–12

[BWOG18]   BHAGAVATHULA, Rajaram ; WILLIAMS, Brian ; OWENS, Justin ;
            GIBBONS, Ronald: The reality of virtual reality: A comparison

of pedestrian behavior in real and virtual environments. In: *Proceedings of the Human Factors and Ergonomics Society Annual Meeting* Bd. 62 SAGE Publications Sage CA: Los Angeles, CA, 2018, S. 2056–2060

[Byr00]   BYRNE, Gerry: Road rage. In: *New Scientist* 168 (2000), Nr. 2268, S. 38–41

[Car03]   CARROLL, John M.: *Making use: scenario-based design of human-computer interactions.* MIT press, 2003

[CBD⁺22]   COLLEY, Mark ; BRITTEN, Julian ; DEMHARTER, Simon ; HISIR, Tolga ; RUKZIO, Enrico: Feedback Strategies for Crowded Intersections in Automated Traffic — A Desirable Future? In: *Proceedings of the 14th International Conference on Automotive User Interfaces and Interactive Vehicular Applications.* New York, NY, USA : Association for Computing Machinery, 2022 (AutomotiveUI '22). – ISBN 9781450394154, 243–252

[CBR21]   COLLEY, Mark ; BELZ, Jan H. ; RUKZIO, Enrico: Investigating the Effects of Feedback Communication of Autonomous Vehicles. In: *13th International Conference on Automotive User Interfaces and Interactive Vehicular Applications.* New York, NY, USA : Association for Computing Machinery, 2021 (AutomotiveUI '21). – ISBN 9781450380638, 263–273

[CBR22a]   COLLEY, Mark ; BAJROVIC, Elvedin ; RUKZIO, Enrico: Effects of pedestrian behavior, time pressure, and repeated exposure on crossing decisions in front of automated vehicles equipped with external communication. In: *CHI Conference on Human Factors in Computing Systems*, 2022, S. 1–11

[CBR22b]   COLLEY, Mark ; BAJROVIC, Elvedin ; RUKZIO, Enrico: Effects of Pedestrian Behavior, Time Pressure, and Repeated Exposure on Crossing Decisions in Front of Automated Vehicles Equipped with External Communication. In: *Proceedings of the 2022 CHI Conference on Human Factors in Computing Systems.* New York, NY, USA : Association for Computing Machinery, 2022 (CHI '22). – ISBN 9781450391573

[CCB⁺20]   CAMARA, Fanta ; COSAR, Serhan ; BELLOTTO, Nicola ; MERAT, Natasha ; FOX, Charles u. a.: Continuous Game Theory Pedestrian Modelling Method for Autonomous Vehicles. (2020)

[CF20]   CAMARA, Fanta ; FOX, Charles: Space Invaders: Pedestrian Proxemic Utility Functions and Trust Zones for Autonomous Vehicle Interactions. In: *International Journal of Social Robotics* (2020), S. 1–21

[CFR22]   COLLEY, Mark ; FABIAN, Tim ; RUKZIO, Enrico: Investigating
             the Effects of External Communication and Automation Behav-
             ior on Manual Drivers at Intersections. In: *Proceedings of the
             ACM on Human-Computer Interaction* 6 (2022), September, Nr.
             MHCI, 1–16. `http://dx.doi.org/10.1145/3546711`. – DOI
             10.1145/3546711. – ISSN 2573–0142

[CHCR03]   CARLO, Gustavo ; HAUSMANN, Anne ; CHRISTIANSEN, Stacie ;
             RANDALL, Brandy A.: Sociocognitive and behavioral correlates
             of a measure of prosocial tendencies for adolescents. In: *The
             journal of early adolescence* 23 (2003), Nr. 1, S. 107–134

[chi23]   CHIARK.GREENEND: *PuTTY: a free SSH and Telnet client.*
             2023. – `https://www.chiark.greenend.org.uk/~sgtatham/`
             `putty/`,[Online; accessed 15-March-2023]

[CL92]   COMREY, Andrew L. ; LEE, Howard B.: *A first course in factor
             analysis, 2nd edn. hillsdale, nj: L.* 1992

[CN16]   CARLSSON, Magnus ; NILSSON, Per: The Smiling Car-concept for
             autonomous cars / Retrieved 2019-03-05. Version: 2016. `https:`
             `//semcon.com/smilingcar`. 2016. – Forschungsbericht

[Coo00]   COOLEY, Mike: Human-centered design. In: *Information design*
             (2000), S. 59–81

[CPD+18]   CURRANO, Rebecca ; PARK, So Y. ; DOMINGO, Lawrence ;
             GARCIA-MANCILLA, Jesus ; SANTANA-MANCILLA, Pedro C. ;
             GONZALEZ, Victor M. ; JU, Wendy: ¡ Vamos! Observations of
             pedestrian interactions with driverless cars in Mexico. In: *Pro-
             ceedings of the 10th international conference on automotive user
             interfaces and interactive vehicular applications*, 2018, S. 210–220

[CRM+18]   CAMARA, Fanta ; ROMANO, Richard ; MARKKULA, Gustav ;
             MADIGAN, Ruth ; MERAT, Natasha ; FOX, Charles: Empiri-
             cal game theory of pedestrian interaction for autonomous vehi-
             cles. In: *Proceedings of measuring behavior 2018* Manchester
             Metropolitan University, 2018, S. 238–244

[CTSI17]   CHANG, Chia-Ming ; TODA, Koki ; SAKAMOTO, Daisuke ;
             IGARASHI, Takeo: Eyes on a Car: an Interface Design for Com-
             munication between an Autonomous Car and a Pedestrian. In:
             *Proceedings of the 9th International Conference on Automotive
             User Interfaces and Interactive Vehicular Applications*, 2017, S.
             65–73

[CWR19]   COLLEY, Mark ; WALCH, Marcel ; RUKZIO, Enrico: For a better (simulated) world: considerations for VR in external communication research. In: *Proceedings of the 11th International Conference on Automotive User Interfaces and Interactive Vehicular Applications: Adjunct Proceedings*, 2019, S. 442–449

[CWR20]   COLLEY, Mark ; WALCH, Marcel ; RUKZIO, Enrico: Unveiling the lack of scalability in research on external communication of autonomous vehicles. In: *Extended abstracts of the 2020 chi conference on human factors in computing systems*, 2020, S. 1–9

[DAE+05]   DYM, Clive L. ; AGOGINO, Alice M. ; ERIS, Ozgur ; FREY, Daniel D. ; LEIFER, Larry J.: Engineering design thinking, teaching, and learning. In: *Journal of engineering education* 94 (2005), Nr. 1, S. 103–120

[DCDNV+19a] DE CLERCQ, Koen ; DIETRICH, Andre ; NÚÑEZ VELASCO, Juan P. ; DE WINTER, Joost ; HAPPEE, Riender: External human-machine interfaces on automated vehicles: effects on pedestrian crossing decisions. In: *Human factors* 61 (2019), Nr. 8, S. 1353–1370

[DCDNV+19b] DE CLERCQ, Koen ; DIETRICH, Andre ; NÚÑEZ VELASCO, Juan P. ; DE WINTER, Joost ; HAPPEE, Riender: External Human-Machine Interfaces on Automated Vehicles: Effects on Pedestrian Crossing Decisions. In: *Human Factors: The Journal of the Human Factors and Ergonomics Society* 61 (2019), Nr. 8, S. 1353–1370

[DHB+20]   DEY, Debargha ; HOLLÄNDER, Kai ; BERGER, Melanie ; EGGEN, Berry ; MARTENS, Marieke ; PFLEGING, Bastian ; TERKEN, Jacques: Distance-dependent ehmis for the interaction between automated vehicles and pedestrians. In: *12th international conference on automotive user interfaces and interactive vehicular applications*, 2020, S. 192–204

[DHL+20]   DEY, Debargha ; HABIBOVIC, Azra ; LÖCKEN, Andreas ; WINTERSBERGER, Philipp ; PFLEGING, Bastian ; RIENER, Andreas ; MARTENS, Marieke ; TERKEN, Jacques: Taming the eHMI jungle: A classification taxonomy to guide, compare, and assess the design principles of automated vehicles' external human-machine interfaces. In: *Transportation Research Interdisciplinary Perspectives* 7 (2020), S. 100174

[DHP+20]   DEY, Debargha ; HABIBOVIC, Azra ; PFLEGING, Bastian ; MARTENS, Marieke ; TERKEN, Jacques: Color and animation preferences for a light band eHMI in interactions between automated vehicles and pedestrians. In: *Proceedings of the 2020 CHI Conference on Human Factors in Computing Systems*, 2020, S. 1–13

[DLT+20] DOMEYER, Joshua E. ; LEE, John D. ; TOYODA, Heishiro ; MEHLER, Bruce ; REIMER, Bryan: Interdependence in vehicle-pedestrian encounters and its implications for vehicle automation. In: *IEEE Transactions on Intelligent Transportation Systems* 23 (2020), Nr. 5, S. 4122–4134

[DLT+22] DOMEYER, Joshua E. ; LEE, John D. ; TOYODA, Heishiro ; MEHLER, Bruce ; REIMER, Bryan: Driver-Pedestrian Perceptual Models Demonstrate Coupling: Implications for Vehicle Automation. In: *IEEE Transactions on Human-Machine Systems* 52 (2022), Nr. 4, S. 557–566

[DMB+20a] DEY, Debargha ; MATVIIENKO, Andrii ; BERGER, Melanie ; PFLEGING, Bastian ; MARTENS, Marieke ; TERKEN, Jacques: Communicating the intention of an automated vehicle to pedestrians: The contributions of eHMI and vehicle behavior. In: *it-Information Technology* 1 (2020), Nr. ahead-of-print

[DMB+20b] DEY, Debargha ; MATVIIENKO, Andrii ; BERGER, Melanie ; PFLEGING, Bastian ; MARTENS, Marieke ; TERKEN, Jacques: Communicating the Intention of an Automated Vehicle to Pedestrians: the Contributions of eHMI and Vehicle Behavior. In: *Information Technology* Submitted (2020), Nr. Special Issue: Automotive User Interfaces in the Age of Automation, S. 123–141. http://dx.doi.org/10.1515/ITIT-2020-0025. – DOI 10.1515/ITIT–2020–0025

[DML+21] DOMMÈS, Aurelie ; MERLHIOT, Gaëtan ; LOBJOIS, Regis ; DANG, Nguyen-Thong ; VIENNE, Fabrice ; BOULO, Joris ; OLIVER, Anne-Hélène ; CRETUAL, Armel ; CAVALLO, Viola: Young and older adult pedestrians' behavior when crossing a street in front of conventional and self-driving cars. In: *Accident Analysis & Prevention* 159 (2021), S. 106256

[DOL94] DEFFENBACHER, Jerry L. ; OETTING, Eugene R. ; LYNCH, Rebekah S.: Development of a driving anger scale. In: *Psychological reports* 74 (1994), Nr. 1, S. 83–91

[DPSP17] DOVIDIO, John F. ; PILIAVIN, Jane A. ; SCHROEDER, David A. ; PENNER, Louis A.: *The social psychology of prosocial behavior*. East Sussex, United Kingdom : Psychology Press, 2017

[DSC⁺17]   DEB, Shuchisnigdha ; STRAWDERMAN, Lesley ; CARRUTH,
            Daniel W. ; DUBIEN, Janice ; SMITH, Brian ; GARRISON,
            Teena M.: Development and validation of a questionnaire to as-
            sess pedestrian receptivity toward fully autonomous vehicles. In:
            Transportation research part C: emerging technologies 84 (2017),
            S. 178–195

[DSD⁺17]   DEB, Shuchisnigdha ; STRAWDERMAN, Lesley ; DUBIEN, Janice
            ; SMITH, Brian ; CARRUTH, Daniel W. ; GARRISON, Teena M.:
            Evaluating pedestrian behavior at crosswalks: Validation of a
            pedestrian behavior questionnaire for the US population. In:
            Accident Analysis & Prevention 106 (2017), S. 191–201

[DT17]   DEY, Debargha ; TERKEN, Jacques: Pedestrian interaction with
            vehicles: roles of explicit and implicit communication. In: *Pro-
            ceedings of the 9th international conference on automotive user
            interfaces and interactive vehicular applications*, 2017, S. 109–113

[DTB20]   DIETRICH, André ; TONDERA, M ; BENGLER, K: Automated
            vehicles in urban traffic: the effect ofkinematics and eHMIs on
            pedestrian crossing behavior. In: *Advances in Transportation
            Studies* (2020)

[DVC⁺21]   DEY, Debargha ; VASTENHOVEN, Arjen van ; CUIJPERS, Ray-
            mond H. ; MARTENS, Marieke ; PFLEGING, Bastian: Towards
            Scalable eHMIs: Designing for AV-VRU Communication Beyond
            One Pedestrian. In: *13th International Conference on Automo-
            tive User Interfaces and Interactive Vehicular Applications*, 2021,
            S. 274–286

[DWMT19]   DEY, Debargha ; WALKER, Francesco ; MARTENS, Marieke ;
            TERKEN, Jacques: Gaze patterns in pedestrian interaction with
            vehicles: towards effective design of external human-machine in-
            terfaces for automated vehicles. In: *Proceedings of the 11th In-
            ternational Conference on Automotive User Interfaces and Inter-
            active Vehicular Applications*, 2019, S. 369–378

[EAKA19]   EZZATI AMINI, Roja ; KATRAKAZAS, Christos ; ANTONIOU, Con-
            stantinos: Negotiation and decision-making for a pedestrian
            roadway crossing: A literature review. In: *Sustainability* 11
            (2019), Nr. 23, S. 6713

[EHL⁺16]   ECKOLDT, Kai ; HASSENZAHL, Marc ; LASCHKE, Matthias ;
            SCHNEIDER, Thies ; SCHUMANN, Josef ; KÖNSGEN, Stefan: The
            Gentleman. A prosocial assistance system to promote considerate
            driving. In: *Proceedings on the 10th Conference on Design and*

Emotion. The Netherlands : Design & Emotion Society, 2016, S. 307–314

[Eps15]   EPSKAMP, Sacha: semPlot: Unified visualizations of structural equation models. In: *Structural Equation Modeling: a multidisciplinary journal* 22 (2015), Nr. 3, S. 474–483

[Eva91]   EVANS, Leonard: *Traffic safety and the driver.* MI, USA : Science Serving Society, 1991

[Fär16]   FÄRBER, Berthold: Communication and communication problems between autonomous vehicles and human drivers. In: *Autonomous driving.* Springer, 2016, S. 125–144

[FBG+19]   FRIDMAN, Lex ; BROWN, Daniel E. ; GLAZER, Michael ; ANGELL, William ; DODD, Spencer ; JENIK, Benedikt ; TERWILLIGER, Jack ; PATSEKIN, Aleksandr ; KINDELSBERGER, Julia ; DING, Li u. a.: MIT advanced vehicle technology study: Large-scale naturalistic driving study of driver behavior and interaction with automation. In: *IEEE Access* 7 (2019), S. 102021–102038

[FCM+18]   FOX, CW ; CAMARA, F ; MARKKULA, G ; ROMANO, RA ; MADIGAN, R ; MERAT, N: When Should the Chicken Cross the Road? - Game Theory for Autonomous Vehicle - Human Interactions. In: *Proceedings of the 4th International Conference on Vehicle Technology and Intelligent Transport Systems* 1 (2018), March, 431–439. https://eprints.whiterose.ac.uk/127403/

[FKB20]   FAAS, Stefanie M. ; KAO, Andrea C. ; BAUMANN, Martin: A longitudinal video study on communicating status and intent for self-driving vehicle–pedestrian interaction. In: *Proceedings of the 2020 CHI Conference on Human Factors in Computing Systems,* 2020, S. 1–14

[FKK10]   FARIA, Jolyon J. ; KRAUSE, Stefan ; KRAUSE, Jens: Collective behavior in road crossing pedestrians: the role of social information. In: *Behavioral ecology* 21 (2010), Nr. 6, S. 1236–1242

[FKSB21]   FAAS, Stefanie M. ; KRAUS, Johannes ; SCHOENHALS, Alexander ; BAUMANN, Martin: Calibrating Pedestrians' Trust in Automated Vehicles. In: *Proceedings of the 2021 CHI Conference on Human Factors in Computing Systems* (2021). http://dx.doi.org/10.1145/3411764.3445738. – DOI 10.1145/3411764.3445738

[FMB20]   FAAS, Stefanie M. ; MATHIS, Lesley-Ann ; BAUMANN, Martin: External HMI for self-driving vehicles: which information shall be displayed? In: *Transportation research part F: traffic psychology and behaviour* 68 (2020), S. 171–186

[FMKB20] FAAS, Stefanie M. ; MATTES, Stefan ; KAO, Andrea C. ; BAUMANN, Martin: Efficient paradigm to measure street-crossing onset time of pedestrians in video-based interactions with vehicles. In: *Information* 11 (2020), Nr. 7, S. 360

[FMX⁺19] FRIDMAN, Lex ; MEHLER, Bruce ; XIA, Lei ; YANG, Yangyang ; FACUSSE, Laura Y. ; REIMER, Bryan: *To Walk or Not to Walk: Crowdsourced Assessment of External Vehicle-to-Pedestrian Displays.* https://arxiv.org/pdf/1707.02698.pdfhttp://arxiv.org/abs/1707.02698. Version: 2019

[FWR⁺19] FRISON, Anna-Katharina ; WINTERSBERGER, Philipp ; RIENER, Andreas ; SCHARTMÜLLER, Clemens ; BOYLE, Linda N. ; MILLER, Erika ; WEIGL, Klemens: In UX we trust: Investigation of aesthetics and usability of driver-vehicle interfaces and their impact on the perception of automated driving. In: *Proceedings of the 2019 CHI conference on human factors in computing systems.* Glasgow, Scotland : ACM SIGCHI, 2019, S. 1–13

[GBY10] GOODE, E. ; BEN-YEHUDA, N.: *Moral Panics: The Social Construction of Deviance.* Wiley, 2010 https://books.google.de/books?id=SbY2MksilkcC. – ISBN 9781444307931

[GC21] GOLDSTEIN, E B. ; CACCIAMANI, Laura: *Sensation and perception.* Boston, Massachusetts, United States : Cengage Learning, 2021

[GDM⁺93] GLENDON, AI ; DORN, Lisa ; MATTHEWS, Gerald ; GULIAN, E ; DAVIES, DR ; DEBNEY, LM: Reliability of the driving behaviour inventory. In: *Ergonomics* 36 (1993), Nr. 6, S. 719–726

[GH90] GOODWIN, Charles ; HERITAGE, John: Conversation analysis. In: *Annual review of anthropology* 19 (1990), Nr. 1, S. 283–307

[GKH⁺15] GOLD, Christian ; KÖRBER, Moritz ; HOHENBERGER, Christoph ; LECHNER, David ; BENGLER, Klaus: Trust in automation–before and after the experience of take-over scenarios in a highly automated vehicle. In: *Procedia Manufacturing* 3 (2015), S. 3025–3032

[GME15] GUÉGUEN, Nicolas ; MEINERI, Sébastien ; EYSSARTIER, Chloé: A pedestrian's stare and drivers' stopping behavior: A field experiment at the pedestrian crossing. In: *Safety science* 75 (2015), S. 87–89

[GMG⁺89]   GULIAN, E ; MATTHEWS, G ; GLENDON, Aleck I. ; DAVIES, DR ; DEBNEY, LM: Dimensions of driver stress. In: *Ergonomics* 32 (1989), Nr. 6, S. 585–602

[GPG13]   GRANIÉ, Marie-Axelle ; PANNETIER, Marjorie ; GUEHO, Ludivine: Developing a self-reporting method to measure pedestrian behaviors at all ages. In: *Accident Analysis & Prevention* 50 (2013), S. 830–839

[GWL⁺19]   GRUENEFELD, Uwe ; WEISS, Sebastian ; LÖCKEN, Andreas ; VIRGILIO, Isabella ; KUN, Andrew L. ; BOLL, Susanne: VRoad: gesture-based interaction between pedestrians and automated vehicles in virtual reality. In: *Proceedings of the 11th International Conference on Automotive User Interfaces and Interactive Vehicular Applications: Adjunct Proceedings*, 2019, S. 399–404

[HA78]   HELMERS, G ; ABERG, L: Driver behavior in intersections as related to priority rules and road design. In: *An exploratory study. Linkoping, Sweden: VTI* (1978)

[HCM⁺19]   HOLLÄNDER, Kai ; COLLEY, Ashley ; MAI, Christian ; HÄKKILÄ, Jonna ; ALT, Florian ; PFLEGING, Bastian: Investigating the influence of external car displays on pedestrians' crossing behavior in virtual reality. In: *Proceedings of the 21st International Conference on Human-Computer Interaction with Mobile Devices and Services*, 2019, S. 1–11

[HCRB21a]   HOLLÄNDER, Kai ; COLLEY, Mark ; RUKZIO, Enrico ; BUTZ, Andreas: A taxonomy of vulnerable road users for hci based on a systematic literature review. In: *Proceedings of the 2021 CHI Conference on Human Factors in Computing Systems*, 2021, S. 1–13

[HCRB21b]   HOLLÄNDER, Kai ; COLLEY, Mark ; RUKZIO, Enrico ; BUTZ, Andreas: A taxonomy of vulnerable road users for hci based on a systematic literature review. In: *Proceedings of the 2021 CHI conference on human factors in computing systems*, 2021, S. 1–13

[HG94]   HIRSCHI, T. ; GOTTFREDSON, M.R.: *The Generality of Deviance.* Transaction Publishers, 1994 `https://books.google.de/books?id=tfmUOrZCY7gC`. – ISBN 9781412836968

[HHL10]   HEATH, Christian ; HINDMARSH, Jon ; LUFF, Paul: *Video in qualitative research.* Sage Publications, 2010

[HHN03]   HOUSTON, John M. ; HARRIS, Paul B. ; NORMAN, Marcia: The Aggressive Driving Behavior Scale: Developing a self-report measure of unsafe driving practices. In: *North American Journal of Psychology* 5 (2003), Nr. 2, S. 269–278. – ISSN 1527–7143

[HHV+14]   HARRIS, Paul B. ; HOUSTON, John M. ; VAZQUEZ, Jose A. ; SMITHER, Janan A. ; HARMS, Amanda ; DAHLKE, Jeffrey A. ; SACHAU, Daniel A.: The Prosocial and Aggressive Driving Inventory (PADI): A self-report measure of safe and unsafe driving behaviors. In: *Accident Analysis & Prevention* 72 (2014), S. 1–8

[Hir69]   HIRSCHI, T.: *Causes of Delinquency.* University of California Press, 1969 (Campus (Berkeley, Calif.)). https://books.google.de/books?id=53MNtMqyOfIC. – ISBN 9780520019010

[HjATB98]   HAIR JR, JF ; ANDERSON, RE ; TATHAM, RL ; BLACK, WC: *Multivariate Data Analysis (Fifth Eds. ed.).* 1998

[HLA+18]   HABIBOVIC, Azra ; LUNDGREN, Victor M. ; ANDERSSON, Jonas ; KLINGEGÅRD, Maria ; LAGSTRÖM, Tobias ; SIRKKA, Anna ; FAGERLÖNN, Johan ; EDGREN, Claes ; FREDRIKSSON, Rikard ; KRUPENIA, Stas u. a.: Communicating intent of automated vehicles to pedestrians. In: *Frontiers in psychology* 9 (2018), S. 1336

[HLVK16]   HERGETH, Sebastian ; LORENZ, Lutz ; VILIMEK, Roman ; KREMS, Josef F.: Keep your scanners peeled: Gaze behavior as a measure of automation trust during highly automated driving. In: *Human factors* 58 (2016), Nr. 3, S. 509–519

[HMC23]   HUO, Dongchao ; MA, Jinfei ; CHANG, Ruosong: The development and application of the drivers' attitudes of right-of-way questionnaire (DARQ). In: *Transportation research part F: traffic psychology and behaviour* 94 (2023), S. 67–82

[HR14]   HADDINGTON, Pentti ; RAUNIOMAA, Mirka: Interaction between road users: Offering space in traffic. In: *Space and culture* 17 (2014), Nr. 2, S. 176–190

[HWB19a]   HOLLÄNDER, Kai ; WINTERSBERGER, Philipp ; BUTZ, Andreas: Overtrust in external cues of automated vehicles: an experimental investigation. In: *Proceedings of the 11th international conference on automotive user interfaces and interactive vehicular applications*, 2019, S. 211–221

[HWB+19b]   HOLTHAUSEN, Brittany E. ; WINTERSBERGER, Philipp ; BECERRA, Zoe ; MIRNIG, Alexander G. ; KUNZE, Alexander ; WALKER, Bruce N.: Third workshop on trust in automation: how does trust influence interaction. In: *Proceedings of the 11th*

International Conference on Automotive User Interfaces and Interactive Vehicular Applications: Adjunct Proceedings. Utrecht, Netherlands : ACM SIGCHI, 2019, S. 13–18

[HWWR20] HOLTHAUSEN, Brittany E. ; WINTERSBERGER, Philipp ; WALKER, Bruce N. ; RIENER, Andreas: Situational trust scale for automated driving (STS-AD): Development and initial validation. In: *12th International Conference on Automotive User Interfaces and Interactive Vehicular Applications*, 2020, S. 40–47

[JAS20] JASP TEAM: *JASP (Version 0.14.0)[Computer software].* https://jasp-stats.org/. Version: 2020

[JCT+19] JAYARAMAN, Suresh K. ; CREECH, Chandler ; TILBURY, Dawn M. ; YANG, X J. ; PRADHAN, Anuj K. ; TSUI, Katherine M. ; ROBERT JR, Lionel P.: Pedestrian trust in automated vehicles: Role of traffic signal and av driving behavior. In: *Frontiers in Robotics and AI* (2019), S. 117

[KB18] KEIJSERS, Merel ; BARTNECK, Christoph: Mindless robots get bullied. In: *2018 13th ACM/IEEE International Conference on Human-Robot Interaction (HRI)* IEEE, 2018, S. 205–214

[Kec19] KECK, Catie: Waymo's Autonomous Vehicles Are Reportedly Facing Ongoing Attacks in Arizona. In: *Gizmodo* (2019)

[KF21] KALATIAN, Arash ; FAROOQ, Bilal: Decoding pedestrian and automated vehicle interactions using immersive virtual reality and interpretable deep learning. In: *Transportation research part C: emerging technologies* 124 (2021), S. 102962

[KHM+13] KNOBEL, Martin ; HASSENZAHL, Marc ; MÄNNLEIN, Simon ; LAMARA, Melanie ; SCHUMANN, Josef ; ECKOLDT, Kai ; LASCHKE, Matthias ; BUTZ, Andreas: Become a Member of the Last Gentlemen: Designing for Prosocial Driving. In: *Proceedings of the 6th International Conference on Designing Pleasurable Products and Interfaces.* New York, NY, USA : Association for Computing Machinery, 2013 (DPPI '13). – ISBN 9781450321921, 60–66

[KLS08] KEIZER, Kees ; LINDENBERG, Siegwart ; STEG, Linda: The spreading of disorder. In: *science* 322 (2008), Nr. 5908, S. 1681–1685

[KML+20] KALEEFATHULLAH, Anees A. ; MERAT, Natasha ; LEE, Yee M. ; EISMA, Yke B. ; MADIGAN, Ruth ; GARCIA, Jorge ; WINTER, Joost d.: External Human–Machine Interfaces Can Be Misleading: An Examination of Trust Development and Misuse in a

CAVE-Based Pedestrian Simulation Environment. In: *Human factors* (2020), S. 0018720820970751

[Kor24]   KOROSEC,   Kirsten: *A   Waymo   robotaxi was   vandalized   and   burned   in   San   Francisco.*   https://techcrunch.com/2024/02/12/ a-waymo-robotaxi-was-vandalized-and-burned-in-san-francisco/ ?guccounter=1. Version: Feb 2024

[KS23]   KNUT   SAUER,   PhD: *How   far   are   we   from   level 5   autonomy?*   https://blog.guardknox.com/ how-far-are-we-from-level-5-autonomy.   Version: Aug 2023

[KTVDH96]   KAPTEIN, Nico A. ; THEEUWES, Jan ; VAN DER HORST, Richard: Driving simulator validity: Some considerations. In: *Transportation research record* 1550 (1996), Nr. 1, S. 30–36

[KW15]   KEUSCHNIGG, Marc ; WOLBRING, Tobias: Disorder, social capital, and norm violation: Three field experiments on the broken windows thesis. In: *Rationality and Society* 27 (2015), Nr. 1, 96-126. http://dx.doi.org/10.1177/1043463114561749. – DOI 10.1177/1043463114561749

[Lar96]   LARSON, John A.: *Steering clear of highway madness: A driver's guide to curbing stress and strain.* Sao Paulo, Brazil : BookPartners, 1996

[Lau19]   LAURIER, Eric: Civility and mobility: drivers (and passengers) appreciating the actions of other drivers. In: *Language & Communication* 65 (2019), S. 79–91

[LBSP+21]   LÜDECKE, Daniel ; BEN-SHACHAR, Mattan S. ; PATIL, Indrajeet ; WAGGONER, Philip ; MAKOWSKI, Dominique: performance: An R Package for Assessment, Comparison and Testing of Statistical Models. In: *Journal of Open Source Software* 6 (2021), Nr. 60, S. 3139. http://dx.doi.org/10.21105/joss.03139. – DOI 10.21105/joss.03139

[LBY+20]   LANZER, Mirjam ; BABEL, Franziska ; YAN, Fei ; ZHANG, Bihan ; YOU, Fang ; WANG, Jianmin ; BAUMANN, Martin: Designing communication strategies of autonomous vehicles with pedestrians: an intercultural study. In: *12th International Conference on Automotive User Interfaces and Interactive Vehicular Applications.* New York, NY, USA : ACM, 2020, S. 122–131

[LDWDY20]   LIU, Peng ; DU, Yong ; WANG, Lin ; DA YOUNG, Ju: Ready to
             bully automated vehicles on public roads? In: *Accident Analysis*
             & Prevention 137 (2020), S. 105457

[Lei14]   LEINER, DJ: SoSci Survey (Version 3.2. 33). In: *SoSci Survey*
             (2014)

[LGR19]   LÖCKEN, Andreas ; GOLLING, Carmen ; RIENER, Andreas: How
             should automated vehicles interact with pedestrians? A com-
             parative analysis of interaction concepts in virtual reality. In:
             Proceedings of the 11th international conference on automotive
             user interfaces and interactive vehicular applications, 2019, S.
             262–274

[LHW21]   LIU, Hailong ; HIRAYAMA, Takatsugu ; WATANABE, Masaya: Im-
             portance of instruction for pedestrian-automated driving vehicle
             interaction with an external human machine interface: Effects
             on pedestrians' situation awareness, trust, perceived risks and
             decision making. In: *2021 IEEE Intelligent Vehicles Symposium*
             (IV). Nagoya, Japan : Institute of Electrical and Electronics
             Engineers (IEEE), 2021, S. 748–754

[Li16]   LI, Cheng-Hsien: Confirmatory factor analysis with ordinal data:
             Comparing robust maximum likelihood and diagonally weighted
             least squares. In: *Behavior research methods* 48 (2016), S. 936–
             949

[LMG+21]   LEE, Yee M. ; MADIGAN, Ruth ; GILES, Oscar ; GARACH-
             MORCILLO, Laura ; MARKKULA, Gustav ; FOX, Charles ; CA-
             MARA, Fanta ; ROTHMUELLER, Markus ; VENDELBO-LARSEN,
             Signe A. ; RASMUSSEN, Pernille H. u. a.: Road users rarely use
             explicit communication when interacting in today's traffic: im-
             plications for automated vehicles. In: *Cognition, Technology &*
             Work 23 (2021), S. 367–380

[LS04]   LEE, John D. ; SEE, Katrina A.: Trust in automation: Designing
             for appropriate reliance. In: *Human factors* 46 (2004), Nr. 1, S.
             50–80

[Lüd18]   LÜDECKE, Daniel: ggeffects: Tidy data frames of marginal effects
             from regression models. In: *Journal of Open Source Software* 3
             (2018), Nr. 26, S. 772

[M+04]   MAYRING, Philipp u. a.: Qualitative content analysis. In: *A*
             companion to qualitative research 1 (2004), Nr. 2, S. 159–176

[Mac22]   MACKENZIE, Angus: *Mercedes-Benz Drive Pilot Au-*
          tonomous first "drive":   We try a world's first driver-
          less system.   https://www.motortrend.com/news/
          mercedes-benz-drive-pilot-eqs-autonomous-driverless-first-drive-review/.
          Version: May 2022

[MAH11]   MURPHY, Ryan O. ; ACKERMANN, Kurt A. ; HANDGRAAF,
          Michel J.:   Measuring social value orientation. In: *Judgment*
          and Decision making 6 (2011), Nr. 8, S. 771–781

[Mai18]   MAIR, Patrick: *Modern psychometrics with R.* Cham : Springer,
          2018

[Man18]   MANGOLD, Pascal: Das Unsichtbare entdecken durch
          werkzeuggestützte wissenschaftliche Beobachtung. In: *Böttger,*
          H., Jensen, K. & Jensen T. Mindful Evolution. Konferenzband.
          Bad Heilbrunn: Klinkhardt (2018)

[MAX23]   MAXQDA: *The #1 software for qualitative and mixed meth-*
          ods data analysis. 2023. – https://www.maxqda.com/, [Online;
          accessed 17-March-2023]

[MB18]   MILLARD-BALL, Adam: Pedestrians, autonomous vehicles, and
          cities. In: *Journal of planning education and research* 38 (2018),
          Nr. 1, S. 6–12

[MCSH15] MORRONGIELLO, Barbara A. ; CORBETT, Michael ; SWITZER,
          Jessica ; HALL, Tom: Using a virtual environment to study
          pedestrian behaviors: How does time pressure affect children's
          and adults' street crossing behaviors? In: *Journal of pediatric*
          psychology 40 (2015), Nr. 7, S. 697–703

[MCSS20] MOORE, Dylan ; CURRANO, Rebecca ; SHANKS, Michael ;
          SIRKIN, David: Defense against the dark cars: Design princi-
          ples for griefing of autonomous vehicles. In: *Proceedings of the*
          2020 ACM/IEEE International Conference on Human-Robot In-
          teraction, 2020, S. 201–209

[MD97]   MOYANO DÍAZ, Emilio: Teoría del Comportamiento Planificado
          e intención de infringir normas de tránsito en peatones. In: *Es-*
          tudos de Psicologia (Natal) 2 (1997), S. 335–348

[MGF⁺22] MIRNIG, Alexander G. ; GÄRTNER, Magdalena ; FRÖHLICH, Pe-
          ter ; WALLNER, Vivien ; DAHLMAN, Anna S. ; ANUND, Anna ;
          POKORNY, Petr ; HAGENZIEKER, Marjan ; BJØRNSKAU, Torkel ;

AASVIK, Ole u. a.: External communication of automated shuttles: Results, experiences, and lessons learned from three European long-term research projects. In: *Frontiers in Robotics and AI* 9 (2022), S. 239

[MH07] MAIR, P. ; HATZINGER, R.: Extended Rasch modeling: The eRm package for the application of IRT models in R. In: *Journal of Statistical Software* 20 (2007), Nr. 9, 1-20. https://www.jstatsoft.org/v20/i09

[MKKB22] MILLER, Linda ; KONIAKOWSKY, Ina M. ; KRAUS, Johannes ; BAUMANN, Martin: The Impact of Expectations about Automated and Manual Vehicles on Drivers' Behavior: Insights from a Mixed Traffic Driving Simulator Study. In: *Proceedings of the 14th International Conference on Automotive User Interfaces and Interactive Vehicular Applications*. Seoul Republic of Korea : ACM, September 2022. – ISBN 978–1–4503–9415–4, 150–161

[MLKB22] MILLER, Linda ; LEITNER, Jasmin ; KRAUS, Johannes ; BAUMANN, Martin: Implicit intention communication as a design opportunity for automated vehicles: Understanding drivers' interpretation of vehicle trajectory at narrow passages. In: *Accident Analysis & Prevention* 173 (2022), August, 106691. http://dx.doi.org/10.1016/j.aap.2022.106691. – DOI 10.1016/j.aap.2022.106691. – ISSN 00014575

[MM19] MERLINO, Sara ; MONDADA, Lorenza: Crossing the street: How pedestrians interact with cars. In: *Language & Communication* 65 (2019), S. 131–147

[MMN+20] MARKKULA, Gustav ; MADIGAN, Ruth ; NATHANAEL, Dimitris ; PORTOULI, Evangelia ; LEE, Yee M. ; DIETRICH, André ; BILLINGTON, Jac ; SCHIEBEN, Anna ; MERAT, Natasha: Defining interactions: A conceptual framework for understanding interactive behaviour in human and automated road traffic. In: *Theoretical Issues in Ergonomics Science* (2020), S. 1–24

[MNF+19] MADIGAN, Ruth ; NORDHOFF, Sina ; FOX, Charles ; AMINI, Roja E. ; LOUW, Tyron ; WILBRINK, Marc ; SCHIEBEN, Anna ; MERAT, Natasha: Understanding interactions between Automated Road Transport Systems and other road users: A video analysis. In: *Transportation research part F: traffic psychology and behaviour* 66 (2019), S. 196–213

[Mon18] MONDADA, Lorenza: Multiple temporalities of language and body in interaction: Challenges for transcribing multimodality.

In: *Research on language and social interaction* 51 (2018), Nr. 1, S. 85–106

[Mor20] MORIUCHI, Emi: "Social credit effect" in a sharing economy: A theory of mind and prisoner's dilemma game theory perspective on the two-way review and rating system. In: *Psychology & Marketing* 37 (2020), Nr. 5, S. 641–662

[MSS18] MAHADEVAN, Karthik ; SOMANATH, Sowmya ; SHARLIN, Ehud: Communicating awareness and intent in autonomous vehicle-pedestrian interaction. In: *Proceedings of the 2018 CHI Conference on Human Factors in Computing Systems*, 2018, S. 1–12

[MSS+19] MAHADEVAN, Karthik ; SANOUBARI, Elaheh ; SOMANATH, Sowmya ; YOUNG, James E. ; SHARLIN, Ehud: AV-Pedestrian interaction design using a pedestrian mixed traffic simulator. In: *Proceedings of the 2019 on designing interactive systems conference*, 2019, S. 475–486

[NPP+18] NATHANAEL, Dimitris ; PORTOULI, Evangelia ; PAPAKOSTOPOU-LOS, Vassilis ; GKIKAS, Kostas ; AMDITIS, Angelos: Naturalistic observation of interactions between car drivers and pedestrians in high density urban settings. In: *Congress of the International Ergonomics Association* Springer, 2018, S. 389–397

[NVVF+20] NUÑEZ VELASCO, Juan P. ; VRIES, Anouk de ; FARAH, Haneen ; AREM, Bart van ; HAGENZIEKER, Marjan P.: Cyclists' crossing intentions when interacting with automated vehicles: A virtual reality study. In: *Information* 12 (2020), Nr. 1, S. 7

[NW72] NELDER, John A. ; WEDDERBURN, Robert W.: Generalized linear models. In: *Journal of the Royal Statistical Society: Series A (General)* 135 (1972), Nr. 3, S. 370–384

[ÖL05] ÖZKAN, Türker ; LAJUNEN, Timo: A new addition to DBQ: Positive driver behaviours scale. In: *Transportation Research Part F: Traffic Psychology and Behaviour* 8 (2005), Nr. 4-5, S. 355–368

[P+81] PILIAVIN, Jane A. u. a.: *Emergency intervention.* Cambridge, Massachusetts, USA : Academic Press, 1981

[Pat11] PATRY, Jean-Luc: Methodological consequences of situation specificity: biases in assessments. In: *Frontiers in psychology* 2 (2011), S. 18

[PMPDA+18] PRATI, Gabriele ; MARÍN PUCHADES, Víctor ; DE ANGELIS, Marco ; FRABONI, Federico ; PIETRANTONI, Luca: Factors contributing to bicycle–motorised vehicle collisions: A systematic literature review. In: *Transport reviews* 38 (2018), Nr. 2, S. 184–208

[PRMP09]   PRYOR, John B. ; REEDER, Glenn D. ; MONROE, Andrew E. ; PATEL, Arati: Stigmas and prosocial behavior. In: *The Psychology of Prosocial Behavior: Group processes, intergroup relations, and helping* (2009), S. 59–80

[PSB18a]   PETZOLDT, Tibor ; SCHLEINITZ, Katja ; BANSE, Rainer: Potential safety effects of a frontal brake light for motor vehicles. In: *IET Intelligent Transport Systems* 12 (2018), Nr. 6, S. 449–453

[PSB18b]   PETZOLDT, Tibor ; SCHLEINITZ, Katja ; BANSE, Rainer: Potential safety effects of a frontal brake light for motor vehicles. In: *IET Intelligent Transport Systems* 12 (2018), August, 449-453(4). https://digital-library.theiet.org/content/journals/10.1049/iet-its.2017.0321. – ISSN 1751–956X

[RAB20a]   RETTENMAIER, Michael ; ALBERS, Deike ; BENGLER, Klaus: After you?! – Use of external human-machine interfaces in road bottleneck scenarios. In: *Transportation Research Part F: Traffic Psychology and Behaviour* 70 (2020), April, 175–190. http://dx.doi.org/10.1016/j.trf.2020.03.004. – DOI 10.1016/j.trf.2020.03.004. – ISSN 13698478

[RAB20b]   RETTENMAIER, Michael ; ALBERS, Deike ; BENGLER, Klaus: After You?!–Use of External Human-Machine Interfaces in Road Bottleneck Scenarios. In: *Transportation research part F* 70 (2020), S. 175–190

[RB20]   RETTENMAIER, Michael ; BENGLER, Klaus: Modeling the Interaction with Automated Vehicles in Road Bottleneck Scenarios. In: *Proceedings of the Human Factors and Ergonomics Society Annual Meeting* 64 (2020), Dezember, Nr. 1, 1615–1619. http://dx.doi.org/10.1177/1071181320641391. – DOI 10.1177/1071181320641391. – ISSN 2169–5067, 1071–1813

[RB21]   RETTENMAIER, Michael ; BENGLER, Klaus: The Matter of How and When: Comparing Explicit and Implicit Communication Strategies of Automated Vehicles in Bottleneck Scenarios. In: *IEEE Open Journal of Intelligent Transportation Systems* 2 (2021), 282–293. http://dx.doi.org/10.1109/OJITS.2021.3107678. – DOI 10.1109/OJITS.2021.3107678. – ISSN 2687–7813

[RC66]   RAPOPORT, Anatol ; CHAMMAH, Albert M.: The game of chicken. In: *American Behavioral Scientist* 10 (1966), Nr. 3, S. 10–28

[RDB21a]   RETTENMAIER, Michael ; DINKEL, Sabrina ; BENGLER, Klaus:
             Communication via motion–Suitability of automated vehicle
             movements to negotiate the right of way in road bottleneck sce-
             narios. In: *Applied ergonomics* 95 (2021), S. 103438

[RDB21b]   RETTENMAIER, Michael ; DINKEL, Sabrina ; BENGLER, Klaus:
             Communication via motion – Suitability of automated vehicle
             movements to negotiate the right of way in road bottleneck sce-
             narios. In: *Applied Ergonomics* 95 (2021), September, 103438.
             `http://dx.doi.org/10.1016/j.apergo.2021.103438`. – DOI
             10.1016/j.apergo.2021.103438. – ISSN 00036870

[Rea90]   REASON, James: *Human error.* UK : Cambridge university press,
             1990

[REV⁺17]   RISTO, Malte ; EMMENEGGER, Colleen ; VINKHUYZEN, Erik ;
             CEFKIN, Melissa ; HOLLAN, Jim: Human-vehicle interfaces: the
             power of vehicle movement gestures in human road user coordi-
             nation. (2017)

[Rev19]   REVELLE, William ; NORTHWESTERN UNIVERSITY (Hrsg.):
             *psych: Procedures for Psychological, Psychometric, and Person-
             ality Research.* Evanston, Illinois: Northwestern University, 2019.
             `https://CRAN.R-project.org/package=psych`. – R package
             version 1.9.12

[Ris85]   RISSER, Ralf: Behavior in traffic conflict situations. In: *Accident
             Analysis & Prevention* 17 (1985), Nr. 2, S. 179–197

[RJW16]   REN, Zeheng ; JIANG, Xiaobei ; WANG, Wuhong: Analysis of the
             influence of pedestrians' eye contact on drivers' comfort boundary
             during the crossing conflict. In: *Procedia engineering* 137 (2016),
             S. 399–406

[RKT17a]   RASOULI, Amir ; KOTSERUBA, Iuliia ; TSOTSOS, John K.: Agree-
             ing to cross: How drivers and pedestrians communicate. In: *2017
             IEEE Intelligent Vehicles Symposium (IV).* Redondo Beach, Cal-
             ifornia, USA : Institute of Electrical and Electronics Engineers
             (IEEE), 2017, S. 264–269

[RKT17b]   RASOULI, Amir ; KOTSERUBA, Iuliia ; TSOTSOS, John K.: Un-
             derstanding pedestrian behavior in complex traffic scenes. In:
             IEEE Transactions on Intelligent Vehicles 3 (2017), Nr. 1, S.
             61–70

[RLS⁺15]   ROTHENBÜCHER, Dirk ; LI, Jamy ; SIRKIN, David ; MOK, Brian
             ; JU, Wendy: Ghost driver: a platform for investigating in-

teractions between pedestrians and driverless vehicles. In: *Adjunct Proceedings of the 7th International Conference on Automotive User Interfaces and Interactive Vehicular Applications*. New York, NY, USA : Association for Computing Machinery, 2015, S. 44–49

[RM22]   RAONIAR, Rahul ; MAURYA, Akhilesh K.: Pedestrian red-light violation at signalised intersection crosswalks: Influence of social and non-social factors. In: *Safety science* 147 (2022), S. 105583

[RMS⁺90]   REASON, James ; MANSTEAD, Antony ; STRADLING, Stephen ; BAXTER, James ; CAMPBELL, Karen: Errors and violations on the roads: a real distinction? In: *Ergonomics* 33 (1990), Nr. 10-11, S. 1315–1332

[Ros96]   ROSS, Edward A.: Social Control. In: *American Journal of Sociology* 1 (1896), Nr. 5, 513–535. http://www.jstor.org/stable/2761903. – ISSN 00029602, 15375390

[Ros09]   ROSENBLOOM, Tova: Crossing at a red light: Behaviour of individuals and groups. In: *Transportation Research Part F: Traffic Psychology and Behaviour* 12 (2009), Nr. 5, 389-394. http://dx.doi.org/https://doi.org/10.1016/j.trf.2009.05.002. – DOI https://doi.org/10.1016/j.trf.2009.05.002. – ISSN 1369–8478

[Ros14]   ROSSEEL, Yves: *The lavaan tutorial.* 2014

[RPSB19]   RETTENMAIER, Michael ; PIETSCH, Moritz ; SCHMIDTLER, Jonas ; BENGLER, Klaus: Passing through the Bottleneck - The Potential of External Human-Machine Interfaces. In: *2019 IEEE Intelligent Vehicles Symposium (IV)*. Paris, France : IEEE, Juni 2019. – ISBN 978-1-72810-560-4, 1687–1692

[RR18]   *Kapitel 7.* In: RANDALL, Dave ; ROUNCEFIELD, Mark: *Ethnographic Approach to Design.* John Wiley Sons, Ltd, 2018. – ISBN 9781118976005, 125-141

[RSt20]   RSTUDIO TEAM ; RSTUDIO, PBC. (Hrsg.): *RStudio: Integrated Development Environment for R.* Boston, MA: RStudio, PBC., 2020. http://www.rstudio.com/

[RT18a]   RAHMATI, Yalda ; TALEBPOUR, Alireza: Learning-based game theoretical framework for modeling pedestrian motion. In: *Physical Review E* 98 (2018), Nr. 3, S. 032312

[RT18b]   RASOULI, Amir ; TSOTSOS, John K.: Joint attention in driver-pedestrian interaction: from theory to practice. In: *arXiv preprint arXiv:1802.02522* (2018)

[RT19]   RASOULI, Amir ; TSOTSOS, John K.:   Autonomous vehicles
              that interact with pedestrians: A survey of theory and practice.
              In: *IEEE Transactions on Intelligent Transportation Systems* 21
              (2019), Nr. 3, S. 900–918

[RUM⁺17]   RODRIGUES, Johannes ; ULRICH, Natalie ; MUSSEL, Patrick ;
              CARLO, Gustavo ; HEWIG, Johannes: Measuring prosocial ten-
              dencies in Germany: Sources of validity and reliablity of the re-
              vised prosocial tendency measure. In: *Frontiers in psychology* 8
              (2017), S. 2119

[S⁺12]   SCHMITZ, Carsten u. a.:   LimeSurvey: An open source survey
              tool. In: *LimeSurvey Project Hamburg, Germany.* (2012). http:
              //www.limesurvey.org

[SAE16]   SAE, Taxonomy: Definitions for terms related to driving au-
              tomation systems for on-road motor vehicles. In: *SAE Standard
              J* 3016 (2016), S. 2016

[Sch77]   SCHWARTZ, Shalom H.: Normative influences on altruism. In:
              Advances in experimental social psychology Bd. 10. Amsterdam,
              The Netherlands : Elsevier, 1977, S. 221–279

[SCY⁺10]   SALVINI, Pericle ; CIARAVELLA, Gaetano ; YU, Wonpil ; FERRI,
              Gabriele ; MANZI, Alessandro ; MAZZOLAI, Barbara ; LASCHI,
              Cecilia ; OH, Sang-Rok ; DARIO, Paolo: How safe are service
              robots in urban environments? Bullying a robot. In: *19th inter-
              national symposium in robot and human interactive communica-
              tion* IEEE, 2010, S. 1–7

[ŞDMB21]   ŞAHIN, Hatice ; DAUDRICH, Kevin ; MÜLLER, Heiko ; BOLL,
              Susanne C.: Signaling Yielding Intent with eHMIs: the Timing
              Determines an Efficient Crossing. In: *13th International Con-
              ference on Automotive User Interfaces and Interactive Vehicular
              Applications,* 2021, S. 5–9

[SDR17]   SUCHA, Matus ; DOSTAL, Daniel ; RISSER, Ralf: Pedestrian-
              driver communication and decision strategies at marked cross-
              ings. In: *Accident Analysis & Prevention* 102 (2017), S. 41–50

[SEKK01]   SHELDON, Kennon M. ; ELLIOT, Andrew J. ; KIM, Youngmee ;
              KASSER, Tim: What is satisfying about satisfying events? Test-
              ing 10 candidate psychological needs. In: *Journal of personality
              and social psychology* 80 (2001), Nr. 2, S. 325

[SF09]   SCHMIDT, Sarah ; FAERBER, Berthold: Pedestrians at the kerb–
              Recognising the action intentions of humans. In: *Transportation*

research part F: traffic psychology and behaviour 12 (2009), Nr.
4, S. 300–310

[SFR01]   SCHUBERT, Thomas ; FRIEDMANN, Frank ; REGENBRECHT, Hol-
             ger: The experience of presence: Factor analytic insights. In:
             Presence: Teleoperators & Virtual Environments 10 (2001), Nr.
             3, S. 266–281

[SG15]   SCHROEDER, David A. ; GRAZIANO, William G.:   3The
             Field of Prosocial Behavior: An Introduction and Overview.
             Version: 05 2015.   http://dx.doi.org/10.1093/oxfordhb/
             9780195399813.013.32. In: *The Oxford Handbook of Proso-
             cial Behavior*.   Oxford, UK : Oxford University Press, 05
             2015. – DOI 10.1093/oxfordhb/9780195399813.013.32. – ISBN
             9780195399813, 3–34

[SG16]   SCHNEEMANN, Friederike ; GOHL, Irene: Analyzing driver-
             pedestrian interaction at crosswalks: A contribution to au-
             tonomous driving in urban environments. In: *2016 IEEE in-
             telligent vehicles symposium (IV)* IEEE, 2016, S. 38–43

[SG20]   STEINER, Markus D. ; GRIEDER, Silvia: EFAtools: An R pack-
             age with fast and flexible implementations of exploratory factor
             analysis tools. In: *Journal of Open Source Software* 5 (2020), Nr.
             53, 2521. http://dx.doi.org/10.21105/joss.02521. – DOI
             10.21105/joss.02521

[SHB22]   SAHIN, Hatice ; HEMESATH, Sebastian ; BOLL, Susanne: De-
             viant Behavior of Pedestrians: A Risk Gamble or Just Against
             Automated Vehicles? How About Social Control? In: *Frontiers
             in Robotics and AI* (2022), S. 177

[SHE20a]   SADEGHIAN, Shadan ; HASSENZAHL, Marc ; ECKOLDT, Kai: An
             Exploration of Prosocial Aspects of Communication Cues be-
             tween Automated Vehicles and Pedestrians. In: *12th Interna-
             tional Conference on Automotive User Interfaces and Interac-
             tive Vehicular Applications*. New York, NY, USA : Association
             for Computing Machinery, 2020 (AutomotiveUI '20). – ISBN
             9781450380652, 205–211

[SHE20b]   SADEGHIAN, Shadan ; HASSENZAHL, Marc ; ECKOLDT, Kai: An
             exploration of prosocial aspects of communication cues between
             automated vehicles and pedestrians. In: *12th International Con-
             ference on Automotive User Interfaces and Interactive Vehicular
             Applications*, 2020, S. 205–211

[ŞİDD+23]   ŞAHIN İPPOLITI, Hatice ; DAUDRICH, Angelique ; DEY, Debargha
             ; WINTERSBERGER, Philipp ; SADEGHIAN, Shadan ; BOLL, Su-
             sanne: A Real Bottleneck Scenario with a Wizard of Oz Auto-
             mated Vehicle-Role of eHMIs. In: *Proceedings of the 15th Inter-
             national Conference on Automotive User Interfaces and Interac-
             tive Vehicular Applications*, 2023, S. 280–290

[SITKB23]   SAHIN IPPOLITI, Hatice ; TRILCK, Nina ; KOELLE, Marion ;
             BOLL, Susanne: Please, Go Ahead! Fostering Prosocial Driving
             with Sympathy-Eliciting Automated Vehicle External Displays.
             In: *Proceedings of the ACM on Human-Computer Interaction* 7
             (2023), Nr. MHCI, S. 1–18

[SMS+21]   SAHIN, Hatice ; MÜLLER, Heiko ; SADEGHIAN, Shadan ; DEY,
             Debargha ; LÖCKEN, Andreas ; MATVIIENKO, Andrii ; COLLEY,
             Mark ; HABIBOVIC, Azra ; WINTERSBERGER, Philipp: Workshop
             on Prosocial Behavior in Future Mixed Traffic. In: *13th Interna-
             tional Conference on Automotive User Interfaces and Interactive
             Vehicular Applications*. New York, NY, USA : Association for
             Computing Machinery, 2021, S. 167–170

[SPAM+19]   SCHWARTING, Wilko ; PIERSON, Alyssa ; ALONSO-MORA, Javier
             ; KARAMAN, Sertac ; RUS, Daniela: Social behavior for au-
             tonomous vehicles. In: *Proceedings of the National Academy of
             Sciences* 116 (2019), Nr. 50, S. 24972–24978

[SRB19]   SCHNEIDER, Sonja ; RATTER, Madeleine ; BENGLER, Klaus:
             Pedestrian behavior in virtual reality: effects of gamification and
             distraction. In: *Proceedings of the Road Safety and Simulation
             Conference 2019*, 2019

[SRE+19]   SCHADE, Jens ; RÖSSGER, Lars ; EGGS, Johannes ; FOLLMER,
             Robert ; SCHLAG, Bernhard: *Entwicklung und Überprüfung eines
             Instruments zur kontinuierlichen Erfassung des Verkehrsklimas.*
             2019

[SRF12]   SCHROETER, Ronald ; RAKOTONIRAINY, Andry ; FOTH, Marcus:
             The social car: new interactive vehicular applications derived
             from social media and urban informatics. In: *Proceedings of the
             4th International Conference on Automotive User Interfaces and
             Interactive Vehicular Applications*, 2012, S. 107–110

[ST15]   SIKKENK, Marin ; TERKEN, Jacques: Rules of conduct for au-
             tonomous vehicles. In: *Proceedings of the 7th international con-
             ference on automotive user interfaces and interactive vehicular
             applications*. New York, NY, USA : ACM, 2015, S. 19–22

[Šuc14]   ŠUCHA, Matúš: Road users' strategies and communication: driver-pedestrian interaction. In: *Transport Research Arena (TRA)* (2014), S. 1

[SWRG19]   SAWITZKY, Tamara von ; WINTERSBERGER, Philipp ; RIENER, Andreas ; GABBARD, Joseph L.: Increasing trust in fully automated driving: Route indication on an augmented reality head-up display. In: *Proceedings of the 8th ACM International Symposium on Pervasive Displays*. New York, NY, USA : Association for Computing Machinery, 2019, S. 1–7

[T$^+$15]   TEAM, RStudio u. a.: RStudio: integrated development for R. In: *RStudio, Inc., Boston, MA URL http://www. rstudio. com* 42 (2015), Nr. 14, S. 84

[TBAMG04]   TAUBMAN-BEN-ARI, Orit ; MIKULINCER, Mario ; GILLATH, Omri: The multidimensional driving style inventory—scale construct and validation. In: *Accident Analysis & Prevention* 36 (2004), Nr. 3, S. 323–332

[TFU13]   TABACHNICK, Barbara G. ; FIDELL, Linda S. ; ULLMAN, Jodie B.: *Using multivariate statistics*. Bd. 6. Boston, MA, USA : Pearson, 2013

[TGS$^+$19]   TERWILLIGER, Jack ; GLAZER, Michael ; SCHMIDT, Henri ; DOMEYER, Josh ; TOYODA, Heishiro ; MEHLER, Bruce ; REIMER, Bryan ; FRIDMAN, Lex: Dynamics of pedestrian crossing decisions based on vehicle trajectories in large-scale simulated and real-world data. In: *arXiv preprint arXiv:1904.04202* (2019)

[Tho06]   THOMAS, David R.: A general inductive approach for analyzing qualitative evaluation data. In: *American journal of evaluation* 27 (2006), Nr. 2, S. 237–246

[Tho23]   THONNY: *Thonny: Python IDE for beginners*. 2023. – https://thonny.org/,[Online; accessed 15-March-2023]

[TK10]   TRAUTMAN, Peter ; KRAUSE, Andreas: Unfreezing the robot: Navigation in dense, interacting crowds. In: *2010 IEEE/RSJ International Conference on Intelligent Robots and Systems* IEEE, 2010, S. 797–803

[TVKBS05]   TE VELDE, Arenda F. ; KAMP, John van d. ; BARELA, José A ; SAVELSBERGH, Geert J.: Visual timing and adaptive behavior in a road-crossing simulation study. In: *Accident Analysis & Prevention* 37 (2005), Nr. 3, S. 399–406

[Urr06]   URRY, John: Inhabiting the car. In: *The Sociological Review* 54 (2006), Nr. 1_suppl, S. 17–31

[Var98]   VARHELYI, Andras: Drivers' speed behaviour at a zebra crossing: a case study. In: *Accident Analysis & Prevention* 30 (1998), Nr. 6, S. 731–743

[VC16]   VINKHUYZEN, Erik ; CEFKIN, Melissa: Developing socially acceptable autonomous vehicles. In: *Ethnographic Praxis in Industry Conference Proceedings* Bd. 2016 Wiley Online Library, 2016, S. 522–534

[VGJ⁺22]   VANDROUX, Romane ; GRANIÉ, Marie-Axelle ; JAY, Mathilde ; SUEUR, Cédric ; PELÉ, Marie: The pedestrian behaviour scale: A systematic review of its validation around the world. In: *Accident Analysis & Prevention* 165 (2022), S. 106509

[VPV⁺09]   VIOLENCE, World Health Organization. D. ; PREVENTION, Injury ; VIOLENCE, World Health O. ; PREVENTION, Injury ; ORGANIZATION, World H.: *Global status report on road safety: time for action.* World Health Organization, 2009

[WD22]   WINTER, Joost de ; DODOU, Dimitra: External Human-Machine Interfaces: Gimmick or Necessity. In: *Delft University of Technology, Delft, The Netherlands* (2022)

[Wer18]   WERNER, Annette: New colours for autonomous driving: An evaluation of chromaticities for the external lighting equipment of autonomous vehicles. In: *Colour Turn* (2018), Nr. 1

[WFO⁺20]   WARD, Nicholas J. ; FINLEY, Kari ; OTTO, Jay ; KACK, David ; GLEASON, Rebecca ; LONSDALE, T: Traffic safety culture and prosocial driver behavior for safer vehicle-bicyclist interactions. In: *Journal of safety research* 75 (2020), S. 24–31

[WFRS18]   WINTERSBERGER, Philipp ; FRISON, Anna-Katharina ; RIENER, Andreas ; SAWITZKY, Tamara v.: Fostering user acceptance and trust in fully automated vehicles: Evaluating the potential of augmented reality. In: *PRESENCE: Virtual and Augmented Reality* 27 (2018), Nr. 1, S. 46–62

[WK82]   WILSON, J ; KELLING, George L.: BROKEN WINDOWS: THE POLICE AND NEIGHBOURHOOD SAFETY. In: *The Atlantic Monthly* 249 (1982), S. 0–0

[WK16]   WOBBROCK, Jacob O. ; KIENTZ, Julie A.: Research contributions in human-computer interaction. In: *interactions* 23 (2016), Nr. 3, S. 38–44

[WMB⁺15]   WEISS, Astrid ; MIRNIG, Nicole ; BRUCKENBERGER, Ulrike ;
            STRASSER, Ewald ; TSCHELIGI, Manfred ; (GONSIOR), Bar-
            bara K. ; WOLLHERR, Dirk ; STANCZYK, Bartlomiej: The Inter-
            active Urban Robot: User-centered development and final field
            trial of a direction requesting robot. In: *Paladyn, Journal of
            Behavioral Robotics* 6 (2015), Nr. 1, 000010151520150005. `http:
            //dx.doi.org/doi:10.1515/pjbr-2015-0005`, Abruf: 2023-09-
            01. – DOI doi:10.1515/pjbr–2015–0005

[WSS⁺21]   WINTERSBERGER, Philipp ; SCHARTMÜLLER, Clemens ;
            SADEGHIAN, Shadan ; FRISON, Anna-Katharina ; RIENER, An-
            dreas: *Evaluation of imminent take-over requests with real au-
            tomation on a test track.* 2021

[WTHR16]   WANG, Chao ; TERKEN, Jacques ; HU, Jun ; RAUTERBERG,
            Matthias: "Likes" and "Dislikes" on the Road: A Social Feedback
            System for Improving Driving Behavior. In: *Proceedings of the
            8th International Conference on Automotive User Interfaces and
            Interactive Vehicular Applications.* New York, NY, USA : ACM,
            2016, S. 43–50

[Zel23]   ZELLER, Henner: *Controlling RGB LED display with Rasp-
            berry Pi GPIO.* 2023. – `https://github.com/hzeller/
            rpi-rgb-led-matrix`,[Online; accessed 15-March-2023]